# RELIGION AND UNDERSTANDING

# RELIGION AND
# UNDERSTANDING

Edited by
## D. Z. PHILLIPS

THE MACMILLAN COMPANY : NEW YORK

Published in the United States by
The Macmillan Company, New York, 1967

Library of Congress Card Number : 67-22156

PRINTED AND BOUND IN GREAT BRITAIN

# CONTENTS

*For I do not seek to understand that I may believe, but I believe in order to understand. For this also I believe, that unless I believed, I should not understand.* St. Anselm

# PREFACE

APART from the third paper, all the papers in this volume have been published previously. My thanks are due to the following for permission to reprint the articles:

To Professor Gilbert Ryle for permission to reprint 'Birth, Suicide and the Doctrine of Creation: An Exploration of Analogies', by W. H. Poteat (*Mind*, Vol. LXVIII, 1959) and my paper, 'Moral and Religious Conceptions of Duty: An Analysis' (*Mind*, Vol. LXXIII, 1964); to Professor Nicholas Rescher for permission to reprint 'Understanding a Primitive Society' by Peter Winch (*American Philosophical Quarterly*, Vol. I, 1964), and 'The Miraculous' by R. F. Holland (*American Philosophical Quarterly*, Vol. II, 1965); to Professor Norman Malcolm and the Editors of *The Philosophical Review* for permission to reprint his paper, 'Anselm's Ontological Arguments' (*The Philosophical Review*, Vol. LXIX, No. 1, Jan. 1960); to Professor A. K. Stout for permission to reprint 'Four Men Talk about God' by R. P. Anschutz (*Australasian Journal of Psychology and Philosophy*, Vol. 12, 1934); to Professor G. P. Henderson for permission to reprint 'I Will Die' by W. H. Poteat (*Philosophical Quarterly*, Vol. 9, 1959); to the University College of Swansea for permission to reprint 'Love as Perception of Meaning' by J.R. Jones (an address delivered on October 4th, 1957, on the occasion of the College Service for the beginning of the thirty-eighth Academic Session); to Canon J. S. Bezzant for permission to reprint 'The Devil' by R. G. Collingwood as it appeared in *Concerning Prayer* ed. B. H. Streeter, Macmillan, 1931; and finally to the Literary Executors of Norman Kemp Smith and the British Academy for permission to reprint 'Is Divine Existence Credible?' (*Proceedings of the British Academy*, 1931). Much of the Introduction appeared as 'Meaning and Belief' in *The Listener*, October 14th, 1965. I am grateful for permission to use the material here.

I am grateful to Mr. Reynold Jones for helping me with the proof-reading, and to Mrs. F. G. Hughes, Mrs. E. Read and Miss G. Davies for typing many of the papers. The Staff Research Fund of the University College of North Wales, Bangor, enabled me to make photostat copies of the remaining papers.

Swansea, July 1966          D. Z. P.

# INTRODUCTION

IN his book, *On Understanding Physics*, W. H. Watson expresses what he takes to be the kernel of Wittgenstein's later teaching as follows, 'Look to see what men do with things, with words and with ideas, and observe their behaviour'. Watson's comment certainly deserves to be taken seriously in any philosophical reflection on religion. A lot of irrelevant talk and needless confusion could be avoided if philosophers did appeal to the actual use of religious language.

Having said this, however, one must confess that the appeal to actual usage has resulted in little agreement among philosophers of religion. Most of them, to a greater or lesser extent, claim to base their observations on the actual beliefs of religious believers. Nevertheless, philosophers who say they believe in God give widely different accounts of their beliefs. Some of them say that to believe in God is to believe in an ultimate order of fact; that ultimately a certain state of affairs is going to be the case. To trust in God is to trust that this state of affairs will come about. The truth or falsity of religion is determined by whether or not this ultimate hope, this eschatological expectation, is to be realized or not. Other philosophers deny that this account has anything to do with religion, and hold that in fact it blinds one to its true nature. To say that religious faith is an expectation of certain states of affairs being the case is to confuse it with idolatry. The strength of religion is in its independence of the way things go. The love of God is that which will not let one go no matter what happens to one. This view was expressed by Simone Weil when she said, 'No event is a favour on the part of God; only grace is that'. By contrast, other philosophers see everything as part of a divine plan. We do not see all of the plan now, and hence we think that many of the things that happen in the world are evil and unjust. A day will dawn when all shall be made known, when all the intricacies of the plan shall be revealed, showing us why everything happened as it did. Yet again, other philosophers see morality as the essence of religion. Morality, we are told, is essentially a matter of resolving to lead a certain way of life, and religious stories act as a psychological aid to such moral endeavour.

These examples are by no means exhaustive. I have confined myself to accounts of the Christian religion. If one were to widen the perspective

1

to include other religions, the position would be far more complicated. It must not be supposed, however, that the disagreement I have illustrated is confined to philosophers who would call themselves religious believers. On the contrary, similar disagreements exist between philosophers who would not describe themselves in this way. Some among these say that religious beliefs are intelligible but false. It is like believing in fairies when in fact there are none. Other philosophers say that religious beliefs are not false, but inherently meaningless. The necessary existence of God, for example, is said to be a self-contradiction. Some philosophers might agree with some of their colleagues in the believers' camp that religious beliefs are psychological aids to moral endeavour, but, unlike them, conclude that if this is so, one ought to have the courage to embrace atheism. Yet again, other philosophers might attempt to give Freudian explanations of religion.

My point is that philosophers, believers and non-believers alike, have appealed to actual religious usage, but have not come to any general agreement in their accounts of religious belief. Why is this so? In an attempt to answer this question, let us make a closer examination of the philosopher's appeal to religious language. He appeals to what is said. But this apparently simple phrase, 'what is said', is far more troublesome than one might suppose. It is essential here to take account of Wittgenstein's important distinction between surface grammar and depth grammar. The surface grammar of 'There is a table in the room' and 'There is a God in heaven' is similar, but their depth grammar is very different. One finds out the latter by exploring the limits of what can and what cannot be said in each case. Two believers may pray for a friend about to undertake a dangerous journey, 'God be with him'. The words they utter are the same, but they may mean something quite different by them. Or again, two mothers place a garland on the statue of the Virgin Mary: one may be making a genuine act of devotion, and the other engaging in a superstitious belief. Looking at the overt act will not tell one what is being said about it. How would one find out what is being said in these situations? Well, one would have to look at the role the prayers play in the life of the believer. Someone might wonder why this should be necessary. Why not ask the believer what his prayers mean? The answer is that this might leave one with exactly the same problem on one's hands. Two believers may give the same account of prayer, and yet mean something different from each other by prayer. The ability to pray is not the same as the ability to give an account of prayer. Just because someone gives a naïve account of the existence of God, it does not follow that this is the God he believes in. To find out what belief in God did mean to him one would have to consider the role of such a belief in his life.

The philosopher, then, in appealing to religious language, is faced with this difficulty: he cannot take the believer's expression of faith or his account of faith at face value. The utterances in the expression of faith and in the account of faith may be the same in the case of two believers, and yet, as we have seen, what is said might be quite different. What has to be recognized is that there is a great diversity of belief even within a single religion. Faced with the diversity I have described, it would be tempting at this point to assume that the philosopher has in his possession rational criteria by means of which he can place the various beliefs into some kind of hierarchical order. But if one notes the contemporary scene in the philosophy of religion, no such assumption is justified. The philosophers vary in their accounts of religious belief as much as the believers themselves. What is one to say about this philosophical diversity? One might say that the philosopher's account does not do justice to his religious beliefs. This would be to say that religion means more to him than his account reveals. He may lack the ability to give a good philosophical account of his religious beliefs. In this context too, the ability to believe is not the same as the ability to give an account of one's belief. But in order to make this judgement one would have to examine the role of belief in that philosopher's life. On the other hand, one might conclude that a false account of religious belief is a true reflection of what a particular philosopher believes. 'That's all religion *does* mean to him' one might say. In calling his account false in these circumstances, one is not denying that the account is a faithful picture of what he believes, one is judging his beliefs and his account of them by some other religious standards.

What are the implications of what I have been saying for the relation of philosophy to religion? To begin with, it ought to be clear how superficial it is to regard conceptual analysis as some kind of philosophical technique quite cut off from the religious insights we may or may not possess. Philosophers, quite rightly, wish to emphasize that it is no part of the philosopher's task either to convert or deconvert anyone. The philosopher does not compete with the preacher or the evangelist. Nevertheless, the philosopher is interested in the concept of reality found in religion. Many philosophers have underestimated the problems of understanding involved in the pursuit of this interest. They have assumed far too readily that everyone understands the kind of claims made by religious belief. The only problem facing us, they would have us believe, is that of determining whether such claims can be substantiated or not. This confident attitude springs from a mistaken epistemology, an epistemology which assumes that there is a certain standard use of language, ordinary language, as it is sometimes called, which is the norm of meaningfulness for all uses of language. As a result of its application, religious language is said to be either meaningless, or meaningful but false. The first task facing anyone who wishes to question this philosophical rejection of religion, is to examine, on epistemological grounds, whether there is any such thing as an all-embracing concept of reality, and to inquire whether the distinction between the real and the unreal comes to the same thing in every context of language. In this collection, Peter Winch's paper serves as such a necessary prolegomenon to the philosophy of religion. There are important epistemological parallels in the issues which arise in attempting to give an account of religious beliefs and in the issues which arise in attempting to give an account of the cultures of 'primitive' societies. In each case, philosophers are tempted to impose an alien account on the concepts in question, an account which ignores the role of such concepts in the forms of life of which they are a part.

When one is concerned to give an account of religious belief, to distinguish religion from other modes of social life with which it can be confused so easily, clarifying conceptual confusions may come to much the same thing as clarifying religious confusions. Sometimes, as R. F. Holland shows with reference to the miraculous, our failure to understand is the result of certain conceptual presuppositions which we bring to our examination of religious beliefs—presuppositions which we think are necessary, but which in fact are not. At other times, the misunderstanding is more complex. For example, consider someone who thinks that the only way to make sense of the death of children is by believing that somewhere there exists a divine plan, a plan which will show us why all these terrible things had to happen. People still seem to think of God's relation to the world as that of artificer to artefact. R. P. Anschutz shows the difficulties involved in holding this belief. I agree with Norman Kemp Smith that this belief is confused, and with his penetrating suggestion that it is often held by people who, having ceased to believe, think of God in utterly anthropomorphic terms under the influence of the language of devotion, a language they no longer use. Perhaps I should want to go further and say that to be in the grip of such a belief is to be in the grip of evil. But what are we to say of this confusion? What sort of confusion is it? Intellectual confusion? Religious confusion? Is it not clear that here there is little point in making this distinction? If we rectify the conceptual confusions involved, do we not rectify the religious confusions at the same time? Of course, one may not be able to predict the result of such clarification on any given individual. If a person comes to see that the idea of belief in God as some kind of super-explanation is false, he may cease to hold any religious beliefs, or his beliefs may undergo a drastic change. What one can predict is that he can no longer view the situation as he did before. One's prediction is negative rather than positive.

It may seem that I am over-emphasizing the diversity of religious belief to be found even within a single religion. I do not think I am. I remember saying to a person once, 'I have no doubt that half-a-dozen gods are worshipped in such-and-such a church', to which he replied, 'Why stop at half-a-dozen? Why not simply count the congregation?' That was going too far, no doubt, but when one considers the different ways in which religious believers react to birth, death, bereavement, good fortune or disaster, one has to conclude that religion means very different things to different people. Some will be close to each other; others wide apart. For example, W. H. Poteat and J. R. Jones give very different accounts of religious attitudes to life from those offered by the advocates of a divine plan. One is tempted to say, considering these extremes, that they do not refer to the same activity.

The philosopher is as immersed in this diversity as the religious believer. His intellect is not some kind of protective clothing which keeps him above the maze of various insights, loves and hates. Various philosophical writings on religion show an awareness of many 'gods', and sometimes a complete ignorance or blindness where certain religious beliefs are concerned. Again, let us ask what kind of ignorance this is? Intellectual ignorance? Religious ignorance? I cannot see how the two can be kept apart in this context. What a philosopher says about religion may show how much religion means to him, or whether, for him, it means anything at all. Once this is recognized one can see why philosophical accounts of religion will always be different. They will be different because people are different; they do not possess the same insights or the same beliefs. What would have to happen for a philosopher for whom religion was meaningless to come to see something of the meaning it has? What sort of change would have to occur?

In what sense would his understanding be increased? But, of course, to answer even these questions one is presupposing some understanding of religion in the person who asks them; one is taking for granted that the questioner can see what sort of change a change from faith to loss of faith or from lack of faith to faith is. It is all too evident from contemporary philosophy of religion that where philosophers are concerned, this presupposition cannot be made. In listening to many philosophers of religion, it would be natural to conclude that coming to see that there is a God after all, is like discovering that an object which one thought did not exist did in fact exist. If this conclusion were correct, in coming to see that there is a God one would increase one's knowledge of facts, but not one's understanding. The reality of God, as Norman Malcolm shows, cannot be construed in this way, and neither for that matter, as R. G. Collingwood illustrates, can the reality of the Devil. Malcolm stresses that if one wishes to give an account of belief in God, one must take the distinction between existence and eternity seriously. In my first paper, I try to show the kind of thing coming to see meaning in the eternal is, and in my second paper, I stress that it is the background of belief in an eternal God which marks the important distinction between morality and religion.

I do not claim that the contributors to this collection agree or would have agreed with my remarks in this introduction. But I did see as a common thread in all the papers, the centrality of the concept of understanding in relation to religion. Furthermore, the analyses of religious beliefs given by these philosophers seem to me to show what true religion is. I realize that many will be prepared to pounce on my use of 'true' in this context. What do I mean by 'true religion'? It seems to me that the question of truth here cannot be answered in isolation from the content of religious beliefs and philosophical accounts of them. For example, if someone tells me that the barbaric practices of the early Hebrews reflect true religion more than the Passion of Christ, I can only ask him to look again. This does not mean that I have some independent criterion of judgement, some so-called rational standard. What it does mean is that I know something of the Passion of Christ, and that what I know makes me want to call this divine. A request for a further justification is simply misunderstanding masquerading as rationality.

Whether one is satisfied with accounts of religious belief being given by philosophers will depend to a large extent on the kind of religious belief one has insight into. This being so, one might say, looking at what is said by most philosophers of religion today, 'Faith in God is as strong as ever', or 'God is dead', or 'Most people seem to be turning away from God'. No doubt this collection will provoke similar reactions. As I have tried to show, that is inevitable.

D. Z. PHILLIPS.

# I

# UNDERSTANDING A PRIMITIVE SOCIETY

## By Peter Winch

THIS essay will pursue further some questions raised in my book, *The Idea of a Social Science*.[1] That book was a general discussion of what is involved in the understanding of human social life. I shall here be concerned more specifically with certain issues connected with social anthropology. In the first part I raise certain difficulties about Professor E. E. Evans-Pritchard's approach in his classic, *Witchcraft, Oracles and Magic among the Azande*.[2] In the second part, I attempt to refute some criticisms recently made by Mr. Alasdair MacIntyre of Evans-Pritchard and myself, to criticize in their turn MacIntyre's positive remarks, and to offer some further reflections of my own on the concept of learning from the study of a primitive society.

## I. The Reality of Magic

Like many other primitive people, the African Azande hold beliefs that we cannot possibly share and engage in practices which it is peculiarly difficult for us to comprehend. They believe that certain of their members are witches, exercising a malignant occult influence on the lives of their fellows. They engage in rites to counteract witchcraft; they consult oracles and use magic medicines to protect themselves from harm.

An anthropologist studying such a people wishes to make those beliefs and practices intelligible to himself and his readers. This means presenting an account of them that will somehow satisfy the criteria of rationality demanded by the culture to which he and his readers belong: a culture whose conception of rationality is deeply affected by the achievements and methods of the sciences, and one which treats such things as a belief in magic or the practice of consulting oracles as almost a paradigm of the irrational. The strains inherent in this situation are very likely to lead the anthropologist to adopt the following posture: *We* know that Zande beliefs in the influence of witchcraft, the efficacy

---

[1] London and New York, 1958.　　　　[2] Oxford, 1937.

of magic medicines, the role of oracles in revealing what is going on and what is going to happen, are mistaken, illusory. Scientific methods of investigation have shown conclusively that there are no relations of cause and effect such as are implied by these beliefs and practices. All we can do then is to show how such a system of mistaken beliefs and inefficacious practices can maintain itself in the face of objections that seem to us so obvious.[3]

Now although Evans-Pritchard goes a very great deal further than most of his predecessors in trying to present the sense of the institutions he is discussing as it presents itself to the Azande themselves, still, the last paragraph does, I believe, pretty fairly describe the attitude he himself took at the time of writing this book. There is more than one remark to the effect that 'obviously there are no witches'; and he writes of the difficulty he found, during his field work with the Azande, in shaking off the 'unreason' on which Zande life is based and returning to a clear view of how things really are. This attitude is not an unsophisticated one but is based on a philosophical position ably developed in a series of papers published in the 1930's in the unhappily rather inaccessible *Bulletin of the Faculty of Arts* of the University of Egypt. Arguing against Lévy-Bruhl, Evans-Pritchard here rejects the idea that the scientific understanding of causes and effects which leads us to reject magical ideas is evidence of any superior intelligence on our part. Our scientific approach, he points out, is as much a function of our culture as is the magical approach of the 'savage' a function of his:

> The fact that we attribute rain to meteorological causes alone while savages believe that Gods or ghosts or magic can influence the rainfall is no evidence that our brains function differently from their brains. It does not show that we 'think more logically' than savages, at least not if this expression suggests some kind of hereditary psychic superiority. It is no sign of superior intelligence on my part that I attribute rain to physical causes. I did not come to this conclusion myself by observation and inference and have, in fact, little knowledge of the meteorological processes that lead to rain. I merely accept what everybody else in my society accepts, namely that rain is due to natural causes. This particular idea formed part of my culture long before I was born into it and little more was required of me than sufficient linguistic ability to learn it. Likewise a savage who

---

[3] At this point the anthropologist is very likely to start speaking of the 'social function' of the institution under examination. There are many important questions that should be raised about functional explanations and their relations to the issues discussed in this essay; but these questions cannot be pursued further here.

believes that under suitable natural and ritual conditions the rainfall can be influenced by use of appropriate magic is not on account of this belief to be considered of inferior intelligence. He did not build up this belief from his own observations and inferences but adopted it in the same way as he adopted the rest of his cultural heritage, namely, by being born into it. He and I are both thinking in patterns of thought provided for us by the societies in which we live.

It would be absurd to say that the savage is thinking mystically and that we are thinking scientifically about rainfall. In either case like mental processes are involved and, moreover, the content of thought is similarly derived. But we can say that the social content of our thought about rainfall is scientific, is in accord with objective facts, whereas the social content of savage thought about rainfall is unscientific since it is not in accord with reality and may also be mystical where it assumes the existence of supra-sensible forces.[4]

In a subsequent article on Pareto, Evans-Pritchard distinguishes between 'logical' and 'scientific'.

Scientific notions are those which accord with objective reality both with regard to the validity of their premisses and to the inferences drawn from their propositions. . . . Logical notions are those in which according to the rules of thought inferences would be true were the premisses true, the truth of the premisses being irrelevant. . . .
A pot has broken during firing. This is probably due to grit. Let us examine the pot and see if this is the cause. That is logical and scientific thought. Sickness is due to witchcraft. A man is sick. Let us consult the oracles to discover who is the witch responsible. That is logical and unscientific thought.[5]

I think that Evans-Pritchard is right in a great deal of what he says here, but wrong, and crucially wrong, in his attempt to characterize the scientific in terms of that which is 'in accord with objective reality'. Despite differences of emphasis and phraseology, Evans-Pritchard is in fact hereby put into the same metaphysical camp as Pareto: for both of them the conception of 'reality' must be regarded as intelligible and applicable *outside* the context of scientific reasoning itself, since it is that to which scientific notions do, and unscientific notions do not, have a relation. Evans-Pritchard, although he emphasizes that a member of scientific culture has a different conception of reality from that of a

[4] E. E. Evans-Pritchard, 'Lévy-Bruhl's Theory of Primitive Mentality', *Bulletin of the Faculty of Arts*, University of Egypt, 1934.
[5] 'Science and Sentiment', *Bulletin of the Faculty of Arts*, ibid., 1935.

Zande believer in magic, wants to go beyond merely registering this fact and making the differences explicit, and to say, finally, that the scientific conception agrees with what reality actually is like, whereas the magical conception does not.

It would be easy, at this point, to say simply that the difficulty arises from the use of the unwieldy and misleadingly comprehensive expression 'agreement with reality'; and in a sense this is true. But we should not lose sight of the fact that the idea that men's ideas and beliefs must be checkable by reference to something independent—some reality— is an important one. To abandon it is to plunge straight into an extreme Protagorean relativism, with all the paradoxes that involves. On the other hand great care is certainly necessary in fixing the precise role that this conception of the independently real does play in men's thought. There are two related points that I should like to make about it at this stage.

In the first place we should notice that the check of the independently real is not peculiar to science. The trouble is that the fascination science has for us makes it easy for us to adopt its scientific form as a paradigm against which to measure the intellectual respectability of other modes of discourse. Consider what God says to Job out of the whirlwind: 'Who is this that darkeneth counsel by words without knowledge? . . . Where wast thou when I laid the foundations of the earth? declare, if thou hast understanding. Who hath laid the measures thereof, if thou knowest? or who hath stretched the line upon it. . . . Shall he that contendeth with the Almighty instruct him? he that reproveth God, let him answer it.' Job is taken to task for having gone astray by having lost sight of the reality of God; this does not, of course, mean that Job has made any sort of theoretical mistake, which could be put right, perhaps, by means of an experiment.[6] God's reality is certainly independent of what any man may care to think, but what that reality amounts to can only be seen from the religious tradition in which the concept of God is used, and this use is very unlike the use of scientific concepts, say of theoretical entities. The point is that it is *within* the religious use of language that the conception of God's reality has its place, though, I repeat, this does not mean that it is at the mercy of what anyone cares to say; if this were so, God would have no reality.

---

[6] Indeed, one way of expressing the point of the story of Job is to say that in it Job is shown as going astray by being induced to make the reality and goodness of God contingent on what happens.

My second point follows from the first. Reality is not what gives language sense. What is real and what is unreal shows itself *in* the sense that language has. Further, both the distinction between the real and the unreal and the concept of agreement with reality themselves belong to our language. I will not say that they are concepts of the language like any other, since it is clear that they occupy a commanding, and in a sense a limiting, position there. We can imagine a language with no concept of, say, wetness, but hardly one in which there is no way of distinguishing the real from the unreal. Nevertheless we could not in fact distinguish the real from the unreal without understanding the way this distinction operates in the language. If then we wish to understand the significance of these concepts, we must examine the use they actually do have—*in* the language.

Evans-Pritchard, on the contrary, is trying to work with a conception of reality which is *not* determined by its actual use in language. He wants something against which that use can itself be appraised. But this is not possible; and no more possible in the case of scientific discourse than it is in any other. We may ask whether a particular scientific hypothesis agrees with reality and test this by observation and experiment. Given the experimental methods, and the established use of the theoretical terms entering into the hypothesis, then the question whether it holds or not is settled by reference to something independent of what I, or anybody else, care to think. But the general nature of the data revealed by the experiment can only be specified in terms of criteria built into the methods of experiment employed and these, in turn, make sense only to someone who is conversant with the kind of scientific activity within which they are employed. A scientific illiterate, asked to describe the results of an experiment which he 'observes' in an advanced physics laboratory, could not do so in terms relevant to the hypothesis being tested; and it is really only in such terms that we can sensibly speak of the 'results of the experiment' at all. What Evans-Pritchard wants to be able to say is that the criteria applied in scientific experimentation constitute a true link between our ideas and an independent reality, whereas those characteristic of other systems of thought—in particular, magical methods of thought—do not. It is evident that the expressions 'true link' and 'independent reality' in the previous sentence cannot themselves be explained by reference to the scientific universe of discourse, as this would beg the question. We have then to ask how, by reference to what established universe of discourse, the use of those expressions *is* to be explained; and it is clear that Evans-Pritchard has not answered this question.

Two questions arise out of what I have been saying. First, is it in fact the case that a primitive system of magic, like that of the Azande, constitutes a coherent universe of discourse like science, in terms of which an intelligible conception of reality and clear ways of deciding what beliefs are and are not in agreement with this reality can be discerned? Second, what are we to make of the possibility of understanding primitive social institutions, like Zande magic, if the situation is as I have outlined? I do not claim to be able to give a satisfactory answer to the second question. It raises some very important and fundamental issues about the nature of human social life, which require conceptions different from, and harder to elucidate than, those I have hitherto introduced. I shall offer some tentative remarks about these issues in the second part of this essay. At present I shall address myself to the first question.

It ought to be remarked here that an affirmative answer to my first question would not commit me to accepting as rational all beliefs couched in magical concepts or all procedures practiced in the name of such beliefs. This is no more necessary than is the corresponding proposition that all procedures 'justified' in the name of science are immune from rational criticism. A remark of Collingwood's is apposite here:

> Savages are no more exempt from human folly than civilized men, and are no doubt equally liable to the error of thinking that they, or the persons they regard as their superiors, can do what in fact cannot be done. But this error is not the essence of magic; it is a perversion of magic. And we should be careful how we attribute it to the people we call savages, who will one day rise up and testify against us.[7]

It is important to distinguish a system of magical beliefs and practices like that of the Azande, which is one of the principal foundations of their whole social life and, on the other hand, magical beliefs that might be held, and magical rites that might be practiced, by persons belonging to our own culture. These have to be understood rather differently. Evans-Pritchard is himself alluding to the difference in the following passage: 'When a Zande speaks of witchcraft he does not speak of it as we speak of the weird witchcraft of our own history. Witchcraft is to him a commonplace happening and he seldom passes a day without

[7] R. G. Collingwood, *Principles of Art*, Oxford (Galaxy Books), 1958, p. 67.

mentioning it. . . . To us witchcraft is something which haunted and disgusted our credulous forefathers. But the Zande expects to come across witchcraft at any time of the day or night. He would be just as surprised if he were not brought into daily contact with it as we would be if confronted by its appearance. To him there is nothing miraculous about it.'[8]

The difference is not merely one of degree of familiarity, however, although, perhaps, even this has more importance than might at first appear. Concepts of witchcraft and magic in our culture, at least since the advent of Christianity, have been parasitic on, and a perversion of other orthodox concepts, both religious and, increasingly, scientific. To take an obvious example, you could not understand what was involved in conducting a Black Mass, unless you were familiar with the conduct of a proper Mass and, therefore, with the whole complex of religious ideas from which the Mass draws its sense. Neither would you understand the relation between these without taking account of the fact that the Black practices are rejected as *irrational* (in the sense proper to religion) in the system of beliefs on which these practices are thus parasitic. Perhaps a similar relation holds between the con- temporary practice of astrology and astronomy and technology. It is impossible to keep a discussion of the rationality of Black Magic or of astrology within the bounds of concepts peculiar to them; they have an essential reference to something outside themselves. The position is like that which Socrates, in Plato's *Gorgias*, showed to be true of the Sophists' conception of rhetoric: namely, that it is parasitic on rational discourse in such a way that its irrational character can be shown in terms of this dependence. Hence, when we speak of such practices as 'superstitious', 'illusory', 'irrational', we have the weight of our culture behind us; and this is not just a matter of being on the side of the big battalions, because those beliefs and practices belong to, and derive such sense as they seem to have, from that same culture. This enables us to show that the sense is only apparent, in terms which are culturally relevant.

It is evident that our relation to Zande magic is quite different. If we wish to understand it, we must seek a foothold elsewhere. And while there may well be room for the use of such critical expressions as 'superstition' and 'irrationality', the kind of rationality with which such terms might be used to point a contrast remains to be elucidated.

8 *Witchcraft, Oracles and Magic among the Azande*, p. 64.

The remarks I shall make in Part II will have a more positive bearing on this issue. In the rest of this Part, I shall develop in more detail my criticisms of Evans-Pritchard's approach to the Azande.

Early in this book he defines certain categories in terms of which his descriptions of Zande customs are couched.

MYSTICAL NOTIONS . . . are patterns of thought that attribute to phenomena supra-sensible qualities which, or part of which, are not derived from observation or cannot be logically inferred from it, *and which they do not possess.*[9] COMMON-SENSE NOTIONS . . . attribute to phenomena only what men observe in them or what can logically be inferred from observation. So long as a notion does not assert something which has not been observed, it is not classed as mystical even though it is mistaken on account of incomplete observation. . . . SCIENTIFIC NOTIONS. Science has developed out of common-sense but is far more methodical and has better techniques of observation and reasoning. Common sense uses experience and rules of thumb. Science uses experiment and rules of Logic. . . . *Our body of scientific knowledge and Logic are the sole arbiters of what are mystical, common sense, and scientific notions.* Their judgments are never absolute. RITUAL BEHAVIOUR. Any behaviour that is accounted for by mystical notions. *There is no objective nexus* between the behaviour and the event it is intended to cause. Such behaviour is usually intelligible to us only when we know the mystical notions associated with it. EMPIRICAL BEHAVIOUR. Any behaviour that is accounted for by common-sense notions.[10]

It will be seen from the phrases which I have italicized that Evans-Pritchard is doing more here than just defining certain terms for his own use. Certain metaphysical claims are embodied in the definitions: identical in substance with the claims embodied in Pareto's way of distinguishing between 'logical' and 'non-logical' conduct.[11] There is a very clear implication that those who use mystical notions and perform ritual behaviour are making some sort of mistake, detectable with the aid of science and logic. I shall now examine more closely some of the institutions described by Evans-Pritchard to determine how far his claims are justified.

*Witchcraft* is a power possessed by certain individuals to harm other individuals by 'mystical' means. Its basis is an inherited organic condition, 'witchcraft-substance' and it does not involve any special magical

---

[9] The italics are mine throughout this quotation.    [10] Op. cit., p. 12.
[11] For further criticism of Pareto see Peter Winch, *The Idea of a Social Science,* pp. 95–111.

ritual or medicine. It is constantly appealed to by Azande when they are afflicted by misfortune, not so as to exclude explanation in terms of natural causes, which Azande are perfectly able to offer themselves within the limits of their not inconsiderable natural knowledge, but so as to supplement such explanations. 'Witchcraft explains *why*[12] events are harmful to man and not *how*[12] they happen. A Zande perceives how they happen just as we do. He does not see a witch charge a man but an elephant. He does not see a witch push over the granary, but termites gnawing away its supports. He does not see a psychical flame igniting thatch, but an ordinary lighted bundle of straw. His perception of how events occur is as clear as our own.'[13]

The most important way of detecting the influence of witchcraft and of identifying witches is by the revelations of oracles, of which in turn the most important is the 'poison oracle'. This name, though convenient, is significantly misleading insofar as, according to Evans-Pritchard, Azande do not have our concept of a poison and do not think of, or behave toward, *benge*—the substance administered in the consultation of the oracle—as we do of and toward poisons. The gathering, preparation, and administering of *benge* is hedged with ritual and strict taboos. At an oracular consultation *benge* is administered to a fowl, while a question is asked in a form permitting a yes or no answer. The fowl's death or survival is specified beforehand as giving the answer 'yes' or 'no'. The answer is then checked by administering *benge* to another fowl and asking the question the other way round. 'Is Prince Ndoruma responsible for placing bad medicines in the roof of my hut? The fowl DIES giving the answer "Yes". . . . Did the oracle speak truly when it said that Ndoruma was responsible? The fowl SURVIVES giving the answer "Yes".' The poison oracle is all-pervasive in Zande life and all steps of any importance in a person's life are settled by reference to it.

A Zande would be utterly lost and bewildered without his oracle. The mainstay of his life would be lacking. It is rather as if an engineer, in our society, were to be asked to build a bridge without mathematical calculation, or a military commander to mount an extensive co-ordinated attack without the use of clocks. These analogies are mine, but a reader may well think that they beg the question at issue. For, he may argue, the Zande practice of consulting the oracle, unlike my

[12] Evans-Pritchard's italics.  [13] Op. cit., p. 72.

technological and military examples, is completely unintelligible and rests on an obvious illusion. I shall now consider this objection.

First I must emphasize that I have so far done little more than note the *fact*, conclusively established by Evans-Pritchard, that the Azande *do* in fact conduct their affairs to their own satisfaction in this way and are at a loss when forced to abandon the practice—when, for instance, they fall into the hands of European courts. It is worth remarking too that Evans-Pritchard himself ran his household in the same way during his field researches and says: 'I found this as satisfactory a way of running my home and affairs as any other I know of.'

Further, I would ask in my turn: *to whom* is the practice alleged to be unintelligible? Certainly it is difficult for us to understand what the Azande are about when they consult their oracles; but it might seem just as incredible to them that the engineer's motions with his slide rule could have any connection with the stability of his bridge. But this riposte of course misses the intention behind the objection, which was not directed to the question whether anyone in fact understands, or claims to understand, what is going on, but rather whether what is going on actually does make sense: i.e., in itself. And it may seem obvious that Zande beliefs in witchcraft and oracles cannot make any sense, however satisfied the Azande may be with them.

What criteria have we for saying that something does, or does not, make sense? A partial answer is that a set of beliefs and practices cannot make sense insofar as they involve contradictions. Now it appears that contradictions are bound to arise in at least two ways in the consultation of the oracle. On the one hand two oracular pronouncements may contradict each other; and on the other hand a self-consistent oracular pronouncement may be contradicted by future experience. I shall examine each of these apparent possibilities in turn.

Of course, it does happen often that the oracle first says 'yes' and then 'no' to the same question. This does not convince a Zande of the futility of the whole operation of consulting oracles: obviously, it cannot, since otherwise the practice could hardly have developed and maintained itself at all. Various explanations may be offered, whose possibility, it is important to notice, is built into the whole network of Zande beliefs and may, therefore, be regarded as belonging to the concept of an oracle. It may be said, for instance, that bad *benge* is being used; that the operator of the oracle is ritually unclean; that the oracle is being itself influenced by witchcraft or sorcery; or it may be that the oracle is showing that the question cannot be answered straightforwardly in its present form, as with 'Have you stopped beating your wife yet?' There are various ways in which the behaviour of the fowl under the influence of *benge* may be ingeniously interpreted by those wise in the ways of the poison oracle. We might compare this situation perhaps with the interpretation of dreams.

In the other type of case: where an internally consistent oracular revelation is apparently contradicted by subsequent experience, the situation may be dealt with in a similar way, by references to the influence of witchcraft, ritual uncleanliness, and so on. But there is another important consideration we must take into account here too. The chief function of oracles is to reveal the presence of 'mystical' forces—I use Evans-Pritchard's term without committing myself to his denial that such forces really exist. Now though there are indeed ways of determining whether or not mystical forces are operating, these ways do not correspond to what we understand by 'empirical' confirmation or refutation. This indeed is a tautology, since such differences in 'confirmatory' procedures are the main criteria for classifying something as a mystical force in the first place. Here we have one reason why the possibilities of 'refutation by experience' are very much fewer than might at first sight be supposed.

There is also another closely connected reason. The spirit in which oracles are consulted is very unlike that in which a scientist makes experiments. Oracular revelations are not treated as hypotheses and, since their sense derives from the way they are treated in their context, they therefore *are not* hypotheses. They are not a matter of intellectual interest but the main way in which Azande decide how they should act. If the oracle reveals that a proposed course of action is fraught with mystical dangers from witchcraft or sorcery, that course of action will not be carried out; and then the question of refutation or confirmation just does not arise. We might say that the revelation has the logical status of an unfulfilled hypothetical, were it not that the context in which this logical term is generally used may again suggest a misleadingly close analogy with scientific hypotheses.

I do not think that Evans-Pritchard would have disagreed with what I have said so far. Indeed, the following comment is on very similar lines:

Azande observe the action of the poison oracle as we observe it, but their observations are always subordinated to their beliefs and are incorporated into their beliefs and made to explain them and justify them. Let the reader consider any argument that would utterly demolish all Zande claims for the power of the oracle. If it were translated into Zande modes of thought it would serve to support their entire structure of belief. For their mystical notions are eminently coherent, being interrelated by a network of logical ties, and are so ordered that they never too crudely contradict sensory experience but, instead, experience seems to justify them. The Zande is immersed in a sea of mystical notions, and if he speaks about his poison oracle he must speak in a mystical idiom.[14]

To locate the point at which the important philosophical issue does arise, I shall offer a parody, composed by changing round one or two expressions in the foregoing quotation.

Europeans observe the action of the poison oracle just as Azande observe it, but their observations are always subordinated to their beliefs and are incorporated into their beliefs and made to explain them and justify them. Let a Zande consider any argument that would utterly refute all European scepticism about the power of the oracle. If it were translated into European modes of thought it would serve to support their entire structure of belief. For their scientific notions are eminently coherent, being interrelated by a network of logical ties, and are so ordered that they never too crudely contradict mystical experience but, instead, experience seems to justify them. The European is immersed in a sea of scientific notions, and if he speaks about the Zande poison oracle he must speak in a scientific idiom.

Perhaps this too would be acceptable to Evans-Pritchard. But it is clear from other remarks in the book to which I have alluded, that at the time of writing it he would have wished to add: and the European is right and the Zande wrong. This addition I regard as illegitimate and my reasons for so thinking take us to the heart of the matter.

It may be illuminating at this point to compare the disagreement between Evans-Pritchard and me to that between the Wittgenstein of the *Philosophical Investigations* and his earlier *alter ego* of the *Tractatus Logico-Philosophicus*. In the *Tractatus* Wittgenstein sought 'the general form of propositions': what made propositions possible. He said that this general form is: 'This is how things are'; the proposition was an articulated model, consisting of elements standing in a definite relation to each other. The proposition was true when there existed a corresponding arrangement of elements in reality. The proposition was

[14] Ibid., p. 319.

capable of saying something because of the identity of structure, of logical form, in the proposition and in reality.

By the time Wittgenstein composed the *Investigations* he had come to reject the whole idea that there must be a general form of propositions. He emphasized the indefinite number of different uses that language may have and tried to show that these different uses neither need, nor in fact do, all have something in common, in the sense intended in the *Tractatus*. He also tried to show that what counts as 'agreement or disagreement with reality' takes on as many different forms as there are different uses of language and cannot, therefore, be taken as given *prior* to the detailed investigation of the use that is in question.

The *Tractatus* contains a remark strikingly like something that Evans-Pritchard says.

*The limits of my language mean the limits of my world.* Logic fills the world: the limits of the world are also its limits. We cannot therefore say in logic: This and this there is in the world, and that there is not.

For that would apparently presuppose that we exclude certain possibilities, and this cannot be the case since otherwise logic must get outside the limits of the world: that is, if it could consider these limits from the other side also.[15]

Evans-Pritchard discusses the phenomena of belief and scepticism, as they appear in Zande life. There *is* certainly widespread scepticism about certain things, for instance, about some of the powers claimed by witchdoctors or about the efficacy of certain magic medicines. But, he points out, such scepticism does not begin to overturn the mystical way of thinking, since it is necessarily expressed in terms belonging to that way of thinking.

In this web of belief every strand depends on every other strand, and a Zande cannot get outside its meshes because this is the only world he knows. The web is not an external structure in which he is enclosed. It is the texture of his thought and he cannot think that his thought is wrong.[16]

Wittgenstein and Evans-Pritchard are concerned here with much the same problem, though the difference in the directions from which they approach it is important too. Wittgenstein, at the time of the *Tractatus*, spoke of 'language', as if all language is fundamentally of the

15 Wittgenstein, *Tractatus Logico-Philosophicus*, paras. 5. 6–5. 61.
16 Evans-Pritchard, op. cit., p. 194.

same kind and must have the same kind of 'relation to reality'; but
Evans-Pritchard is confronted by two languages which he recognizes
as fundamentally different in kind, such that much of what may be
expressed in the one has no possible counterpart in the other. One
might, therefore, have expected this to lead to a position closer to that
of the *Philosophical Investigations* than to that of the *Tractatus*. Evans-
Pritchard is not content with elucidating the differences in the two
concepts of reality involved; he wants to go further and say: our
concept of reality is the correct one, the Azande are mistaken. But the
difficulty is to see what 'correct' and 'mistaken' can mean in this context.

Let me return to the subject of contradictions. I have already noted
that many contradictions we might expect to appear in fact do not in
the context of Zande thought, where provision is made for avoiding
them. But there are some situations of which this does not seem to be
true, where what appear to us as obvious contradictions are left where
they are, apparently unresolved. Perhaps this may be the foothold we
are looking for, from which we can appraise the 'correctness' of the
Zande system.[17]

Consider Zande notions about the inheritance of witchcraft. I have
spoken so far only of the role of oracles in establishing whether or not
someone is a witch. But there is a further and, as we might think, more
'direct' method of doing this, namely by post-mortem examination of
a suspect's intestines for 'witchcraft-substance'. This may be arranged
by his family after his death in an attempt to clear the family name of
the imputation of witchcraft. Evans-Pritchard remarks: 'To our minds
it appears evident that if a man is proven a witch the whole of his
clan are *ipso facto* witches, since the Zande clan is a group of persons
related biologically to one another through the male line. Azande see
the sense of this argument but they do not accept its conclusions, and
it would involve the whole notion of witchcraft in contradiction were
they to do so.'[18] Contradiction would presumably arise because a few
positive results of post-mortem examinations, scattered among all the
clans, would very soon prove that everybody was a witch, and a few
negative results, scattered among the same clans, would prove that
nobody was a witch. Though, in particular situations, individual
Azande may avoid personal implications arising out of the presence of
witchcraft-substance in deceased relatives, by imputations of bastardy
and similar devices, this would not be enough to save the generally

---

[17] I shall discuss this point in a more general way in Part II.        [18] Ibid., p. 24.

contradictory situation I have sketched. Evans-Pritchard comments: 'Azande do not perceive the contradiction as we perceive it because they have no theoretical interest in the subject, and those situations in which they express their belief in witchcraft do not force the problem upon them.'[19]

It might now appear as though we had clear grounds for speaking of the superior rationality of European over Zande thought, insofar as the latter involves a contradiction which it makes no attempt to remove and does not even recognize: one, however, which is recognizable as such in the context of European ways of thinking. But does Zande thought on this matter really involve a contradiction? It appears from Evans-Pritchard's account that Azande do not press their ways of thinking about witches to a point at which they would be involved in contradictions.

Someone may now want to say that the irrationality of the Azande in relation to witchcraft shows itself in the fact that they do not press their thought about it 'to its logical conclusion'. To appraise this point we must consider whether the conclusion we are trying to force on them is indeed a logical one; or perhaps better, whether someone who does press this conclusion is being more rational than the Azande, who do not. Some light is thrown on this question by Wittgenstein's discussion of a game,

> such that whoever begins can always win by a particular simple trick. But this has not been realized—so it is a game. Now someone draws our attention to it—and it stops being a game.
>
> What turn can I give this, to make it clear to myself?—For I want to say: "and it stops being a game"—not: "and now we see that it wasn't a game."
>
> That means, I want to say, it can also be taken like this: the other man did not *draw our attention* to anything; he taught us a different game in place of our own. But how can the new game have made the old one obsolete? We now see something different, and can no longer naively go on playing.
>
> On the one hand the game consisted in our actions (our play) on the board; and these actions I could perform as well now as before. But on the other hand it was essential to the game that I blindly tried to win; and now I can no longer do that.[20]

19 Ibid., p. 25.
20 L. Wittgenstein, *Remarks on the Foundations of Mathematics*, Pt. II, § 77. Wittgenstein's whole discussion of 'contradiction' in mathematics is directly relevant to the point I am discussing.

There are obviously considerable analogies between Wittgenstein's example and the situation we are considering. But there is an equally important difference. Both Wittgenstein's games: the old one without the trick that enables the starter to win and the new one with the trick, are in an important sense on the same level. They are both *games*, in the form of a contest where the aim of a player is to beat his opponent by the exercise of skill. The new trick makes this situation impossible and this is why it makes the old game obsolete. To be sure, the situation could be saved in a way by introducing a new rule, forbidding the use by the starter of the trick which would ensure his victory. But our intellectual habits are such as to make us unhappy about the artificiality of such a device, rather as logicians have been unhappy about the introduction of a Theory of Types as a device for avoiding Russell's paradoxes. It is noteworthy in my last quotation from Evans-Pritchard, however, that the Azande, when the possibility of this contradiction about the inheritance of witchcraft is pointed out to them, do *not* then come to regard their old beliefs about witchcraft as obsolete. 'They have no theoretical interest in the subject.' This suggests strongly that the context from which the suggestion about the contradiction is made, the context of our scientific culture, is not on the same level as the context in which the beliefs about witchcraft operate. Zande notions of witchcraft do not constitute a theoretical system in terms of which Azande try to gain a quasi-scientific understanding of the world.[21] This in its turn suggests that it is the European, obsessed with pressing Zande thought where it would not naturally go—to a contradiction—who is guilty of misunderstanding, not the Zande. The European is in fact committing a category-mistake.

Something else is also suggested by this discussion: the forms in which rationality expresses itself in the culture of a human society cannot be elucidated *simply* in terms of the logical coherence of the rules according to which activities are carried out in that society. For, as we have seen, there comes a point where we are not even in a position to determine what is and what is not coherent in such a context of rules, without raising questions about the point which following those rules has in the society. No doubt it was a realization of this fact which led Evans-Pritchard to appeal to a residual 'correspondence with reality' in distinguishing between 'mystical' and 'scientific' notions.

---

[21] Notice that I have *not* said that Azande conceptions of witchcraft have nothing to do with understanding the world at all. The point is that a different form of the concept of understanding is involved here.

The conception of reality is indeed indispensable to any understanding of the point of a way of life. But it is not a conception which can be explicated as Evans-Pritchard tries to explicate it, in terms of what science reveals to be the case; for a form of the conception of reality must already be presupposed before we can make any sense of the expression 'what science reveals to be the case'.

## II. OUR STANDARDS AND THEIRS

In Part I, I attempted, by analysing a particular case, to criticize by implication a particular view of how we can understand a primitive institution. In this Part I shall have two aims. First, I shall examine in a more formal way a general philosophical argument, which attempts to show that the approach I have been criticizing is in principle the right one. This argument has been advanced by Mr. Alasdair MacIntyre in two places: (a) in a paper entitled Is Understanding Religion Compatible with Believing? read to the Sesquicentennial Seminar of the Princeton Theological Seminar in 1962.[22] (b) In a contribution to Philosophy, Politics and Society (Second Series),[23] entitled A Mistake about Causality in Social Science. Next, I shall make some slightly more positive suggestions about how to overcome the difficulty from which I started: how to make intelligible in our terms institutions belonging to a primitive culture, whose standards of rationality and intelligibility are apparently quite at odds with our own.

The relation between MacIntyre, Evans-Pritchard, and myself is a complicated one. MacIntyre takes Evans-Pritchard's later book, Nuer Religion, as an application of a point of view like mine in The Idea of a Social Science; he regards it as an object lesson in the absurd results to which such a position leads, when applied in practice. My own criticisms of Evans-Pritchard, on the other hand, have come from precisely the opposite direction. I have tried to show that Evans-Pritchard did not at the time of writing The Azande agree with me enough; that he did not take seriously enough the idea that the concepts used by primitive peoples can only be interpreted in the context of the way of life of those peoples. Thus I have in effect argued that Evans-Pritchard's account of the Azande is unsatisfactory precisely to the extent that he agrees with MacIntyre and not me.

[22] To be published along with other papers, by the Macmillan Company. [Faith and the Philosophers, ed. John Hick—Ed.]
[23] Edited by Peter Laslett and W. G. Runciman, Oxford, 1962.

C

The best point at which to start considering McIntyre's position is that at which he agrees with me—in emphasizing the importance of possibilities of *description* for the concept of human action. An agent's action 'is identified fundamentally as what it is by the description under which he deems it to fall'. Since, further, descriptions must be intelligible to other people, an action 'must fall under some description which is socially recognizable as the description of an action'.[24] 'To identify the limits of social action in a given period', therefore, 'is to identify the stock of descriptions current in that age'.[25] MacIntyre correctly points out that descriptions do not exist in isolation, but occur 'as constituents of beliefs, speculations and projects'. As these in turn 'are continually criticized, modified, rejected, or improved, the stock of descriptions changes. The changes in human action are thus intimately linked to the thread of rational criticism in human history.'

This notion of rational criticism, MacIntyre points out, requires the notion of choice between alternatives, to explain which 'is a matter of making clear what the agent's criterion was and why he made use of this criterion rather than another and to explain why the use of this criterion appears rational to those who invoke it'.[26] Hence 'in explaining the rules and conventions to which action in a given social order conform (*sic*) we cannot omit reference to the rationality or otherwise of those rules and conventions'. Further, 'the beginning of an explanation of why certain criteria are taken to be rational in some societies is that they *are* rational. And since this has to enter into our explanation we cannot explain social behaviour independently of our own norms of rationality.'

I turn now to criticism of this argument. Consider first MacIntyre's account of changes in an existing 'stock' of available descriptions of actions. How does a candidate for inclusion *qualify* for admission to the stock? Unless there are limits, all MacIntyre's talk about possibilities of description circumscribing possibilities of action becomes nugatory, for there would be nothing to stop anybody inventing some arbitrary verbal expression, applying it to some arbitrary bodily movement, and thus adding that expression to the stock of available descriptions. But of course the new description must be an *intelligible* one. Certainly, its intelligibility cannot be decided by whether or not it belongs to an *existing* stock of descriptions, since this would rule out precisely what is being discussed: the addition of *new* descriptions to the stock. 'What

[24] Ibid., p. 58          [25] Ibid., p. 60.          [26] Ibid., p. 61.

can intelligibly be said' is not equivalent to 'what has been intelligibly said', or it would never be possible to say anything new. *Mutatis mutandis* it would never be possible to *do* anything new. Nevertheless the intelligibility of anything new said or done does depend in a certain way on what already has been said or done and understood. The crux of this problem lies in how we are to understand that 'in a certain way'.

In *Is Understanding Religion Compatible with Believing?* MacIntyre asserts that the development through criticism of the standards of intelligibility current in a society is ruled out by my earlier account (in *The Idea of a Social Science*) of the origin in social institutions themselves of such standards. I shall not now repeat my earlier argument, but simply point out that I did, in various passages,[27] emphasize the *open* character of the 'rules' which I spoke of in connection with social institutions: i.e. the fact that in changing social situations, reasoned decisions have to be made about what is to count as 'going on in the same way'. MacIntyre's failure to come to terms with this point creates difficulties for him precisely analogous to those which he mistakenly attributes to my account.

It is a corollary of his argument up to this point, as well as being intrinsically evident, that a new description of action must be intelligible to the members of the society in which it is introduced. On my view the point is that what determines this is the further development of rules and principles already implicit in the previous ways of acting and talking. To be emphasized are not the actual members of any 'stock' of descriptions; but the *grammar* which they express. It is through this that we understand their structure and sense, their mutual relations, and the sense of new ways of talking and acting that may be introduced. These new ways of talking and acting may very well at the same time involve modifications in the grammar, but we can only speak thus if the new grammar is (to its users) intelligibly related to the old.

But what of the intelligibility of such changes to observers from another society with a different culture and different standards of intelligibility? MacIntyre urges that such observers must make clear 'what the agent's criterion was and why he made use of this criterion rather than another and why the use of this criterion appears rational to those who invoke it'. Since what is at issue is the precise relation between the concepts of rationality current in these different societies it is obviously of first importance to be clear about *whose* concept of

[27] Pp. 57–65; 91–94; 121–123.

rationality is being alluded to in this quotation. It seems that it must be that which is current in the society in which the criterion is invoked. Something can appear rational to someone only in terms of *his* understanding of what is and is not rational. If *our* concept of rationality is a different one from his, then it makes no sense to say that anything either does or does not appear rational to *him* in *our* sense.

When MacIntyre goes on to say that the observer 'cannot omit reference to the rationality or otherwise of those rules and conventions' followed by the alient agent, whose concept of rationality is now in question: ours or the agent's? Since the observer must be understood now as addressing himself to members of his own society, it seems that the reference must here be to the concept of rationality current in the observer's society. Thus there is a *non sequitur* in the movement from the first to the second of the passages just quoted.

MacIntyre's thought here and in what immediately follows, seems to be this. The explanation of why, in Society S, certain actions are taken to be rational, has got to be an explanation for *us*; so it must be in terms of concepts intelligible to us. If then, in the explanation, we say that in fact those criteria *are* rational, we must be using the word '*rational*' in *our* sense. For this explanation would require that we had previously carried out an independent investigation into the actual rationality or otherwise of those criteria, and we could do this only in terms of an understood concept of rationality—*our* understood concept of rationality. The explanation would run: members of Society S have seen to be the case something that we know to be the case. If 'what is seen to be the case' is common to us and them, it must be referred to under the same concept for each of us.

But obviously this explanation is not open to us. For we start from the position that standards of rationality in different societies do not always coincide; from the possibility, therefore, that the standards of rationality current in S are different from our own. So we cannot assume that it will make sense to speak of members of S as discovering something which we have also discovered; such discovery presupposes initial conceptual agreement.

Part of the trouble lies in MacIntyre's use of the expression, 'the rationality of criteria', which he does not explain. In the present context to speak thus is to cloak the real problem, since what we are concerned with are differences in *criteria of rationality*. MacIntyre seems to be saying that certain standards are taken as criteria of rationality because they *are* criteria of rationality. But whose?

There are similar confusions in MacIntyre's other paper: *Is Understanding Religion Compatible with Believing?* There he argues that when we detect an internal incoherence in the standards of intelligiblity current in an alien society and try to show why this does not appear, or is made tolerable to that society's members, 'we have already invoked our standards'. In what sense is this true? Insofar as *we* 'detect' and 'show' something, obviously we do so in a sense intelligible to us; so we are limited by what *counts* (for us) as 'detecting', 'showing' something. Further, it may well be that the interest in showing and detecting such things is peculiar to our society—that we are doing something in which members of the studied society exhibit no interest, because the institutions in which such an interest could develop are lacking. Perhaps too the pursuit of that interest in our society has led to the development of techniques of inquiry and modes of argument which again are not to be found in the life of the studied society. But it cannot be guaranteed in advance that the methods and techniques we have used in the past— e.g., in elucidating the logical structure of arguments in our own language and culture—are going to be equally fruitful in this new context. They will perhaps need to be extended and modified. No doubt, if they are to have a logical relation to our previous forms of investigation, the new techniques will have to be recognizably continuous with previously used ones. But they must also so extend our conception of intelligibility as to make it possible for us to see what intelligibility amounts to in the life of the society we are investigating.

The task MacIntyre says we must undertake is to make intelligible (*a*) (to us) why it is that members of *S* think that certain of their practices are intelligible (*b*) (to them), when in fact they are not. I have introduced differentiating letters into my two uses of 'intelligible', to mark the complexity that MacIntyre's way of stating the position does not bring out: the fact that we are dealing with two different senses of the word 'intelligible'. The relation between these is precisely the question at issue. MacIntyre's task is not like that of making intelligible a natural phenomenon, where we are limited only by what counts as intelligibility for us. We must somehow bring *S*'s conception of intelligibility (*b*) into (intelligible!) relation with our own conception of intelligibility (*a*). That is, we have to create a new unity for the concept of intelligibility, having a certain relation to our old one and perhaps requiring a considerable realignment of our categories. We are not seeking a state in which things will appear to us just as they do to members of $S$, and perhaps such a state is unattainable anyway. But we *are* seeking a way of looking at things which goes beyond our previous way in that it has in some way taken account of and incorporated the other way that members of $S$ have of looking at things. Seriously to study another way of life is necessarily to seek to extend our own—not simply to bring the other way within the already existing boundaries of our own, because the point about the latter in their present form, is that they *ex hypothesi* exclude that other.

There is a dimension to the notions of rationality and intelligibility which may make it easier to grasp the possibility of such an extension. I do not think that MacIntyre takes sufficient account of this dimension and, indeed, the way he talks about 'norms of rationality' obscures it. Rationality is not *just* a concept *in* a language like any other; it is this too, for, like any other concept it must be circumscribed by an established use: a use, that is, established in the language. But I think it is not a concept which a language may, as a matter of fact, have and equally well may not have, as is, for instance, the concept of politeness. It is a concept necessary to the existence of any language: to say of a society that it has a language[28] is also to say that it has a concept of rationality. There need not perhaps be any *word* functioning in its language as 'rational' does in ours, but at least there must be features of its members' use of language analogous to those features of *our* use of language which are connected with our use of the word 'rational'. Where there is language it must make a difference what is said and this is only possible where the saying of one thing rules out, on pain of failure to communicate, the saying of something else. So in one sense MacIntyre is right in saying that we have already invoked our concept of rationality in saying of a collection of people that they constitute a society with a language: in the sense, namely, that we imply formal analogies between their behaviour and that behaviour in our society which we refer to in distinguishing between rationality and irrationality. This, however, is so far to say nothing about what in particular constitutes rational behaviour in that society; that would require more particular knowledge about the norms they appeal to in living their lives. In other words, it is not so much a matter of invoking 'our own norms of rationality' as of invoking our notion of rationality in speaking of their behaviour in terms of 'conformity to norms'. But how precisely this notion is to be applied to them will depend on our

[28] I shall not discuss here what justifies us in saying *this* in the first place.

reading of their conformity to norms—what counts for them as conformity and what does not.

Earlier I criticized MacIntyre's conception of a 'stock of available descriptions'. Similar criticisms apply to his talk about 'our norms of rationality', if these norms are taken as forming some finite set. Certainly we learn to think, speak, and act rationally *through* being trained to adhere to particular norms. But having learned to speak, etc., rationally does not *consist* in having been trained to follow those norms; to suppose that would be to overlook the importance of the phrase 'and so on' in any description of what someone who follows norms does. We must, if you like, be open to new possibilities of what could be invoked and accepted under the rubric of 'rationality'— possibilities which are perhaps suggested and limited by what we have hitherto so accepted, but not uniquely determined thereby.

This point can be applied to the possibilities of our grasping forms of rationality different from ours in an alien culture. First, as I have indicated, these possibilities are limited by certain formal requirements centering round the demand for consistency. But these formal requirements tell us nothing about what in particular is to *count* as consistency, just as the rules of the propositional calculus limit, but do not themselves determine what are to be proper values of $p$, $q$, etc. We can only determine this by investigating the wider context of the life in which the activities in question are carried on. This investigation will take us beyond merely specifying the rules governing the carrying out of those activities. For, as MacIntyre quite rightly says, to note that certain rules are followed is so far to say nothing about the *point* of the rules; it is not even to decide whether or not they have a point at all.

MacIntyre's recipe for deciding this is that 'in bringing out this feature of the case one shows also whether the use of this concept is or is not a possible one for people who have the standards of intelligibility in speech and action which we have'.[29] It is important to notice that his argument, contrary to what he supposes, does not in fact show that our *own* standards of rationality occupy a peculiarly central position. The appearance to the contrary is an optical illusion engendered by the fact that MacIntyre's case has been advanced in the English language and in the context of 20th century European culture. But a formally similar argument could be advanced in *any* language containing concepts playing a similar role in that language to those of 'intelligibility'

[29] *Is Understanding Religion Compatible with Believing?*

and 'rationality' in ours. This shows that, so far from overcoming relativism, as he claims, MacIntyre himself falls into an extreme form of it. He disguises this from himself by committing the very error of which, wrongly as I have tried to show, he accuses me: the error of overlooking the fact that 'criteria and concepts have a history'. While he emphasizes this point when he is dealing with the concepts and criteria governing action in particular social contexts, he forgets it when he comes to talk of the *criticism* of such criteria. Do not the criteria appealed to in the criticism of existing institutions equally have a history? And in whose society do they have that history? MacIntyre's implicit answer is that it is in ours; but if we are to speak of difficulties and incoherencies appearing and being detected in the way certain practices have hitherto been carried on in a society, surely this can only be understood in connection with problems arising *in* the carrying on of the activity. Outside that context we could not begin to grasp what was problematical.

Let me return to the Azande and consider something which Mac-Intyre says about them, intended to support the position I am criticizing.

The Azande believe that the performance of certain rites in due form affects their common welfare; this belief cannot in fact be refuted. For they also believe that if the rites are ineffective it is because someone present at them had evil thoughts. Since this is always possible, there is never a year when it is unavoidable for them to admit that the rites were duly performed, but they did not thrive. Now the belief of the Azande is not unfalsifiable in principle (we know perfectly well what would falsify it—the conjunction of the rite, no evil thoughts and disasters). But in fact it cannot be falsified. Does this belief stand in need of rational criticism? And if so by what standards? It seems to me that one could only hold the belief of the Azande rational *in the absence of* any practice of science and technology in which criteria of effectiveness, ineffectiveness and kindred notions had been built up. But to say this is to recognize the appropriateness of scientific criteria of judgment from our standpoint. The Azande do not intend their belief either as a piece of science or as a piece of non-science. They do not possess these categories. It is only *post eventum*, in the light of later and more sophisticated understanding that their belief and concepts can be classified and evaluated at all.[30]

Now in one sense classification and evaluation of Zande beliefs and concepts does require 'a more sophisticated understanding' than is

[30] Ibid.

found in Zande culture; for the sort of classification and evaluation that are here in question are sophisticated philosophical activities. But this is not to say that Zande forms of life are to be classified and evaluated in the way MacIntyre asserts: in terms of certain specific forms of life to be found in our culture, according as they do or do not measure up to what is required within these. MacIntyre confuses the sophistication of the interest in classification with the sophistication of the concepts employed in our classificatory work. It is of interest to us to understand how Zande magic is related to science; the concept of such a comparison is a very sophisticated one; but this does not mean that we have to see the unsophisticated Zande practice in the light of more sophisticated practices in our own culture, like science—as perhaps a more primitive form of it. MacIntyre criticizes, justly, Sir James Frazer for having imposed the image of his own culture on more primitive ones; but that is exactly what MacIntyre himself is doing here. It is extremely difficult for a sophisticated member of a sophisticated society to grasp a very simple and primitive form of life: in a way he must jettison his sophistication, a process which is itself perhaps the ultimate in sophistication. Or, rather, the distinction between sophistication and simplicity becomes unhelpful at this point.

It may be true, as MacIntyre says, that the Azande do not have the categories of science and non-science. But Evans-Pritchard's account shows that they do have a fairly clear working distinction between the technical and the magical. It is neither here nor there that individual Azande may sometimes confuse the categories, for such confusions may take place in any culture. A much more important fact to emphasize is that *we* do not initially have a category that looks at all like the Zande category of magic. Since it is we who want to understand the Zande category, it appears that the onus is on us to extend our understanding so as to make room for the Zande category, rather than to insist on seeing it in terms of our own ready-made distinction between science and non-science. Certainly the sort of understanding we seek requires that we see the Zande category in relation to our own already understood categories. But this neither means that it is right to 'evaluate' magic in terms of criteria belonging to those other categories; nor does it give any clue as to *which* of our existing categories of thought will provide the best point of reference from which we can understand the point of the Zande practices.

MacIntyre has no difficulty in showing that *if* the rites which the Azande perform in connection with their harvests are 'classified and evaluated' by reference to the criteria and standards of science or technology, then they are subject to serious criticism. He thinks that the Zande 'belief' is a sort of *hypothesis* like, e.g., an Englishman's belief that all the heavy rain we have been having is due to atomic explosions.[31] MacIntyre believes that he is applying as it were a neutral concept of '*A* affecting *B*', equally applicable to Zande magic and western science. In fact, however, he is applying the concept with which *he* is familiar, one which draws its significance from its use in scientific and technological contexts. There is no reason to suppose that the Zande magical concept of '*A* affecting *B*' has anything like the same significance. On the contrary, since the Azande do, in the course of their practical affairs, apply something very like our technical concept—though perhaps in a more primitive form—and since their attitude to and thought about their magical rites are quite different from those concerning their technological measures, there is every reason to think that their concept of magical 'influence' is quite different. This may be easier to accept if it is remembered that, even in our own culture, the concept of causal influence is by no means monolithic: when we speak, for example, of 'what made Jones get married', we are not saying the same kind of thing as when we speak of 'what made the aeroplane crash'; I do not mean simply that the events of which we speak are different in kind but that the relation between the events is different also. It should not then be difficult to accept that in a society with quite different institutions and ways of life from our own, there may be concepts of 'causal influence' which behave even more differently.

But I do not want to say that we are quite powerless to find ways of thinking in our own society that will help us to see the Zande institution in a clearer light. I only think that the direction in which we should look is quite different from what MacIntyre suggests. Clearly the nature of Zande life is such that it is of very great importance to them that their crops should thrive. Clearly too they take all kinds of practical 'technological' steps, within their capabilities, to ensure that they *do* thrive. But that is no reason to see their magical rites as a further, misguided such step. A man's sense of the importance of something to him shows itself in all sorts of ways: not merely in precautions to

---

[31] In what follows I have been helped indirectly, but greatly, by some unpublished notes made by Wittgenstein on Frazer, which Mr. Rush Rhees was kind enough to show me; and also by various scattered remarks on folklore in *The Notebooks* of Simone Weil, London, 1963.

safeguard that thing. He may want to come to terms with its importance to him in quite a different way: to contemplate it, to gain some sense of his life in relation to it. He may wish thereby, in a certain sense, to *free* himself from dependence on it. I do not mean by making sure that it does not let him down, because the point is that, *whatever* he does, he may still be let down. The important thing is that he should understand *that* and come to terms with it. Of course, merely to understand that is not to come to terms with it, though perhaps it is a necessary condition for so doing, for a man may equally well be transfixed and terrorized by the contemplation of such a possibility. He must see that he can still go on even if he is let down by what is vitally important to him; and he must so order his life that he still *can* go on in such circumstances. I stress once again that I do not mean this in the sense of becoming 'technologically independent', because from the present point of view technological independence is yet another form of dependence. Technology destroys some dependencies but always creates new ones, which may be fiercer—because harder to understand—than the old. This should be particularly apparent to *us*.[32]

In Judaeo-Christian cultures the conception of 'If it be Thy Will', as developed in the story of Job, is clearly central to the matter I am discussing. Because this conception is central to Christian prayers of supplication, they may be regarded from one point of view as freeing the believer from dependence on what he is supplicating for.[33] Prayers cannot play this role if they are regarded as a means of influencing the outcome for in that case the one who prays is still dependent on the outcome. He frees himself from this by acknowledging his complete dependence on God; and this is totally unlike any dependence on the outcome precisely because God is eternal and the outcome contingent.

I do not say that Zande magical rites are at all like Christian prayers of supplication in the positive attitude to contingencies which they express. What I do suggest is that they are alike in that they do, or may, express an attitude to contingencies; one, that is, which involves recognition that one's life is subject to contingencies, rather than an attempt to control these. To characterize this attitude more specifically one should note how Zande rites emphasize the importance of certain

[32] The point is beautifully developed by Simone Weil in her essay on 'The Analysis of Oppression' in *Oppression and Liberty*, London, Routledge & Kegan Paul, 1958.
[33] I have been helped to see this point by a hitherto unpublished essay on the concept of prayer by Mr. D. Z. Phillips. [See *The Concept of Prayer*, London and New York, 1965—*Ed.*]

fundamental features of their life which MacIntyre ignores. MacIntyre concentrates implicitly on the relation of the rites to consumption, but of course they are also fundamental to social relations and this seems to be emphasized in Zande notions of witchcraft. We have a drama of resentments, evil-doing, revenge, expiation, in which there are ways of dealing (symbolically) with misfortunes and their disruptive effect on a man's relations with his fellows, with ways in which life can go on despite such disruptions.

How is my treatment of this example related to the general criticisms I was making of MacIntyre's account of what it is for us to see the *point* of the rules and conventions followed in an alien form of life? MacIntyre speaks as though our own rules and conventions are somehow a paradigm of what it is for rules and conventions to have a point, so that the only problem that arises is in accounting for the point of the rules and conventions in some other society. But in fact, of course, the problem is the same in relation to our own society as it is in relation to any other; no more than anyone else's are *our* rules and conventions immune from the danger of being or becoming pointless. So an account of this matter cannot be given simply in terms of any set of rules and conventions at all: our own or anyone else's; it requires us to consider the relation of a set of rules and conventions to something else. In my discussion of Zande magical rites just now what I tried to relate the magical rites to was a sense of the significance of human life. This notion is, I think, indispensable to any account of what is involved in understanding and learning from an alien culture; I must now try to say more about it.

In a discussion of Wittgenstein's philosophical use of language games[34] Mr. Rush Rhees points out that to try to account for the meaningfulness of language solely in terms of isolated language games is to omit the important fact that ways of speaking are not insulated from each other in mutually exclusive systems of rules. What can be said in one context by the use of a certain expression depends for its sense on the uses of that expression in other contexts (different language games). Language games are played by men who have lives to live—lives involving a wide variety of different interests, which have all kinds of different bearings on each other. Because of this, what a man says or does may make a difference not merely to the performance of the activity upon which he is at present engaged, but to his *life* and to the

---

[34] Rush Rhees, 'Wittgenstein's Builders', *Proceedings of the Aristotelian Society*, vol. 20 (1960), pp. 171–186.

lives of other people. Whether a man sees point in what he is doing will then depend on whether he is able to see any unity in his multi-farious interests, activities, and relations with other men; what sort of sense he sees in his life will depend on the nature of this unity. The ability to see this sort of sense in life depends not merely on the indivi-dual concerned, though this is not to say it does not depend on him at all; it depends also on the possibilities for making such sense which the culture in which he lives does, or does not, provide.

What we may learn by studying other cultures are not merely possibilities of different ways of doing things, other techniques. More importantly we may learn different possibilities of making sense of human life, different ideas about the possible importance that the carrying out of certain activities may take on for a man, trying to contemplate the sense of his life as a whole. This dimension of the matter is precisely what MacIntyre misses in his treatment of Zande magic: he can see in it only a (misguided) technique for producing consumer goods. But a Zande's crops are not just potential objects of consumption: the life he lives, his relations with his fellows, his chances for acting decently or doing evil, may all spring from his relation to his crops. Magical rites constitute a form of expression in which these possibilities and dangers may be contemplated and reflected on—and perhaps also thereby transformed and deepened. The difficulty we find in understanding this is not merely its remoteness from science, but an aspect of the general difficulty we find, illustrated by MacIntyre's procedure, of thinking about such matters at all except in terms of 'efficiency of production'—production, that is, for consumption. This again is a symptom of what Marx called the 'alienation' characteristic of man in industrial society, though Marx's own confusions about the relations between production and consumption are further symptoms of that same alienation. Our blindness to the point of primitive modes of life is a corollary of the pointlessness of much of our own life.

I have now explicitly linked my discussion of the 'point' of a system of conventions with conceptions of good and evil. My aim is not to engage in moralizing, but to suggest that the concept of *learning from* which is involved in the study of other cultures is closely linked with the concept of *wisdom*. We are confronted not just with different techniques, but with new possibilities of good and evil, in relation to which men may come to terms with life. An investigation into this dimension of a society may indeed require a quite detailed inquiry into alternative techniques (e.g., of production), but an inquiry conducted for the light it throws on those possibilities of good and evil. A very good example of the kind of thing I mean is Simone Weil's analysis of the techniques of modern factory production in *Oppression and Liberty*, which is not a contribution to business management, but part of an inquiry into the peculiar form which the evil of oppression takes in our culture.

In saying this, however, I may seem merely to have lifted to a new level the difficulty raised by MacIntyre of how to relate our own conceptions of rationality to those of other societies. Here the difficulty concerns the relation between our own conceptions of good and evil and those of other societies. A full investigation would thus require a discussion of ethical relativism at this point. I have tried to show some of the limitations of relativism in an earlier paper.[35] I shall close the present essay with some remarks which are supplementary to that.

I wish to point out that the very conception of human life involves certain fundamental notions—which I shall call 'limiting notions'—which have an obvious ethical dimension, and which indeed in a sense determine the 'ethical space', within which the possibilities of good and evil in human life can be exercised. The notions which I shall discuss very briefly here correspond closely to those which Vico made the foundation of his idea of natural law, on which he thought the possibility of understanding human history rested: birth, death, sexual relations. Their significance here is that they are inescapably involved in the life of all known human societies in a way which gives us a clue where to look, if we are puzzled about the point of an alien system of institutions. The specific forms which these concepts take, the particular institutions in which they are expressed, vary very considerably from one society to another; but their central position within a society's institutions is and must be a constant factor. In trying to understand the life of an alien society, then, it will be of the utmost importance to be clear about the way in which these notions enter into it. The actual practice of social anthropologists bears this out, although I do not know how many of them would attach the same kind of importance to them as I do.

I speak of a 'limit' here because these notions, along no doubt with others, give shape to what we understand by 'human life'; and because a concern with questions posed in terms of them seems to me constitutive of what we understand by the 'morality' of a society. In saying

[35] Peter Winch, 'Nature and Convention', *Proceedings of the Aristotelian Society*, vol. 20 (1960), pp. 231–252.

this, I am of course disagreeing with those moral philosophers who have made attitudes of approval and disapproval, or something similar, fundamental in ethics, and who have held that the *objects* of such attitudes were conceptually irrelevant to the conception of morality. On that view, there might be a society where the sorts of attitude taken up in *our* society to questions about relations between the sexes were reserved, say, for questions about the length people wear their hair, and *vice versa*. This seems to me incoherent. In the first place, there would be a confusion in *calling* a concern of that sort a 'moral' concern, however passionately felt. The story of Samson in the Old Testament confirms rather than refutes this point, for the interdict on the cutting of Samson's hair is, of course, connected there with much else: and pre-eminently, it should be noted, with questions about sexual relations. But secondly, if that is thought to be merely verbal quibbling, I will say that it does not seem to me a merely conventional matter that T. S. Eliot's trinity of 'birth, copulation and death' happen to be such deep objects of human concern. I do not mean just that they are made such by fundamental psychological and sociological forces, though that is no doubt true. But I want to say further that the very notion of human life is limited by these conceptions.

Unlike beasts, men do not merely live but also have a conception of life. This is not something that is simply added to their life; rather, it changes the very sense which the word 'life' has, when applied to men. It is no longer equivalent to 'animate existence'. When we are speaking of the life of man, we can ask questions about what is the right way to live, what things are most important in life, whether life has any significance, and if so what.

To have a conception of life is also to have a conception of death. But just as the 'life' that is here in question is not the same as animate existence, so the 'death' that is here in question is not the same as the end of animate existence. My conception of the death of an animal is of an event that will take place in the world; perhaps I shall observe it —and my life will go on. But when I speak of 'my death', I am not speaking of a future event in my life;[36] I am not even speaking of an event in anyone else's life. I am speaking of the cessation of my world. That is also a cessation of my ability to do good or evil. It is not just that *as a matter of fact* I shall no longer be able to do good or evil after I am dead; the point is that my very *concept* of what it is to be able to

[36] Cf. Wittgenstein, *Tractatus Logico-Philosophicus*, 6.431–6.4311.

do good or evil is deeply bound up with my concept of my life as ending in death. If ethics is a concern with the right way to live, then clearly the nature of this concern must be deeply affected by the concept of life as ending in death. One's attitude to one's life is at the same time an attitude to one's death.

This point is very well illustrated in an anthropological datum which MacIntyre confesses himself unable to make any sense of.

> According to Spencer and Gillen some aborigines carry about a stick or stone which is treated *as if* it is or embodies the soul of the individual who carries it. If the stick or stone is lost, the individual anoints himself as the dead are anointed. Does the concept of 'carrying one's soul about with one' make sense? Of course we can redescribe what the aborigines are doing and transform it into sense, and perhaps Spencer and Gillen (and Durkheim who follows them) misdescribe what occurs. But if their reports are not erroneous, we confront a blank wall here, so far as meaning is concerned, although it is easy to give the rules for the use of the concept.[37]

MacIntyre does not say why he regards the concept of carrying one's soul about with one in a stick 'thoroughly incoherent'. He is presumably influenced by the fact that it would be hard to make sense of an action like this if performed by a twentieth-century Englishman or American; and by the fact that the soul is not a material object like a piece of paper and cannot, therefore, be carried about in a stick as a piece of paper might be. But it does not seem to me so hard to see sense in the practice, even from the little we are told about it here. Consider that a lover in our society may carry about a picture or lock of hair of the beloved; that this may symbolize for him his relation to the beloved and may, indeed, change the relation in all sorts of ways: for example, strengthening it or perverting it. Suppose that when the lover loses the locket he feels guilty and asks his beloved for her forgiveness: there might be a parallel here to the aboriginal's practice of anointing himself when he 'loses his soul'. And is there necessarily anything irrational about either of these practices? Why should the lover not regard his carelessness in losing the locket as a sort of betrayal of the beloved? Remember how husbands and wives may feel about the loss of a wedding ring. The aborigine is clearly expressing a concern with his life as a whole in this practice; the anointing shows the close connection between such a concern and contemplation of death. Perhaps it is

---

[37] *Is Understanding Religion Compatible with Believing?*

precisely this practice which makes such a concern possible for him, as religious sacraments make certain sorts of concern possible. The point is that a concern with one's life as a whole, involving as it does the limiting conception of one's death, if it is to be expressed *within* a person's life, can necessarily only be expressed quasi-sacramentally. The form of the concern shows itself in the form of the sacrament.

The sense in which I spoke also of sex as a 'limiting concept' again has to do with the concept of a human life. The life of a man is a man's life and the life of a woman is a woman's life: the masculinity or the femininity are not just *components* in the life, they are its *mode*. Adapting Wittgenstein's remark about death, I might say that my masculinity is not an experience in the world, but my way of experiencing the world. Now the concepts of masculininity and femininity obviously require each other. A man is a man in relation to women; and a woman is a woman in relation to men.[38] Thus the form taken by man's relation to women is of quite fundamental importance for the significance he can attach to his own life. The vulgar identification of morality with sexual morality certainly *is* vulgar; but it is a vulgarization of an important truth.

The limiting character of the concept of birth is obviously related to the points I have sketched regarding death and sex. On the one hand, my birth is no more an event in my life than is my death; and through my birth ethical limits are set for my life quite independently of my will: I am, from the outset, in specific relations to other people, from which obligations spring which cannot but be ethically fundamental.[39] On the other hand, the concept of birth is fundamentally linked to that of relations between the sexes. This remains true, however much or little may be known in a society about the contribution of males and females to procreation; for it remains true that man is born of woman, not of man. This, then, adds a new dimension to the ethical institutions in which relations between the sexes are expressed.

I have tried to do no more, in these last brief remarks, than to focus attention in a certain direction. I have wanted to indicate that forms of these limiting concepts will necessarily be an important feature of any human society and that conceptions of good and evil in human life

---

[38] These relations, however, are not simple converses. See Georg Simmel, 'Das Relative und das Absolute im Geschlechter-Problem' in *Philosophische Kultur*, Leipzig, 1911.

[39] For this reason, among others, I think A. I. Melden is wrong to say that parent-child obligations and rights have nothing directly to do with physical genealogy. Cf. Melden, *Rights and Right Conduct*, Oxford, 1959.

D

will necessarily be connected with such concepts. In any attempt to understand the life of another society, therefore, an investigation of the forms taken by such concepts—their role in the life of the society— must always take a central place and provide a basis on which understanding may be built.

Now since the world of nations has been made by men, let us see in what institutions men agree and always have agreed. For these institutions will be able to give us the universal and eternal principles (such as every science must have) on which all nations were founded and still preserve themselves.

We observe that all nations, barbarous as well as civilized, though separately founded because remote from each other in time and space, keep these three human customs: all have some religion, all contract solemn marriages, all bury their dead. And in no nation, however savage and crude, are any human actions performed with more elaborate ceremonies and more sacred solemnity than the rites of religion, marriage and burial. For by the axiom that 'uniform ideas, born among peoples unknown to each other, must have a common ground of truth', it must have been dictated to all nations that from these institutions humanity began among them all, and therefore they must be most devoutly guarded by them all, so that the world should not again become a bestial wilderness. For this reason we have taken these three eternal and universal customs as the first principles of this Science.[40]

[40] Giambattista Vico, *The New Science*, §§ 332–333.

# II

# ANSELM'S ONTOLOGICAL ARGUMENTS

## By NORMAN MALCOLM

## I

I BELIEVE that in Anselm's *Proslogion* and *Responsio editoris* there are two different pieces of reasoning which he did not distinguish from one another, and that a good deal of light may be shed on the philosophical problem of 'the ontological argument' if we do distinguish them. In Chapter 2 of the *Proslogion*[1] Anselm says that we believe that God is *something a greater than which cannot be conceived*. (The Latin is *aliquid quo nihil maius cogitari possit*. Anselm sometimes uses the alternative expressions *aliquid quo maius nihil cogitari potest, id quo maius cogitari nequit, aliquid quo maius cogitari non valet*.) Even the fool of the Psalm who says in his heart there is no God, when he hears this very thing that Anselm says, namely, 'something a greater than which cannot be conceived', understands what he hears, and what he understands is in his understanding though he does not understand that it exists.

Apparently Anselm regards it as tautological to say that whatever is understood is in the understanding (*quidquid intelligitur in intellectu est*): he uses *intelligitur* and *in intellectu est* as interchangeable locutions. The same holds for another formula of his: whatever is thought is in thought (*quidquid cogitatur in cogitatione est*).[2]

Of course many things may exist in the understanding that do not exist in reality; for example, elves. Now, says Anselm, something a greater than which cannot be conceived exists in the understanding. But it cannot exist *only* in the understanding, for to exist in reality is greater. Therefore that thing a greater than which cannot be conceived cannot exist only in the understanding, for then a greater thing could

---

[1] I have consulted the Latin text of the *Proslogion*, of *Gaunilonis Pro Insipiente*, and of the *Responsio editoris*, in S. Anselmi, *Opera Omnia*, edited by F. C. Schmitt, Secovii, 1938, Vol. I. With numerous modifications, I have used the English translation by S. N. Deane: *St. Anselm*, La Salle, Ill.: Open Court Publishing Co., 1948.

[2] See *Proslogion* 1 and *Responsio* 2.

be conceived: namely, one that exists both in the understanding and in reality.[3]

Here I have a question. It is not clear to me whether Anselm means that (a) existence in reality by itself is greater than existence in the understanding, or that (b) existence in reality and existence in the understanding together are greater than existence in the understanding alone. Certainly he accepts (b). But he might also accept (a), as Descartes apparently does in *Meditation III* when he suggests that the mode of being by which a thing is 'objectively in the understanding' is *imperfect*.[4] Of course Anselm might accept both (a) and (b). He might hold that in general something is greater if it has both of these 'modes of existence' than if it has either one alone, but also that existence in reality is a more perfect mode of existence than existence in the understanding.

In any case, Anselm holds that something is greater if it exists both in the understanding and in reality than if it exists merely in the understanding. An equivalent way of putting this interesting proposition, in a more current terminology, is: something is greater if it is both conceived of and exists than if it is merely conceived of. Anselm's reasoning can be expressed as follows: *id quo maius cogitari nequit* cannot be merely conceived of and not exist, for then it would not be *id quo maius cogitari nequit*. The doctrine that something is greater if it exists in addition to being conceived of, than if it is only conceived of, could be called the doctrine that *existence is a perfection*. Descartes maintained, in so many words, that existence is a perfection,[5] and presumably he was holding Anselm's doctrine, although he does not, in *Meditation V* or elsewhere, argue in the way that Anselm does in *Proslogion* 2.

When Anselm says 'And certainly, that than which nothing greater can be conceived cannot exist merely in the understanding. For suppose it exists merely in the understanding, then it can be conceived to exist in reality, which is greater,'[6] he is claiming that if I conceived of a being of great excellence, that being would be *greater* (more excellent, more perfect) if it existed than if it did not exist. His supposition that 'it exists merely in the understanding' is the supposition that it is

[3] Anselm's actual words are: 'Et certe id quo maius cogitari nequit, non potest esse in solo intellectu. Si enim vel in solo intellectu est, potest cogitari esse et in re, quod maius est. Si ergo id quo maius cogitari non potest, est in solo intellectu: id ipsum quo maius cogitari non potest, est quo maius cogitari potest. Sed certe hoc esse non potest.' *Proslogion* 2.

[4] Haldane and Ross, *The Philosophical Works of Descartes*, 2 vols. (Cambridge, 1931), I, 163.     [5] Op. cit., p. 182.     [6] *Proslogion* 2; Deane, p. 8.

conceived of but does not exist. Anselm repeated this claim in his reply to the criticism of the monk Gaunilo. Speaking of the being a greater than which cannot be conceived, he says:

I have said that if it exists merely in the understanding it can be conceived to exist in reality, which is greater. Therefore, if it exists merely in the understanding obviously the very being a greater than which cannot be conceived, is one a greater than which can be conceived. What, I ask, can follow better than that? For if it exists merely in the understanding, can it not be conceived to exist in reality? And if it can be so conceived does not he who conceives of this conceive of a thing greater than it, if it does exist merely in the understanding? Can anything follow better than this: that if a being a greater than which cannot be conceived exists merely in the understanding, it is something a greater than which can be conceived? What could be plainer?[7]

He is implying, in the first sentence, that if I conceive of something which does not exist then it is possible for it to exist, and *it will be greater if it exists than if it does not exist.*

The doctrine that existence is a perfection is remarkably queer. It makes sense and is true to say that my future house will be a better one if it is insulated than if it is not insulated; but what could it mean to say that it will be a better house if it exists than if it does not? My future child will be a better man if he is honest than if he is not; but who would understand the saying that he will be a better man if he exists than if he does not? Or who understands the saying that if God exists He is more perfect than if He does not exist? One might say, with some intelligibility, that it would be better (for oneself or for mankind) if God exists than if He does not—but that is a different matter.

A king might desire that his next chancellor should have knowledge, wit, and resolution; but it is ludicrous to add that the king's desire is to have a chancellor who exists. Suppose that two royal councillors, A and B, were asked to draw up separately descriptions of the most perfect chancellor they could conceive, and that the descriptions they produced were identical except that A included existence in his list of attributes of a perfect chancellor and B did not. (I do not mean that B put non-existence in his list.) One and the same person could satisfy both descriptions. More to the point, any person who satisfied A's description would *necessarily* satisfy B's description and *vice versa*! This

[7] *Responsio* 2; Deane, pp. 157–158.

is to say that A and B did not produce descriptions that differed in any way but rather one and the same description of necessary and desirable qualities in a chancellor. A only made a show of putting down a desirable quality that B had failed to include.

I believe I am merely restating an observation that Kant made in attacking the notion that 'existence' or 'being' is a 'real predicate'. He says:

> By whatever and by however many predicates we may think a thing—even if we completely determine it—we do not make the least addition to the thing when we further declare that this thing *is*. Otherwise, it would not be exactly the same thing that exists, but something more than we had thought in the concept; and we could not, therefore, say that the exact object of my concept exists.[8]

Anselm's ontological proof of *Proslogion* 2 is fallacious because it rests on the false doctrine that existence is a perfection (and therefore that 'existence' is a 'real predicate'). It would be desirable to have a rigorous refutation of the doctrine but I have not been able to provide one. I am compelled to leave the matter at the more or less intuitive level of Kant's observation. In any case, I believe that the doctrine does not belong to Anselm's other formulation of the ontological argument. It is worth noting that Gassendi anticipated Kant's criticism when he said, against Descartes:

> Existence is a perfection neither in God nor in anything else; it is rather that in the absence of which there is no perfection. . . . Hence neither is existence held to exist in a thing in the way that perfections do, nor if the thing lacks existence is it said to be imperfect (or deprived of a perfection), so much as to be nothing.[9]

## II

I take up now the consideration of the second ontological proof, which Anselm presents in the very next chapter of the *Proslogion*. (There is no evidence that he thought of himself as offering two different proofs.) Speaking of the being a greater than which cannot be conceived, he says:

> And it so truly exists that it cannot be conceived not to exist. For it is possible to conceive of a being which cannot be conceived not to

---

[8] *The Critique of Pure Reason*, tr. by Norman Kemp Smith, London, 1929, p. 505.
[9] Haldane and Ross, II, 186.

exist; and this is greater than one which can be conceived not to exist. Hence, if that, than which nothing greater can be conceived, can be conceived not to exist, it is not that than which nothing greater can be conceived. But this is a contradiction. So truly, therefore, is there something than which nothing greater can be conceived, that it cannot even be conceived not to exist. And this being thou art, O Lord, our God.[10]

Anselm is saying two things: first, that a being whose non-existence is logically impossible is 'greater' than a being whose non-existence is logically possible (and therefore that a being a greater than which cannot be conceived must be one whose non-existence is logically impossible); second, that *God* is a being than which a greater cannot be conceived.

In regard to the second of these assertions, there certainly is *a* use of the word 'God', and I think far the more common use, in accordance with which the statements 'God is the greatest of all beings', 'God is the most perfect being', 'God is the supreme being', are *logically* necessary truths, in the same sense that the statement 'A square has four sides' is a logically necessary truth. If there is a man named 'Jones' who is the tallest man in the world, the statement 'Jones is the tallest man in the world' is merely true and is not a logically necessary truth. It is a virtue of Anselm's unusual phrase, 'a being a greater than which cannot be conceived',[11] to make it explicit that the sentence 'God is the greatest of all beings' expresses a logically necessary truth and not a mere matter of fact such as the one we imagined about Jones.

With regard to Anselm's first assertion (namely, that a being whose non-existence is logically impossible is greater than a being whose non-existence is logically possible) perhaps the most puzzling thing about it is the use of the word 'greater'. It appears to mean exactly the same as 'superior', 'more excellent', 'more perfect'. This equivalence by itself is of no help to us, however, since the latter expressions would be equally puzzling here. What is required is some explanation of their use.

We do think of *knowledge*, say, as an excellence, a good thing. If *A* has more knowledge of algebra than *B* we express this in common language by saying that *A* has a better knowledge of algebra than *B*, or

---

[10] *Proslogion* 3, Deane, pp. 8–9.
[11] Professor Robert Calhoun has pointed out to me that a similar locution had been used by Augustine. In *De moribus Manichaeorum* (Bk. II, ch. 11, sec. 24), he says that God is a being *quo esse aut cogitari melius nihil possit* (*Patrologiae Patrum Latinorum*, J. P. Migne, ed. Paris, 1841–1845, Vol. 32; *Augustinus*, Vol. 1).

that $A$'s knowledge of algebra is *superior* to $B$'s, whereas we should not say that $B$ has a better or superior *ignorance* of algebra than $A$. We do say 'greater ignorance', but here the word 'greater' is used purely quantitatively.

Previously I rejected *existence* as a perfection. Anselm is maintaining in the remarks last quoted, not that existence is a perfection, but that *the logical impossibility of non-existence is a perfection*. In other words, *necessary existence is a perfection*. His first ontological proof uses the principle that a thing is greater if it exists than if it does not exist. His second proof employs the different principle that a thing is greater if it necessarily exists than if it does not necessarily exist.

Some remarks about the notion of *dependence* may help to make this latter principle intelligible. Many things depend for their existence on other things and events. My house was built by a carpenter: its coming into existence was dependent on a certain creative activity. Its continued existence is dependent on many things: that a tree does not crush it, that it is not consumed by fire, and so on. If we reflect on the common meaning of the word 'God' (no matter how vague and confused this is), we realize that it is incompatible with this meaning that God's existence should *depend* on anything. Whether we believe in Him or not we must admit that the 'almighty and everlasting God' (as several ancient prayers begin), the 'Maker of heaven and earth, and of all things visible and invisible' (as is said in the Nicene Creed), cannot be thought of as being brought into existence by anything or as depending for His continued existence on anything. To conceive of anything as dependent upon something else for its existence is to conceive of it as a lesser being than God.

If a housewife has a set of extremely fragile dishes, then as dishes they are *inferior* to those of another set like them in all respects except that they are *not* fragile. Those of the first set are *dependent* for their continued existence on gentle handling; those of the second set are not. There is a definite connection in common language between the notions of dependency and inferiority, and independence and superiority. To say that something which was dependent on nothing whatever was superior to ('greater than') anything that was dependent in any way upon anything is quite in keeping with the everyday use of the terms 'superior' and 'greater'. Correlative with the notions of dependence and independence are the notions of *limited* and *unlimited*. An engine requires fuel and this is a limitation. It is the same thing to say that an engine's operation is *dependent* on as that it is *limited* by its fuel supply. An engine that could accomplish the same work in the same time and was in other respects satisfactory, but did not require fuel, would be a *superior* engine.

God is usually conceived of as an *unlimited* being. He is conceived of as a being who *could not* be limited, that is, as an absolutely unlimited being. This is no less than to conceive of Him as *something a greater than which cannot be conceived*. If God is conceived to be an absolutely unlimited being He must be conceived to be unlimited in regard to His existence as well as His operation. In this conception it will not make sense to say that He depends on anything for coming into or continuing in existence. Nor, as Spinoza observed, will it make sense to say that something could *prevent* Him from existing.[12] Lack of moisture can prevent trees from existing in a certain region of the earth. But it would be contrary to the concept of God as an unlimited being to suppose that anything other than God Himself could prevent Him from existing, and it would be self-contradictory to suppose that He Himself could do it.

Some may be inclined to object that although nothing could prevent God's existence, still it might just *happen* that He did not exist. And if He did exist that too would be by chance. I think, however, that from the supposition that it could happen that God did not exist it would follow that, if He existed, He would have mere duration and not eternity. It would make sense to ask, 'How long has He existed?', 'Will He still exist next week?', 'He was in existence yesterday but how about today?', and so on. It seems absurd to make God the subject of such questions. According to our ordinary conception of Him, He is an eternal being. And eternity does not mean endless duration, as Spinoza noted. To ascribe eternity to something is to exclude as senseless all sentences that imply that it has duration. If a thing has duration then it would be merely a *contingent* fact, if it was a fact, that its duration was endless. The moon could have endless duration but not eternity. If something has endless duration it will *make sense* (although it will be false) to say that it will cease to exist, and it will make sense (although it will be false) to say that something will *cause* it to cease to exist. A being with endless duration is not, therefore, an absolutely unlimited being. That God is conceived to be eternal follows from the fact that He is conceived to be an absolutely unlimited being.

[12] *Ethics*, Part I, prop. 11.

I have been trying to expand the argument of *Proslogion* 3. In *Responsio* 1 Anselm adds the following acute point: if you can conceive of a certain thing and this thing does not exist then if it *were* to exist its non-existence would be *possible*. It follows, I believe, that if the thing were to exist it would depend on other things both for coming into and continuing in existence, and also that it would have duration and not eternity. Therefore it would not be, either in reality or in conception, an unlimited being, *aliquid quo nihil maius cogitari possit*.

Anselm states his argument as follows:

If it [the thing a greater than which cannot be conceived] can be conceived at all it must exist. For no one who denies or doubts the existence of a being a greater than which is inconceivable, denies or doubts that if it did exist its non-existence, either in reality or in the understanding, would be impossible. For otherwise it would not be a being a greater than which cannot be conceived. But as to whatever can be conceived but does not exist: if it were to exist its non-existence either in reality or in the understanding would be possible. Therefore, if a being a greater than which cannot be conceived, can even be conceived, it must exist.[13]

What Anselm has proved is that the notion of contingent existence or of contingent non-existence cannot have any application to God. His existence must either be logically necessary or logically impossible. The only intelligible way of rejecting Anselm's claim that God's existence is necessary is to maintain that the concept of God, as a being a greater than which cannot be conceived, is self-contradictory or non-sensical.[14] Supposing that this is false, Anselm is right to deduce God's necessary existence from his characterization of Him as a being a greater than which cannot be conceived.

Let me summarize the proof. If God, a being a greater than which cannot be conceived, does not exist then He cannot *come* into existence. For if He did He would either have been *caused* to come into existence or have *happened* to come into existence, and in either case He would be

---

[13] *Responsio* 1, Deane, pp. 154–155.

[14] Gaunilo attacked Anselm's argument on this very point. He would not concede that a being a greater than which cannot be conceived existed in his understanding (*Gaunilonis Pro Insipiente*, secs. 4 and 5; Deane, *St. Anselm*, pp. 148–150). Anselm's reply is: 'I call on your faith and conscience to attest that this is most false' (*Responsio* 1, Deane, *St. Anselm*, p. 154). Gaunilo's faith and conscience will attest that it is false that 'God is not a being a greater than which is inconceivable', and false that 'He is not understood (*intelligitur*) or conceived (*cogitatur*)' (ibid.). Descartes remarks that one would go to 'strange extremes' who denied that we understand the words '*that thing which is the most perfect that we can conceive*; for that is what all men call God' (Haldane and Ross, II, 129).

a limited being, which by our conception of Him He is not. Since He cannot come into existence, if He does not exist His existence is impossible. If He does exist He cannot have come into existence (for the reasons given), nor can He cease to exist, for nothing could cause Him to cease to exist nor could it just happen that He ceased to exist. So if God exists His existence is necessary. Thus God's existence is either impossible or necessary. It can be the former only if the concept of such a being is self-contradictory or in some way logically absurd. Assuming that this is not so, it follows that He necessarily exists.

It may be helpful to express ourselves in the following way: to say, not that *omnipotence* is a property of God, but rather that *necessary omnipotence* is; and to say, not that omniscience is a property of God, but rather that *necessary omniscience* is. We have criteria for determining that a man knows this and that and can do this and that, and for determining that one man has greater knowledge and abilities in a certain subject than another. We could think of various tests to give them. But there is nothing we should wish to describe, seriously and literally, as 'testing' God's knowledge and powers. That God is omniscient and omnipotent has not been determined by the application of criteria: rather these are requirements of our conception of Him. They are internal properties of the concept, although they are also rightly said to be properties of God. *Necessary existence* is a property of God in the *same sense* that *necessary omnipotence* and *necessary omniscience* are His properties. And we are not to think that 'God necessarily exists' means that it follows necessarily from something that God exists *contingently*. The *a priori* proposition 'God necessarily exists' entails the proposition 'God exists', if and only if the latter also is understood as an *a priori* proposition: in which case the two propositions are equivalent. In this sense Anselm's proof is a proof of God's existence.

Descartes was somewhat hazy on the question of whether existence is a property of things that exist, but at the same time he saw clearly

> I do not see to what class of reality you wish to assign existence, nor do I see why it may not be said to be a property as well as omni-potence, taking the word property as equivalent to any attribute or anything which can be predicated of a thing, as in the present case it should be by all means regarded. Nay, necessary existence in the case of God is also a true property in the strictest sense of the word, because it belongs to Him and forms part of His essence alone.[15]

[15] Haldane and Ross, II, 228.

enough that *necessary existence* is a property of God. Both points are illustrated in his reply to Gassendi's remark, which I quoted above:

Elsewhere he speaks of 'the necessity of existence' as being 'that crown of perfections without which we cannot comprehend God'.[16] He is emphatic on the point that necessary existence applies solely to 'an absolutely perfect Being'.[17]

## III

I wish to consider now a part of Kant's criticism of the ontological argument which I believe to be wrong. He says:

If, in an identical proposition, I reject the predicate while retaining the subject, contradiction results; and I therefore say that the former belongs necessarily to the latter. But if we reject subject and predicate alike, there is no contradiction; for nothing is then left that can be contradicted. To posit a triangle, and yet to reject its three angles, is self-contradictory; but there is no contradiction in rejecting the triangle together with its three angles. The same holds true of the concept of an absolutely necessary being. If its existence is rejected, we reject the thing itself with all its predicates; and no question of contradiction can then arise. There is nothing outside it that would then be contradicted, since the necessity of the thing is not supposed to be derived from anything external; nor is there anything internal that would be contradicted, since in rejecting the thing itself we have at the same time rejected all its internal properties. 'God is omnipotent' is a necessary judgement. The omnipotence cannot be rejected if we posit a Deity, that is, an infinite being; for the two concepts are identical. But if we say 'There is no God' neither the omnipotence nor any other of its predicates is given; they are one and all rejected together with the subject, and there is therefore not the least contradiction in such a judgement.[18]

To these remarks the reply is that when the concept of God is correctly understood one sees that one cannot 'reject the subject'. 'There is no God' is seen to be a necessarily false statement. Anselm's demonstration proves that the proposition 'God exists' has the same *a priori* footing as the proposition 'God is omnipotent'.

Many present-day philosophers, in agreement with Kant, declare that existence is not a property and think that this overthrows the ontological argument. Although it is an error to regard existence as a property of things that have contingent existence, it does not follow

[16] Ibid., I, 445.      [17] e.g., ibid., Principle 15, p. 225.      [18] Op. cit., p. 502.

that it is an error to regard necessary existence as a property of God. A recent writer says, against Anselm, that a proof of God's existence 'based on the necessities of thought' is 'universally regarded as fallacious: it is not thought possible to build bridges between mere abstractions and concrete existence'.[19] But this way of putting the matter obscures the distinction we need to make. Does 'concrete existence' mean contingent existence? Then to build bridges between concrete existence and mere abstractions would be like inferring the existence of an island from the concept of a perfect island, which both Anselm and Descartes regarded as absurd. What Anselm did was to give a demonstration that the proposition 'God necessarily exists' is entailed by the proposition 'God is a being a greater than which cannot be conceived' (which is equivalent to 'God is an absolutely unlimited being'). Kant declares that when 'I think a being as the supreme reality, without any defect, the question still remains whether it exists or not'.[20] But once one has grasped Anselm's proof of the necessary existence of a being a greater than which cannot be conceived, no question remains as to whether it exists or not, just as Euclid's demonstration of the existence of an infinity of prime numbers leaves no question on that issue.

Kant says that 'every reasonable person' must admit that 'all existential propositions are synthetic'.[21] Part of the perplexity one has about the ontological argument is in deciding whether or not the proposition 'God necessarily exists' is or is not an 'existential proposition'. But let us look around. Is the Euclidean theorem in number theory, 'There exists an infinite number of prime numbers', an 'existential proposition'? Do we not want to say that *in some sense* it asserts the existence of something? Cannot we say, with equal justification, that the proposition 'God necessarily exists' asserts the existence of something, *in some sense*? What we need to understand, in each case, is the particular sense of the assertion. Neither proposition has the same sort of sense as do the propositions 'A low pressure area exists over the Great Lakes', 'There still exists some possibility that he will survive', 'The pain continues to exist in his abdomen'. One good way of seeing the difference in sense of these various propositions is to see the variously different ways in which they are proved or supported. It is wrong to think that all assertions of existence have the same kind of meaning.

[19] J. N. Findlay, 'Can God's Existence Be Disproved?' *New Essays in Philosophical Theology*, A. N. Flew and A. MacIntyre, eds., London, 1955, p. 47.
[20] Op. cit., pp. 505–506.     [21] Ibid., p. 504.

There are as many kinds of existential propositions as there are kinds of subjects of discourse.

Closely related to Kant's view that all existential propositions are 'synthetic' is the contemporary dogma that all existential propositions are contingent. Professor Gilbert Ryle tells us that 'Any assertion of the existence of something, like any assertion of the occurrence of something, can be denied without logical absurdity'.[22] 'All existential statements are contingent', says Mr. I. M. Crombie.[23] Professor J. J. C. Smart remarks that 'Existence is not a property' and then goes on to assert that 'There can never be any *logical contradiction* in denying that God exists'.[24] He declares that 'The concept of a logically necessary being is a self-contradictory concept, like the concept of a round square. . . . No existential proposition can be logically necessary', he maintains, for 'the truth of a logically necessary proposition depends only on our symbolism, or to put the same thing in another way, on the relationship of concepts' (p. 38). Professor K. E. M. Baier says, 'It is no longer seriously in dispute that the notion of a logically necessary being is self-contradictory. Whatever can be conceived of as existing can equally be conceived of as not existing.'[25] This is a repetition of Hume's assertion, 'Whatever we conceive as existent, we can also conceive as non-existent. There is no being, therefore, whose non-existence implies a contradiction.'[26]

Professor J. N. Findlay ingeniously constructs an ontological *dis*proof of God's existence, based on a 'modern' view of the nature of 'necessity in propositions': the view, namely, that necessity in propositions 'merely reflects our use of words, the arbitrary conventions of our language'.[27] Findlay undertakes to characterize what he calls 'religious attitude', and here there is a striking agreement between his observations and some of the things I have said in expounding Anselm's proof. Religious attitude, he says, presumes *superiority* in its object and superiority so great that the worshipper is in comparison as nothing. Religious attitude finds it 'anomalous to worship anything *limited* in any thinkable manner. . . . And hence we are led on irresistibly to demand that our religious object should have an *unsurpassable* supremacy along all

22 *The Nature of Metaphysics*, D. F. Pears, ed., New York, 1957, p. 150.
23 *New Essays in Philosophical Theology*, p. 114.
24 Ibid., p. 34.
25 *The Meaning of Life*, Inaugural Lecture, Canberra University College, Canberra, 1957, p. 8.
26 *Dialogues Concerning Natural Religion*, Part IX.
27 Findlay, op. cit., p. 154.

avenues, that it should tower *infinitely* above all other objects' (p. 51). We cannot help feeling that 'the worthy object of our worship can never be a thing that merely *happens* to exist, nor one on which all other objects merely *happen* to depend. The true object of religious reverence must not be one, merely, to which no *actual* independent realities stand opposed: it must be one to which such opposition is totally *inconceivable*. . . . And not only must the existence of *other* things be unthinkable without him, but his own non-existence must be wholly unthinkable in any circumstances' (p. 52). And now, says Findlay, when we add up these various requirements, what they entail is 'not only that there isn't a God, but that the Divine Existence is either senseless or impossible' (p. 54). For on the one hand, 'if God is to satisfy religious claims and needs, He must be a being in every way inescapable, One whose existence and whose possession of certain excellences we cannot possibly conceive away'. On the other hand, 'modern views make it self-evidently absurd (if they don't make it ungrammatical) to speak of such a Being and attribute existence to Him. It was indeed an ill day for Anselm when he hit upon his famous proof. For on that day he not only laid bare something that is of the essence of an adequate religious object, but also something that entails its necessary non-existence' (p. 55).

Now I am inclined to hold the 'modern' view that logically necessary truth 'merely reflects our use of words' (although I do not believe that the conventions of language are always *arbitrary*). But I confess that I am unable to see how that view is supposed to lead to the conclusion that 'the Divine existence is either senseless or impossible'. Findlay does not explain how this result comes about. Surely he cannot mean that this view entails that nothing can have necessary properties: for this would imply that mathematics is 'senseless or impossible', which no one wants to hold. Trying to fill in the argument that is missing from his article, the most plausible conjecture I can make is the following: Findlay thinks that the view that logical necessity 'reflects the use of words' implies, not that nothing has necessary properties, but that *existence* cannot be a necessary property of anything. That is to say, every proposition of the form '*x* exists', including the proposition 'God exists', must be *contingent*.[28] At the same time, our concept of God

---

[28] The other philosophers I have just cited may be led to this opinion by the same thinking. Smart, for example, says that 'the truth of a logically necessary proposition depends only on our symbolism, or to put the same thing in another way, on the relationship of concepts' (*supra*). This is very similar to saying that it 'reflects our use of words'.

requires that His existence be *necessary*, that is, that 'God exists' be a necessary truth. Therefore, the modern view of necessity proves that what the concept of God requires *cannot* be fulfilled. It proves that God *cannot* exist.

The correct reply is that the view that logical necessity merely reflects the use of words cannot possibly have the implication that every existential proposition must be contingent. That view requires us to *look at* the use of words and not manufacture *a priori* theses about it. In the Ninetieth Psalm it is said: 'Before the mountains were brought forth, or ever thou hadst formed the earth and the world, even from everlasting to everlasting, thou art God'. Here is expressed the idea of the necessary existence and eternity of God, an idea that is essential to the Jewish and Christian religions. In those complex systems of thought, those 'languages-games', God has the status of a necessary being. Who can doubt that? Here we must say with Wittgenstein, 'This language-game is played!'[29] I believe we may rightly take the existence of those religious systems of thought in which God figures as a necessary being to be a disproof of the dogma, affirmed by Hume and others, that no existential proposition can be necessary.

Another way of criticizing the ontological argument is the following: 'Granted that the concept of necessary existence follows from the concept of a being a greater than which cannot be conceived, this amounts to no more than granting the *a priori* truth of the *conditional* proposition, "If such a being exists then it necessarily exists". This proposition, however, does not entail the *existence of anything*, and one can deny its antecedent without contradiction'. Kant, for example, compares the proposition (or 'judgment', as he calls it) 'A triangle has three angles' with the proposition 'God is a necessary being'. He allows that the former is 'absolutely necessary' and goes on to say:

> The absolute necessity of the judgment is only a conditional necessity of the thing, or of the predicate in the judgment. The above proposition does not declare that three angles are absolutely necessary, but that, under the condition that there is a triangle (that is, that a triangle is given), three angles will necessarily be found in it.[30]

He is saying, quite correctly, that the proposition about triangles is equivalent to the conditional proposition 'If a triangle exists, it has

---

[29] *Philosophical Investigations*, New York, 1953, sec. 654.
[30] Op. cit., pp. 501–502.

three angles'. He then makes the comment that there is no contradiction 'in rejecting the triangle together with its three angles'. He proceeds to draw the alleged parallel: 'The same holds true of the concept of an absolutely necessary being. If its existence is rejected, we reject the thing itself with all its predicates; and no question of contradiction can then arise.'[31] The priest, Caterus, made the same objection to Descartes when he said:

> Though it be conceded that an entity of the highest perfection implies its existence by its very name, yet it does not follow that that very existence is anything actual in the real world, but merely that the concept of existence is inseparably united with the concept of highest being. Hence you cannot infer that the existence of God is anything actual, unless you assume that that highest being actually exists; for then it will actually contain all its perfections, together with this perfection of real existence.[32]

I think that Caterus, Kant, and numerous other philosophers have been mistaken in supposing that the proposition 'God is a necessary being' (or 'God necessarily exists') is equivalent to the conditional proposition 'If God exists then He necessarily exists'.[33] For how do they want the antecedent clause '*If* God exists' to be understood? Clearly

[31] Ibid., p. 502.

[32] Haldane and Ross, *The Philosophical Works of Descartes*, II, 7.

[33] I have heard it said by more than one person in discussion that Kant's view was that it is really a misuse of language to speak of a 'necessary being', on the grounds that necessity is properly predicated only of propositions (judgments) not of *things*. This is not a correct account of Kant. (See his discussion of 'The Postulates of Empirical Thought in General', op. cit., pp. 239–256, esp. p. 239 and pp. 247–248.) But if he had held this, as perhaps the above philosophers think he should have, then presumably his view would not have been that the pseudo-proposition 'God is a necessary being' is equivalent to the conditional 'If God exists then He necessarily exists'. Rather his view would have been that the genuine proposition ' "God exists" is necessarily true' is equivalent to the conditional 'If God exists then He exists' (*not* 'If God exists then He necessarily exists', which would be an illegitimate formulation, on the view imaginatively attributed to Kant).
'If God exists then He exists' is a foolish tautology which says nothing different from the tautology 'If a new earth satellite exists then it exists'. If 'If God exists then He exists' were a correct analysis of ' "God exists" is necessarily true', then 'If a new earth satellite exists then it exists' would be a correct analysis of ' "A new earth satellite exists" is necessarily true'. If the *analysans* is necessarily true then the *analysandum* must be necessarily true, provided the analysis is correct. If this proposed Kantian analysis of ' "God exists" is necessarily true' were correct, we should be presented with the consequence that not only is it necessarily true that God exists, but also it is necessarily true that a new earth satellite exists, which is absurd.

E

they want it to imply that it is *possible* that God does *not* exist.[34] The whole point of Kant's analysis is to try to show that it is possible to 'reject the subject'. Let us make this implication explicit in the conditional proposition, so that it reads: 'If God exists (and it is possible that He does not) then He necessarily exists'. But now it is apparent, I think, that these philosophers have arrived at a self-contradictory position. I do not mean that this conditional proposition, taken alone, is self-contradictory. Their position is self-contradictory in the following way. On the one hand, they agree that the proposition 'God necessarily exists' is an *a priori* truth; Kant implies that it is 'absolutely necessary', and Caterus says that God's existence is implied by His very name. On the other hand, they think that it is correct to analyse this proposition in such a way that it will entail the proposition 'It is possible that God does not exist'. But so far from its being the case that the proposition 'God necessarily exists' entails the proposition 'It is possible that God does not exist', it is rather the case that they are *incompatible* with one another! Can anything be clearer than the conjunction 'God necessarily exists but it is possible that He does not exist' is self-contradictory? Is it not just as plainly self-contradictory as the conjunction 'A square necessarily has four sides but it is possible for a square not to have four sides'? In short, this familiar criticism of the ontological argument is self-contradictory, because it accepts *both* of two incompatible propositions.[35]

One conclusion we may draw from our examination of this criticism is that (contrary to Kant) there is a lack of symmetry, in an important respect, between the propositions 'A triangle has three angles' and 'God has necessary existence', although both are *a priori*. The former can be expressed in the conditional assertion 'If a triangle exists (and it is possible that none does) it has three angles'. The latter cannot be expressed in the corresponding conditional assertion without contradiction.

[34] When summarizing Anselm's proof (in Part II, *supra*) I said: 'If God exists He necessarily exists'. But there I was merely stating an entailment. 'If God exists' did not have the implication that it is possible He does not exist. And of course I was not regarding the conditional as *equivalent* to 'God necessarily exists'.

[35] This fallacious criticism of Anselm is implied in the following remarks by Gilson: 'To show that the affirmation of necessary existence is analytically implied in the idea of God, would be . . . to show that God is necessary if He exists, but would not prove that He does exist' (E. Gilson, *The Spirit of Medieval Philosophy*, New York, 1940, p. 62).

## IV

I turn to the question of whether the idea of a being a greater than which cannot be conceived is self-contradictory. Here Leibniz made a contribution to the discussion of the ontological argument. He remarked that the argument of Anselm and Descartes

> is not a paralogism, but it is an imperfect demonstration, which assumes something that must still be proved in order to render it mathematically evident; that is, it is tacitly assumed that this idea of the all-great or all-perfect being is possible, and implies no contradiction. And it is already something that by this remark it is proved that, assuming that God is possible, he exists, which is the privilege of divinity alone.[36]

Leibniz undertook to give a proof that God is possible. He defined a *perfection* as a simple, positive quality in the highest degree.[37] He argued that since perfections are *simple* qualities they must be compatible with one another. Therefore the concept of a being possessing all perfections is consistent.

I will not review his argument because I do not find his definition of a perfection intelligible. For one thing, it assumes that certain qualities or attributes are 'positive' in their intrinsic nature, and others 'negative' or 'privative', and I have not been able to clearly understand that. For another thing, it assumes that some qualities are intrinsically simple. I believe that Wittgenstein has shown in the *Investigations* that nothing is *intrinsically* simple, but that whatever has the status of a simple, an indefinable, in one system of concepts, may have the status, of a complex thing, a definable thing, in another system of concepts.

I do not know how to demonstrate that the concept of God—that is, of a being a greater than which cannot be conceived—is not self-contradictory. But I do not think that it is legitimate to demand such a demonstration. I also do not know how to demonstrate that either the concept of a material thing or the concept of *seeing* a material thing is not self-contradictory, and philosophers have argued that both of them are. With respect to any particular reasoning that is offered for holding that the concept of seeing a material thing, for example, is self-contradictory, one may try to show the invalidity of the reasoning and thus free the concept from the charge of being self-contradictory

---

[36] *New Essays Concerning the Human Understanding*, Bk. IV, ch. 10; A. G. Langley, ed., La Salle, Ill., 1949, p. 504.

[37] See ibid., Appendix X, p. 714.

*on that ground.* But I do not understand what it would mean to demonstrate *in general,* and not in respect to any particular reasoning, that the concept is not self-contradictory. So it is with the concept of God. I should think there is no more of a presumption that it is self-contradictory than is the concept of seeing a material thing. Both concepts have a place in the thinking and the lives of human beings.

But even if one allows that Anselm's phrase may be free of self-contradiction, one wants to know how it can have any *meaning* for anyone. Why is it that human beings have even *formed* the concept of an infinite being, a being a greater than which cannot be conceived? This is a legitimate and important question. I am sure there cannot be a deep understanding of that concept without an understanding of the phenomena of human life that give rise to it. To give an account of the latter is beyond my ability. I wish, however, to make one suggestion (which should not be understood as autobiographical).

There is the phenomenon of feeling guilt for something that one has done or thought or felt or for a disposition that one has. One wants to be free of this guilt. But sometimes the guilt is felt to be so great that one is sure that nothing one could do oneself, nor any forgiveness by another human being, would remove it. One feels a guilt that is beyond all measure, a guilt 'a greater than which cannot be conceived'. Paradoxically, it would seem, one nevertheless has an intense desire to have this incomparable guilt removed. One requires a forgiveness that is beyond all measure, a forgiveness 'a greater than which cannot be conceived'. Out of such a storm in the soul, I am suggesting, there arises the conception of a forgiving mercy that is limitless, beyond all measure. This is one important feature of the Jewish and Christian conception of God.

I wish to relate this thought to a remark made by Kierkegaard, who was speaking about belief in Christianity but whose remark may have a wider application. He says:

> There is only one proof of the truth of Christianity and that, quite rightly, is from the emotions, when the dread of sin and a heavy conscience torture a man into crossing the narrow line between despair bordering upon madness—and Christendom.[38]

One may think it absurd for a human being to feel a guilt of such magnitude, and even more absurd that, if he feels it, he should *desire* its

[38] *The Journals,* tr. by A. Dru, Oxford, 1938, sec. 926.

removal. I have nothing to say about that. It may also be absurd for people to fall in love, but they do it. I wish only to say that there *is* that human phenomenon of an unbearably heavy conscience and that it is importantly connected with the genesis of the concept of God, that is, with the formation of the 'grammar' of the word 'God'. I am sure that this concept is related to human experience in other ways. If one had the acuteness and depth to perceive these connections one could grasp the *sense* of the concept. When we encounter this concept as a problem in philosophy, we do not consider the human phenomena that lie behind it. It is not surprising that many philosophers believe that the idea of a necessary being is an arbitrary and absurd construction.

What is the relation of Anselm's ontological argument to religious belief? This is a difficult question. I can imagine an atheist going through the argument, becoming convinced of its validity, acutely defending it against objections, yet remaining an atheist. The only effect it could have on the fool of the Psalm would be that he stopped saying in his heart 'There is no God', because he would now realize that this is something he cannot meaningfully say or think. It is hardly to be expected that a demonstrative argument should, in addition, produce in him a living faith. Surely there is a level at which one can view the argument as a piece of logic, following the deductive moves but not being touched religiously? I think so. But even at this level the argument may not be without religious value, for it may help to remove some philosophical scruples that stand in the way of faith. At a deeper level, I suspect that the argument can be thoroughly understood only by one who has a view of that human 'form of life' that gives rise to the idea of an infinitely great being, who views it from the *inside* not just from the outside and who has, therefore, at least some inclination to *partake* in that religious form of life. This inclination, in Kierkegaard's words, is 'from the emotions'. This inclination can hardly be an *effect* of Anselm's argument, but is rather presupposed in the fullest understanding of it. It would be unreasonable to require that the recognition of Anselm's demonstration as valid must produce a conversion.

## III

## FAITH, SCEPTICISM AND RELIGIOUS
## UNDERSTANDING

### By D. Z. Phillips

The relation between religion and philosophical reflection needs to be reconsidered. For the most part, in recent philosophy of religion, philosophers, believers and non-believers alike, have been concerned with discovering *the grounds* of religious belief. Philosophy, they claim, is concerned with reasons; it considers what is to count as good evidence for a belief. In the case of religious beliefs, the philosopher ought to inquire into the reasons anyone could have for believing in the existence of God, for believing that life is a gift from God, or for believing that an action is the will of God. Where can such reasons be found? One class of reasons comes readily to mind. Religious believers, when asked why they believe in God, may reply in a variety of ways. They may say, 'I have had an experience of the living God', 'I believe on the Lord Jesus Christ', 'God saved me while I was a sinner', or, ' I just can't help believing'. Philosophers have not given such reasons very much attention. The so-called trouble is not so much with the content of the replies, as with the fact that the replies are made by believers. The answers come from *within* religion, they presuppose the framework of Faith, and therefore cannot be treated as *evidence* for religious belief. Many philosophers who argue in this way seem to be searching for evidence or reasons for religious beliefs *external* to belief itself. It is assumed that such evidence and reasons would, if found, constitute the grounds of religious belief.

The philosophical assumption behind the ignoring of religious testimony as begging the question, and the search for external reasons for believing in God, is that one could settle the question of whether there is a God or not without referring to the form of life of which belief in God is a fundamental part. What would it be like for a philosopher to settle the question of the existence of God? Could a philosopher say that he believed that God exists and yet, never pray to Him, rebel against Him, lament the fact that he could no longer pray,

63

aspire to deepen his devotion, seek His will, try to hide from Him, or fear and tremble before Him? In short, could a man believe that God exists without his life being touched *at all* by the belief? Norman Malcolm asks with good reason,

> Would a belief that he exists, if it were completely non-affective, really be a belief that he exists? Would it be anything at all? What is 'the form of life' into which it would enter? What difference would it make whether anyone did or did not have this belief?[1]

Yet, many philosophers who search for the grounds of religious belief, claim, to their own satisfaction at least, to understand what a purely theoretical belief in the existence of God would be. But the accounts these philosophers give of what religious believers seem to be saying are often at variance with what many believers say, at least, when *they* are not philosophizing. Every student of the philosophy of religion will have been struck by the amount of talking at crossed purposes within the subject. A philosopher may say that there is no God, but a believer may reply, 'You are creating and then attacking a fiction. The god whose existence you deny is not the God I believe in.' Another philosopher may say that religion is meaningless, but another believer may reply, 'You say that when applied to God, words such as "exists", "love", "will", etc., do not mean what they signify in certain non-religious contexts. I agree. You conclude from this that religion is meaningless, whereas the truth is that you are failing to grasp the meaning religion has.' Why is there this lack of contact between many philosophers and religious believers? One reason is that philosophers who do not believe that God exists assume that they know what it means to say that there is a God. Norman Kemp Smith made a penetrating analysis of this fact when commenting on the widespread belief among American philosophers in his day of the uselessness of philosophy of religion.

> . . . those who are of this way of thinking, however they may have thrown over the religious beliefs of the communities in which they have been nurtured, still continue to be influenced by the phraseology of religious devotion—a phraseology which, in its endeavour to be concrete and universally intelligible, is at little pains to guard against the misunderstandings to which it may so easily give rise. As they

---

[1] 'Is it a Religious Belief that "God Exists"?' in *Faith and the Philosophers*, p. 107, ed. John Hick, London, 1964.

insist upon, and even exaggerate, the merely literal meaning of this phraseology, the God in whom they have ceased to believe is a Being whom they picture in an utterly anthropomorphic fashion....[2]

The distinction between religious believers and atheistical philosophers is not, of course, as clear-cut as I have suggested. It is all too evident in contemporary philosophy of religion that many philosophers who *do* believe in God philosophize about religion in the way which Kemp Smith found to be true of philosophical non-believers. Here, one can say either that their philosophy reflects their belief, in which case they believe in superstition but not in God, or, taking the more charitable view, that they are failing to give a good philosophical account of what they really believe.

Insufficient attention has been paid to the question of what kind of philosophical inquiry the concept of divine reality calls for. Many philosophers assume that everyone knows *what* it means to say that there is a God, and that the only outstanding question is *whether* there is a God. Similarly, it might be thought, everyone knows what it means to say that there are unicorns, although people may disagree over whether in fact there are any unicorns. If there were an analogy between the existence of God and the existence of unicorns, then coming to see that there is a God would be like coming to see that an additional being exists. 'I know what people are doing when they worship', a philosopher might say, 'They praise, they confess, they thank, and they ask for things. The only difference between myself and religious believers is that I do not believe that there is a being who receives their worship.' The assumption, here, is that the meaning of worship is contingently related to the question whether there is a God or not. The assumption might be justified by saying that there need be no consequences of existential beliefs. Just as one can say, 'There is a planet Mars, but I couldn't care less,' so one can say, 'There is a God, but I couldn't care less.' But what is one *saying* here when one says that there is a God? Despite the fact that one need take no interest in the existence of a planet, an account could be given of the kind of difference the existence of the planet makes, and of how one could find out whether the planet exists or not. But all this is foreign to the question whether there is a God. That is not something anyone could *find out*. It has been far too readily assumed that the dispute between the believer and the unbeliever is over a *matter of fact*. Philosophical

[2] 'Is Divine existence credible?' See pp. 105–106.

reflection on the reality of God then becomes the philosophical reflection appropriate to an assertion of a matter of fact. That this is a misrepresentation of the religious concept is made obvious by a brief comparison of talk about facts with talk about God.[3]

When do we say, 'It is a fact that . . .' or ask, 'Is it a fact that. . . .?' Often, we do so where there is some uncertainty. For example, if the police hear that a wanted criminal has died in some remote part of the world, their reaction might be, 'Check the facts'. Again, we often say that something is a fact in order to rule out other possibilities. A student asks, 'Is the professor coming in today?' and receives the reply, 'No, as a matter of fact he never comes in on Mondays.' A fact might not have been: it is conceivable that the wanted criminal had not died, just as it is conceivable that it had been the custom of the professor to come in on Mondays. On the other hand, many religious believers do not think of God as a being who may or may not exist. It is not that as a *matter of fact* God will always exist, but that it *makes no sense* to say that God might not exist.

We decide the truth or falsity of many matters of fact by taking account of the truth or falsity of other matters of fact. What is to count in deciding whether something is a fact is agreed upon in most cases. Refusal to admit that something is a fact even when one is directly confronted by it might be cause for alarm, as in the case of someone who sees chairs in a room which in fact is empty. Is this akin to the dispute between the believer and the unbeliever; one sees God but the other does not? The believer is not like someone who sees objects when they are not there, since his reaction to the absence of factual evidence is not at all like that of a man suffering from hallucinations. In the case of the chairs there is no dispute over the *kind of evidence* needed to settle the issue. When the positivist claims that there is no God because God cannot be located, the believer does not object on the grounds that the investigation has not been thorough enongh, but on the grounds that the investigation fails to understand the grammar of what is being investigated, namely, the reality of God. Of one thing he is certain, whatever *is* located is not God.

It makes as little sense to say that God's existence is not a fact as it does to say that God's existence is a fact. In saying that something is or

[3] The following five paragraphs are more or less an extract from my paper, 'Philosophy, Theology, and the Reality of God', Oct. 1964. I am grateful to the Editor of the *Philosophical Quarterly* for permission to use the material here.

is not a fact in this philosophical context I am not describing the 'something' in question. To say that 'x' is a fact, here, is to say something about the grammar of 'x'; it is to indicate what it would and would not be sensible to say or do in connection with it. To say that the concept of divine reality does not share this grammar is to reject the possibility of talking about God in the way in which one talks about matters of fact. I suggest that more can be gained if one comparss the question, 'What kind of reality is divine reality?' not with the question, 'Is this physical object real or not?' but with the different question, 'What kind of reality is the reality of physical objects?' To ask a question about the reality of physical objects is not like asking whether this appearance is real or not, where often one can find out. I can find out whether unicorns are real or not, but how can I find out whether the physical world is real or not? This latter question is not about the possibility of carrying out an empirical investigation, since the answer to it is presupposed by any experimentation. It is a question of whether it is possible to speak of truth or falsity in the physical world; a question logically prior to that of determining the truth or falsity of any particular matter of fact. Similarly, the question of the reality of God is a question of the possibility of sense and nonsense, truth and falsity, in religion. When God's existence is construed as a matter of fact, it is taken for granted that the concept of God is at home within the conceptual framework of the reality of the physical world. It is as if we said, 'We know where the assertion of God's existence belongs, we understand what kind of assertion it is, all we need do is determine its truth or falsity.' But to ask a question about the reality of God is to ask a question about *a kind of reality*, not about the reality of *this* or *that* being, in much the same way as asking a question about the reality of physical objects is not to ask about the reality of this or that physical object.

What, then, is the appropriate philosophical investigation of the reality of God? Suppose one asks, 'His reality as opposed to what?' The possibility of the unreality of God does not occur *within* any religion, but it might well occur in disputes *between* religions. A believer of one religion might say that the believers of other religions were not worshipping *the same* God. The question how he would decide the identity of God is connected in many ways with what it means to talk of divine reality.

In a dispute over whether two people are discussing the same person there are ways of removing the doubt, but the identity of God is not like the identity of a human being. To say that one worships the same God as someone else is not to point to the same object or to be confronted with it. How did Paul, for example, know that the God he worshipped was also the God of Abraham? What enabled him to say this was not anything like an empirical method of agreement as in the case of two astronomers who check whether they are talking of the same star. What enabled Paul to say that he worshipped the same God as Abraham was the fact that although many changes had taken place in Jewish beliefs about God, there was nevertheless a common religious tradition in which both he and Abraham stood. To say that a god is not the same as one's own God involves saying that those who believe in him are in a radically different religious tradition from one's own. To say that one worships the same God as other people is to say that worship plays a role in their lives similar to the role it plays in one's own. The criteria of what can be sensibly said of God are to be found *within* the religious tradition. This conclusion has important consequences for the question of what account of religion philosophy can give. It follows from my argument that the criteria of intelligibility cannot be found outside religion, since they are given by religious discourse itself. Philosophy can claim justifiably to show what is meaningful in religion only if it is prepared to examine religious concepts in the contexts from which they derive their meaning.

A failure to take account of the above context has led some philosophers to ask religious language to satisfy criteria of meaningfulness alien to it. They say that religion must be rational if it is to be intelligible. Certainly, the distinction between the rational and the irrational must be central in any account one gives of meaning. But this is not to say that there is a paradigm of rationality to which all modes of discourse conform. A necessary prolegomenon to the philosophy of religion, then, is to show the diversity of criteria of rationality; to show that the distinction between the real and the unreal does not come to the same thing in every context. If this were observed, one would no longer wish to construe God's reality as being that of an existent among existents, an object among objects.

Coming to see that there is a God is not like coming to see that an additional being exists. If it were, there would be an extension of one's knowledge of facts, but no extension of one's understanding. Coming to see that there is a God involves seeing a new meaning in one's life, and being given a new understanding. The Hebrew-Christian conception of God is not a conception of a being among beings. Kierkegaard emphasized the point when he said bluntly, 'God does not exist. He is eternal.'[4]

The distinction between eternity and existence has been ignored by many philosophers of religion, and as a result they have singled out particular religious beliefs for discussion, divorcing them from the context of belief in God. Alasdair MacIntyre has pointed out the importance of recognizing the need, not simply to discuss specific religious utterances, but to ask why such utterances are called religious in the first place.

Those linguistic analysts who have turned their attention to theology have begun to examine in detail particular religious utterances and theological concepts. This examination of the logic of religious language has gone with a great variety of religious attitudes on the part of the philosophers concerned. Some have been sceptics, others believers. But what their enterprise has had in common is an examination of *particular* religious forms of speech and utterance, whether such examination has been presented as part of an argument for or as part of an argument against belief. What such examinations may omit is a general consideration of what it means to call a particular assertion or utterance part of a religious belief as distinct from a moral code or a scientific theory.[5]

In his more recent work in the philosophy of religion, MacIntyre has said that the above distinction buys a position at the price of emptiness,[6] but I think his earlier view is the correct one. It stresses the artificiality of separating the love, mercy, or forgiveness of God from His nature. One cannot understand what praising, confessing, thanking, or asking, mean in worship apart from belief in an eternal God. The eternity of the Being addressed determines the meaning of all these activities. One implication of this fact is that philosophers who do not believe in God can no longer think of their rejection as the denial of something *with which they are familiar*. Discovering that there is a God is not like establishing that something is the case within a universe of discourse with which we are already familiar. On the contrary, it is to discover that there *is* a universe of discourse we had been unaware of. The flattering picture that the academic philosopher may have of

---

[4] *Concluding Unscientific Postscript*, trans. David F. Swenson, Princeton University Press, 1944, p. 296.

[5] 'The Logical Status of Religious Belief', in *Metaphysical Beliefs*, ed. A. MacIntyre, London, 1957, p. 172.

[6] See 'Is Understanding Religion Compatible with Believing?' in *Faith and the Philosophers*, ed. John Hick, London, 1964.

himself as possessing the key to reality has to be abandoned. The philosopher, like anyone else, may fail to understand what it means to believe in an eternal God.

In saying that one must take account of the concept of the eternal if one wishes to understand various religious activities, I realize that I am laying myself open to all kinds of misunderstandings. Some religious believers, when they have wanted to turn aside the philosopher's questions, have said, 'Finite understanding cannot understand the eternal', or something similar. This is not what I am saying. There is a proper place to say such things, that God is the inexpressible, for example, but that place is within religious belief. These are religious utterances whose meaning is seen in the role they play in the lives of believers. Sometimes, however, the utterances are used as a form of protectionism against intellectual inquiry. They began as religious utterances, but end up as pseudo-epistemological theories. When this happens, the philosopher's censure is deserved. In saying that human understanding cannot fathom the eternal, the believer is claiming that there is some higher order of things that transcends all human discourse, that religion expresses 'the nature of things'. In saying this, the believer falsifies the facts. Such a position involves upholding what John Anderson calls, 'a hierarchical doctrine of reality'. Anderson has a powerful argument against this brand of religious apologetics. He says that to speak in this way

. . . is to speak on behalf of the principle of authority—and so again (whatever the actual power may be that is thus metaphysically bolstered up) to support a low way of living. It is low, in particular, because it is anti-intellectual, because it is necessarily dogmatic. Some account can be given of the relation of a particular 'rule' or way of behaving to a certain way of life, but it can have no demonstrable relation to 'the nature of things'. To say that something is required by the nature of things is just to say that it is required—to say, without reason, that it 'is to be done'; and, as soon as any specification is attempted, the whole structure breaks down. If, for example, we are told to do something because God commands us to do so, we can immediately ask why we should do what God commands—and any intelligible answer brings us back to *human* relationships, to the struggle between opposing movements.[7]

[7] 'Art and Morality', pp. 256–257, *Australasian Journal of Psychology and Philosophy*, XIX 3, Dec. 1941.

I should like to make it quite clear that I agree with Anderson in the above criticism. In speaking of religion as turning away from the temporal towards the eternal, I am not putting forward any kind of epistemological thesis. On the contrary, I am referring to the way in which the concept of the eternal does play a role in very many human relationships. I am anxious to show that religion is not some kind of technical discourse or esoteric pursuit cut off from the ordinary problems and perplexities, hopes and joys, which most of us experience at some time or other. If it were, it would not have the importance it does have for so many people. By considering one example in detail, namely, eternal love or the love of God, I shall try to show what significance it has in human experience, the kind of circumstances which occasion it, and the kind of human predicament it answers. By so doing I hope to illustrate how seeing that there is a God in this context is synonymous with seeing the possibility of eternal love.[8]

Let me begin by speaking of a distinction with which we are all familiar: the distinction between *mine* and *yours*. The distinction is relevant to the concept of justice. If I take what is yours, or if you take what is mine, justice is thereby transgressed against. Our relationships with other people are pervaded by a wide range of rights and obligations, many of which serve to emphasize the distinction between *mine* and *yours*. But all human relationships are not like this. In erotic love and in friendship, the distinction between *mine* and *yours* is broken down. The lovers or the friends may say, 'All I have is his, and what is his is mine.' Kierkegaard says that the distinction between *mine* and *yours* has been transformed by a relationship in which the key term is *ours*. Nevertheless, he goes on to show that the *mine/yours* distinction is not completely transformed by such relationships, since the *ours* now functions as a new *mine* for the partners in the relationships. The distinguishing factor in the *mine/yours* distinction is now the relation of erotic love or friendship as opposed to the self-love which prevailed previously. *Mine* and *yours* now refer to those who are within and to those who are outside the specific relationship.

Now Christianity wishes to speak of a kind of love which is such that no man is excluded from it. It calls this love, love of one's neighbour. What is more, it claims that this love is internally related to the love of God; that is, that without knowing what this love is, one cannot know what the love of God is either. An attempt to elucidate

---

[8] Anyone acquainted with Kierkegaard's *Works of Love* will recognize in what follows how dependent I am on the Second Part of that work.

what is meant by love of the neighbour will therefore be an attempt to elucidate what is meant by the love of God.

If one considers self-love in its simplest form, namely, as the desire to possess the maximum of what one considers to be good for oneself, it is easy enough to imagine conditions in which such love could be thwarted. War, famine, or some other natural disaster, might upset the normal conditions in which rights and obligations operate. Even given such conditions, the self-lover's ambitions may be thwarted by the greater ingenuity of his competitors. Sooner or later he may be forced to realize that the minimum rather than the maximum is going to be his lot. Self-love might be called temporal love in so far as it depends on states of affairs contingently related to itself. If a man's life revolves around self-love, it is obvious that he is forever dependent on the way things go, since it is the way things go that determines whether his self-love is satisfied or not.

It might be thought that erotic love and friendship avoid the predicament of self-love outlined above. The lovers or the friends may say to one another, 'Come what may, we still have each other.' Yet, such reliance shows that this love too is temporal; it depends on certain states of affairs being realized. To begin with, the point of such love depends on the existence of *the other*. Often, when the lovers or the friends love each other very much, the death of the beloved can rob life of its meaning; for what is love without the beloved? Again, erotic love and friendship depend on the unchangeability of the beloved. But the beloved may change. Friendship can cool, and love can fade. If the relationship is such that it depended on reciprocation, then a change in the beloved or in the friend may rob it of its point. So although erotic love and friendship are far removed from self-love, they too are forms of temporal love in so far as they are dependent on how things go.

Temporal love, then, is marked by certain characteristics: it depends on how things go, it may change, and it may end in failure. Eternal love, it is said, is not dependent on how things go, it cannot change, and it cannot suffer defeat. One must not think that this contrast presents the believer with an either/or. He is not asked to choose between loving God on the one hand, and loving the loved one on the other. What he is asked to do is not to love the loved one in such a way that the love of God becomes impossible. The death of the beloved must not rob life of its meaning, since for the believer, the meaning of life is found in God. The believer claims that there is a love that will not let one go whatever happens. This is the love of God, the independence of which from what happens is closely bound up with the point of calling it eternal.

The object of Christian love is the neighbour. But who is the neighbour? The neighbour is every man. The obligation to love the neighbour does not depend on the particularity of the relationship as in the case of the love which exists between parents and children, lovers or friends. The neighbour is not loved because of his being a parent, lover, or friend, but simply because of his being. In relation to the agent, the love takes the form of self-renunciation. In this self-renunciation, man discovers the Spirit of God. Consider how love of the neighbour exhibits the three characteristics I mentioned earlier: independence of the way things go, unchangeability, and immunity from defeat. Kierkegaard brings out the contrast between love of one's neighbour on the one hand, and erotic love and friendship on the other, in these terms.

The beloved can treat you in such a way that he is lost to you, and you can lose a friend, but whatever a neighbour does to you, you can never lose him. To be sure, you can also continue to love your beloved and your friend no matter how they treat you, but you cannot truthfully continue to call them beloved and friend when they, sorry to say, have really changed. No change, however, can take your neighbour from you, for it is not your neighbour who holds you fast—it is your love which holds your neighbour fast.[9]

For someone with eyes only for the prudential, and common-sense considerations, the love which Kierkegaard is talking about seems to lead inevitably to self-deception, and to a kind of foolishness. On the contrary, Kierkegaard argues, eternal love is precisely the only kind of love which can never deceive one. After a certain stage of unrequited love, no one could be blamed for saying, 'The lover has deceived me.' It becomes intelligible and justifiable to say this because the love in question does not have much point without some degree of reciprocation. At first sight it looks as if the same conclusions apply to love of one's neighbour. But eternal love believes all things, and yet is never deceived! Ordinarily speaking, we say that only a fool believes all things; only a man who ignores the odds could be so stupid. Yet, Christianity says that eternal love cannot be deceived, for if a believer is wrong about a man but continues to love him, in what sense is he

9 Søren Kierkegaard, *Works 'of Love*, translated by Howard and Edna Hong, Wm. Collins, Sons & Co., London, 1962, p. 76.

F

deceived? True, one can enumerate all the ways in which obvious deceptions have taken place: loans unreturned, promises broken, trusts betrayed, etc., but the believer continues to love the neighbour despite all this. Those who see little in the love of the neighbour will say, especially if the believer is reduced to a state which many would call ruin, that the believer has lost all. On the contrary, Kierkegaard tells us, the believer, in the act of self-renunciation possesses all; he possesses love. To possess this love is to possess God. Indeed, the only way in which the believer can be deceived is by ceasing to love. Ordinarily, when we say, 'I shall show no more love towards him,' we envisage the loss as suffered by the person who is the object of one's love. But if the believer says, 'I shall love the neighbour no longer,' he is the victim of deception, since the loss of loving is his loss too. Kierkegaard brings this point out very clearly.

When someone says, 'I have given up my love for this man,' he thinks that it is this person who loses, this person who was the object of his love. The speaker thinks that he himself possesses his love in the same sense as when one who has supported another financially says, 'I have quit giving assistance to him.' In this case the giver keeps for himself the money which the other previously received, he who is the loser, for the giver is certainly far from losing by this financial shift. But it is not like this with love; perhaps the one who was the object of love does lose, but he who 'has given up his love for this man' is the loser. Maybe he does not detect this himself; perhaps he does not detect that the language mocks him, for he says explicitly, 'I have given up my love.' But if he has given up his love, he has then ceased to be loving. True enough, he adds my love 'for this man', but this does not help when love is involved, although in money matters one can manage things this way without loss to oneself. The adjective *loving* does not apply to me when I have given up my love 'for this man'—alas, even though I perhaps imagined that he was the one who lost. It is the same with despairing over another person; it is oneself who is in despair.[10]

In this way, Kierkegaard illustrates the truth that for the believer, love itself is the real object of the relationship between himself and another person. This love is the Spirit of God, and to possess it is to walk with God. Once this is realized, one can see how love and

[10] Ibid., pp. 239–240.

understanding are equated in Christianity. To know God is to love Him. There is no theoretical understanding of the reality of God.

If anyone thinks he is a Christian and yet is indifferent towards his being a Christian, then he really is not one at all. What would we think of a man who affirmed that he was in love and also that it was a matter of indifference to him?[11]

'But, so far,' the non-believer might complain, 'you have simply concealed the advantage entailed in religion, namely, God's love for the sinner. Is not this the reason for love of the neighbour? Unless one loves the neighbour, God will not love one.' There is truth in this *unless*, but not as conceived in the above objection. The love of the neighbour is not the means whereby a further end is realized, namely, one's own forgiveness. On the contrary, there is an internal relation between forgiving another and being forgiven oneself. I cannot hope to emulate Kierkegaard's analysis of this religious truth, so I must ask the reader to forgive a final quotation of two passages where his analysis is particularly forceful.

When we say, 'Love saves from death,' there is straightway a reduplication in thought: the lover saves another human being from death, and in entirely the same or yet in a different sense he saves himself from death. This he does at the same time; it is one and the same; he does not save the other at one moment and at another save himself, but in the moment he saves the other he saves himself from death. Only love never thinks about the latter, about saving oneself, about acquiring confidence itself; the lover in love thinks only about giving confidence and saving another from death. But the lover is not thereby forgotten. No, he who in love forgets himself, forgets his sufferings in order to think of another's, forgets all his wretchedness in order to think of another's, forgets what he himself loses in order lovingly to consider another's loss, forgets his advantage in order lovingly to look after another's advantage: truly, such a person is not forgotten. There is one who thinks of him, God in heaven; or love thinks of him. God is love, and when a human being because of love forgets himself, how then should God forget him! No, while the lover forgets himself and thinks of the other person, God thinks of the lover. The self-lover is busy; he shouts and complains and insists on his rights in order to make sure he is not forgotten—and yet he is forgotten. But the lover, who forgets himself, is remembered

[11] Ibid., p. 42.

by love. There is one who thinks of him, and in this way it comes about that the lover gets what he gives.[12]

And again,

'Forgive, and you will also be forgiven.' Meanwhile, one might nevertheless manage to understand these words in such a way that he imagined it possible to receive forgiveness without his forgiving. Truly this is a misunderstanding. Christianity's view is: forgiveness *is* forgiveness; your forgiveness is your forgiveness; your forgiveness of another is your own forgiveness; the forgiveness which you give you receive, not contrariwise that you give the forgiveness which you receive. It is as if Christianity would say: pray to God humbly and believing in your forgiveness, for he really is compassionate in such a way as no human being is; but if you will test how it is with respect to the forgiveness, then observe yourself. If honestly before God you wholeheartedly forgive your enemy (but remember that if you do, God sees it), then you dare hope also for your forgiveness, for it is one and the same. God forgives you neither more nor less nor otherwise than *as* you forgive your trespassers. It is only an illusion to imagine that one himself has forgiveness, although one is slack in forgiving others.[13]

My purpose in discussing the Christian concept of love was to show how coming to see the possibility of such love amounts to the same thing as coming to see the possibility of belief in God. As I said earlier, to know God is to love Him, and the understanding which such knowledge brings is the understanding of love. Belief, understanding, and love, can all be equated with each other in this context. There are, however, certain objections which can be made against this conclusion. Before ending, I want to consider one of the strongest of these made recently by Alasdair MacIntyre.

And if the believer wishes to he can always claim that we can only disagree with him because we do not understand him. But the implications of this defence of belief are more fatal to it than any attack could be.[14]

One of the fatal implications of identifying understanding and believing, according to MacIntyre, is that one can no longer give an intelligible account of a rejection of religious belief. MacIntyre says

[12] Ibid., p. 262.          [13] Ibid., pp. 351–352.
[14] 'Is Understanding Religion Compatible with Believing?', Faith and the Philosophers, p. 133.

that the Protestant who claims that grace is necessary before one can possess religious understanding is soon convicted of paradox.

For the Protestant will elsewhere deny what is entailed by his position, namely that nobody ever rejects Christianity (since anyone who thinks he has rejected it must have lacked saving grace and so did not understand Christianity and so in fact rejected something else).[15]

Does MacIntyre's point hold for any identification of understanding and believing? I suggest not. To begin with, there is a perfectly natural use of the word *rejection* which is connected with the inability of the person who rejects to make any sense of what is rejected. I can see no objection to saying that the man who says that religion means nothing to him rejects the claims of religion on his life. Apparently, when Oscar Wilde was accused of blasphemy during his trial, he replied, 'Sir, blasphemy is a word I never use.' Wilde is rejecting a certain way of talking. Similarly, the man who says, 'Religion is mumbo-jumbo as far as I am concerned,' is making a wholesale rejection of a way of talking or a way of life. That way of talking and that way of life mean nothing to him, but this does not mean that he cannot reject them.

On the other hand, I agree with MacIntyre that there are difficulties involved in the view I wish to maintain if the rejection of religion in question is not the rejection of the meaningless, but rebellion against God. Camus says of the rebel,

The rebel defies more than he denies. Originally, at least, he does not deny God, he simply talks to Him as an equal. But it is not a polite dialogue. It is a polemic animated by the desire to conquer.[16]

But if the rebel knows God and yet defies Him, how can one say that to know God is to love Him? Clearly, some kind of modification of my thesis is called for. I agree. But what is not called for is a denial of the identification of belief and understanding in religion. The fact of rebellion makes one think otherwise because of a false and unnecessary assimilation of 'I believe in God', to 'I believe in John'. Belief in God has a wider range of application than belief in another person. This point has been made very clearly by Norman Malcolm.

Belief in a person primarily connotes trust or faith: but this is not so of belief in God. A man could properly be said to believe in God

[15] Ibid., p. 116.
[16] *The Rebel*, p. 31. Peregrine Book edn., trans. by Anthony Bower.

whose chief attitude towards God was *fear*. ('A sword is sent upon you, and who may turn it back?') But if you were enormously afraid of another human being you could not be said to believe in him. At least you would not believe in him *in so far* as you were afraid of him: whereas the fear of God is one form of belief in him.

I am suggesting that *belief-in* has a wider meaning when God is the object of it than when a human being is. Belief in God encompasses not only trust but also awe, dread, dismay, resentment, and perhaps even hatred. Belief in God will involve some affective state or attitude, having God as its object, and those attitudes could vary from reverential love to rebellious rejection.[17]

I should still want to argue, however, that the love of God is the primary form of belief in God if only because the intelligibility of all the other attitudes Malcolm mentions is logically dependent on it. The rebel must see the kind of relationship God asks of the believer before he can reject and defy it. He sees the story from the inside, but it is not a story that captivates him. The love of God is active in his life, but in him it evokes hatred. To say that he does not believe in God is absurd, for whom does he hate if not God?

Similar difficulties to those mentioned by MacIntyre might be thought to arise in giving an account of seeking for God. If one must believe before one can know God, how can one know that it is God one is seeking for? The answer to this difficulty has been given by Pascal: 'Comfort yourself, you would not seek me if you had not found me.' One must not think of belief in God as an all-or-nothing affair. Whether the love of God means anything in a man's life can be assessed, not simply by his attainments, but also by his aspirations. So even if a man does not actually love God, his understanding of what it means to love God can be shown by his aspirations towards such love.

On the other hand, it would be a mistake to conclude that in the absence of religious attainments only religious aspirations could be the sign that religion held some meaning for a person. We have seen already in the case of the rebel that belief in God need not entail a worshipful attitude on the part of the believer. Neither need the believer aspire to attain love of God. On the contrary, he may want to flee from it. Instead of feeling sad because he spurns God's love, he may hate the fact that he cannot rid his life of God. If someone were to say

[17] Op. cit., pp. 106–107.

to him, 'You do not believe in God,' he might reply, 'How can you say that when God will not leave me alone?'

What, then, are our conclusions? The assertion that to know God is to love Him is false if it is taken to imply that everyone who believes in God loves Him. What it stresses, quite correctly, is that there is no theoretical knowledge of God. As Malcolm said, 'belief in God involves some affective state or attitude.' I think that love of God is fundamental in religion since all other attitudes can be explained by reference to it. I believe that Kierkegaard says somewhere that in relation to God there are only lovers—happy or unhappy—but lovers. The unhappy or unruly lover has an understanding of what it means to believe in God as well as the happy lover. The man who construes religious belief as a theoretical affair distorts it. Kierkegaard emphasizes that there is no understanding of religion without passion. This is why understanding religion is incompatible with scepticism.

IV

## FOUR MEN TALK ABOUT GOD

By R. P. Anschutz

I

Agnostic. In a case like this, there is only one course open to a reasonable man—suspense of judgment. There is evidence on both sides, but no proof. We must recognize, then, that with our finite intelligence we cannot obtain any certain knowledge whether or not there is an infinite intelligence which creates and sustains the world. We can only weigh the conflicting probabilities furnished by our experience of the world. And in my own experience, and, I believe, in the experience of most other men, the probabilities are too nearly balanced for a definite decision to be possible.

Protestant. But you can't reach God by searching Him out like that. He has to search you out. The living belief in God which is possessed by a Christian, which possesses a Christian, is an immediate conviction which could not possibly be attained by any weighing of probabilities. I am as certain of God's existence as I am of yours or my own—I have a living experience of God.

Agnostic. But what about me? Without any similar conviction of my own, I cannot regard yours as deciding the question. I can only regard it as one of the many bits of evidence that have to be taken into consideration in this matter. And I am afraid that I am not justified, scientifically, in according it any more weight than the conviction of Atheist that there is no God.

Protestant. But surely you cannot weigh his ignorance against my knowledge. What I offer is the evidence of an eye-witness—not one bit of circumstantial evidence to set against other bits. I tell you that I have experienced God as directly and immediately as I have experienced anything—more directly. You say that you haven't and Atheist hasn't. Is your lack of experience to be set against my experience? Will you say that the chances are a thousand to one against the existence of the Pyramids because there are a thousand men that have not seen them for every one that has?

81

ATHEIST. But what precisely is this religious experience of yours, Protestant? It is true that you cannot argue that a thing doesn't exist because a great many men are ignorant of it. And no doubt my ignorance of God and the ignorance of Agnostic cannot be set against your knowledge—if you have knowledge. But that is just the point: how are we to know that you have knowledge? How do you know yourself? After all, you know, error is nearly as common as ignorance.

PROTESTANT. Now you are asking for the impossible. The knowledge of God cannot be certified. But, then, neither can the knowledge of anything else—except to a very limited extent and never in regard to ultimates. In the last resort all knowledge has to be regarded as self-certifying. Why not, then, my knowledge of God? You cannot go outside experience to guarantee what you find within experience. You simply have to accept it.

ATHEIST. That only means that you cannot know without knowing, which doesn't seem to help much. At any rate it doesn't answer my question. How do you know that your experience is an experience *of God* and not, say, the after-effects of a good meal?

PROTESTANT. Well, how do I know when you look at this bit of paint that you are having an experience of red? If you can answer that question, I'll answer yours.

ATHEIST. I am afraid that won't do. Red is not a theory about the universe: God is. What you are saying is that your experience provides a proof of Theism and I am not saying anything like that when I say that paint is red. If you want a parallel to your 'religious experience' you will have to find a physicist with a 'relativity experience' or a biologist with an 'evolutionary experience'.

PROTESTANT. Well, all that I can say is, that if you had had a religious experience, you would know very well how it certifies itself as an experience of God. But since you lack that experience—and, I am afraid, deliberately harden yourself against it—it is useless to talk to you. It is an impossible task—like describing glories of colour to a man who has been blind from birth.

ATHEIST. But that is not the point. You say that you have had an experience. That is all right—no one is going to deny that. But then you go on to say that it is an experience *of God*. And when you say that, you are not merely describing the quality of your experience or its intensity or anything like that. You are saying something quite different. You are saying that, in that experience, you are aware that all the things of this world are the creatures of an infinitely perfect

Creator. And what I want to know is how any single experience could possibly supply you with all that information.

AGNOSTIC. Well, isn't it possible to say that a man's belief that he has had an experience of God is verified by its consequences—like any other hypothesis? Religious faith does work, you know. A man does sometimes manage to pull himself together under its influence when all other influences have failed. And the same thing can sometimes be seen on a larger scale with whole communities—the Pitcairn Islanders, for instance. Don't cases like that prove, or at least tend to confirm, a man's assertion that his experience really was of God?

ATHEIST. No, they don't. All they prove is that a belief in God is sometimes efficacious in promoting the survival of men. And exactly the same thing can be said of any belief that is strongly held—of Communism, for example. But just as the survival effects of a belief in Communism do not prove the truth of Communism, so the survival effects of a belief in God do not prove the existence of God.

AGNOSTIC. But why not? A belief in Communism is really a belief that society is of such and such a nature. And if people act on this assumption and the results agree with their expectations, surely they have verified the hypothesis at least as certainly as a scientist verifies the hypothesis, for example, that an acid neutralizes an alkali. Similarly a belief in God is really a belief that the universe is of such and such a nature, and that should be capable of verification in the same sort of way. The only difficulty seems to be that nobody is very sure just what is implied by this hypothesis.

ATHEIST. I should have distinguished between the survival effects of a belief in Communism when it is held by an individual in a non-communist society and when it is held by a communist society. In the latter case, I agree, the survival of the society will verify the belief of its members in exactly the same way as a successful experiment verifies a chemical hypothesis. But not in the former case, when the individual survives. The survival effects of a belief in Communism in that case would not prove the truth of Communism because the same effects might equally well have been brought about by some other belief— by a belief in Fascism, for example. It is possible—and probable—that the survival effects of beliefs of this sort in these circumstances do not depend at all on *what* is believed, but simply on the fact *that* it is believed. And with regard to a belief in God, I will go further and say that its survival effects cannot possibly depend on anything else in any circumstances. This belief may, and does, enable men to live longer because it gives them something to live for. But from the very nature of the belief it can't enable them to live longer because it is true.

AGNOSTIC. But why not? I admit that in some instances the usefulness of a belief in God depends more or less demonstrably on the fact that it is held with some fervour. And I admit that this is a possible explanation of its usefulness in all instances. But I cannot agree that no other explanation is possible. It may be difficult to verify the other explanation—that it is useful because it is true. That is because it is difficult to see precisely what is asserted by a belief in God and how *that* can be verified. But, if the belief has any significance at all, it must assert something about the universe which can be verified by examination. And if that assertion is true, then, presumably, it is useful to know that it is true.

ATHEIST. But that is just the trouble. A belief in God is not a belief that the universe has a certain nature. It is a belief that the universe is created by a perfect being *who might equally well have left it uncreated.* And that is why it is not merely difficult, but impossible, to verify the hypothesis of God from an examination of the universe. On this hypothesis the universe becomes a sort of epiphenomenon which cannot verify anything.

AGNOSTIC. But surely if the belief in God is a belief that the universe is created by a perfect being, it must be based on some perfection that has been found in the universe.

ATHEIST. No. It is an essential part of God's perfection that He should be absolutely independent of anything else. And so you can't argue to His existence from the existence of anything else.

AGNOSTIC. Well, I am prepared to accept your first point, Atheist, but I don't see how you can possibly be right about the second. I can see that it is necessary to distinguish between the realized expectations which verify an assumption and those which do not. And I am prepared to admit that the survival effects of a belief in God do not *necessarily* imply the existence of God. But I still maintain that there is a *possibility* that men who hold this belief do as a matter of fact survive because this belief is true. And I completely disagree with your assertion that the assumption of God raises *no* expectation about the nature of the universe which would enable the assumption to be verified. If that were true, the term God could mean nothing to us and there would be no possible way of proving His existence.

ATHEIST. Well, Protestant is not the first to maintain that the experience of God is self-certifying. That has been held by a great many philosophers. But then they, unlike Protestant, have also held that in this respect the experience of God is quite unlike the experience of anything else. It is God, and God alone, they have held, whose existence can be proved merely from the idea that we have of Him.

AGNOSTIC. I suppose you mean the 'ontological argument'—that God is a completely perfect being and *therefore* cannot lack existence. Otherwise He would not be perfect.

ATHEIST. Yes. It is true that the experience of God which is pre-supposed in this argument is very much less than the experience which Protestant starts with. It consists only in the apprehension of the meaning of the word 'God'. But from the point of view of philosophy, of course, the less we presuppose the better. And this statement of the religious experience argument has the further advantage that, presupposing less, it goes much further. It can be used against anybody who understands the meaning of the term 'God'. And it is argued with some plausibility that even the fool who denies the existence of God will have to admit that he understands what he is denying.

AGNOSTIC. Well, the fallacy in the ontological argument has been pointed out often enough. I have an idea of God as a completely perfect being. A completely perfect being will also have the perfection of existence. Therefore my idea of God must include the idea of existence. That is all that follows—not that God actually exists, but only that the *idea* of existence is contained in the *idea* of God.

ATHEIST. But all the same, the ontological argument is the only way of proving the existence of God. And if it cannot prove His existence—well, then, it proves His non-existence. It still remains as important as it was ever thought to be by Anselm, Descartes and Hegel, because its consideration provides the quickest and surest way of demonstrating the truth of Atheism. Or at least what comes to the same thing, its failure shows the utter impossibility of obtaining any consistent statement of Theism.

PROTESTANT. How on earth do you make that out?

ATHEIST. God is perfect and therefore self-sufficient. He cannot therefore be proved to exist through the existence of anything else because His existence does not depend on the existence of anything else. Finally, indeed, nothing else exists besides Him. And so He must be proved to exist through Himself alone. Now the ontological argu-ment is the only argument which attempts to do this. Since that fails, then, there can be no case for Theism. If Theism were sound the ontological argument would be sound. Since the ontological argument is not sound, Theism is not sound.

CATHOLIC. I think you've omitted to draw a very important distinction—that, namely, between the system of reality and the system of knowledge. In reality, I agree, the existence of God is demonstrable from the nature of God, since nothing is more certain than that He derives His existence from Himself. And so the ontological argument must not only be a sound argument for His existence, but the soundest argument. So far, then, I agree with you. But it does not follow that we with our limited knowledge should be able to see that it is sound. The divine Existence is demonstrable from the divine Nature only when that Nature is adequately known. And it is not adequately known in this life. Perhaps I might put it that the ontological argument is sound *de jure* but not *de facto*. Nor does it follow—and this is the more important point at the moment—that in default of the ontological argument we are left without any other evidence of the existence of God. We may not be able to comprehend the essence of God in itself, but we can apprehend Him to some extent through His effects. And that apprehension is, in point of fact, sufficient to prove His existence in this life.

ATHEIST. Well, I don't see how you can know that an argument is sound unless you know that it is sound. But never mind that now. What I should like to know now is how you are going to justify the distinction between the essence of God and His effects. If you assume that God's effects exist apart from God Himself, you will be admitting surely, that He may be limited by His effects. And then, ceasing to be omnipotent, He will cease to be God. That is why I say that the ontological argument is the only argument which *could* prove the existence of God—in this life or any other life. It is the only argument which avoids this assumption.

CATHOLIC. Well, this is the position. Theism asserts that the universe is created by a perfect being. And so we can approach the consideration of Theism from two sides: either from the consideration of the nature of this being, or from the consideration of the nature of the universe. The first approach gives us the ontological argument which, as I have explained, I believe to be true in reality but not available to our limited intelligences. And we are left, then, with the second approach which gives us the arguments from motion, from causation, from design, and so on.

ATHEIST. But you don't seem to understand my objection. You say that the first approach fails and therefore we must fall back on the second. But this is just what I am suggesting we cannot do. I am suggesting that there are no alternatives to the ontological argument.

PROTESTANT. Why not? The thing is of no importance. It is a sort of trick which bears no relation to anything that anybody really thinks—least of all to my attempt to state the Christian position. A child can see the absurdity of trying to prove the existence of anything through the fact that someone has an idea of it. And it is obvious that in default of the direct experience which I assert, it can only be proved through the existence of something else.

ATHEIST. I agree, of course, that the ontological argument is invalid. But that is not the point. What I am suggesting is that the failure of the ontological argument involves the failure of Theism.

PROTESTANT. Well that, I think, is the queerest observation I ever heard on this subject.

ATHEIST. It seems straightforward enough to me: The existence of God can only be proved, you seem to admit, through the existence of something else. But the existence of God cannot be proved through the existence of anything else because there are no other existents besides Him. He is the self-subsistent on whom all other things depend for their existence. 'In Him we live and move and have our being', you remember. Well, what is the conclusion? The existence of God can be proved only through the existence of other things. There are no other things. Therefore the existence of God cannot be proved at all. That is the plain consequence of your rejection of the ontological argument. If you throw that over, you throw over Theism.

*       *       *

CATHOLIC. But aren't you confusing Theism with Pantheism? The assumption on which your argument depends is that God alone exists; that is, that God is the formal being of all things. And this is expressly denied in Theism, or at least in Christian Theism. If you want texts, consider these: 'God is high and elevated'—'He is over all things'. God is the creator of all things. But He must not therefore be identified with His creatures. There is, you know, some difference between the philosophies of Saint Thomas and Spinoza.

ATHEIST. Yes, but it is only the difference between a partial and a complete presentation of what is fundamentally the same doctrine. If Thomas had really thought out his Theism to the end, there would have been no need for Spinoza's supplement. All that Spinoza did was to follow the argument for Theism as it had been stated by the Scholastics, notably, of course, by Thomas. And then it turned out to be Pantheism. And that is my reply to your objection. I am not confusing Theism with Pantheism—I am saying that Theism is an unstable position which can only reach some measure of stability by becoming Pantheism. And then I am saying that Pantheism is indistinguishable from Atheism. Spinoza's contemporaries were quite right, and all the modern talk about the 'God-drunken' man is nonsense. If God is everything, He is nothing. And we are left, then, with the things of this world as they appear to be, without any supernatural support.

CATHOLIC. There is no need to convince me of the second part of your thesis—that Pantheism is Atheism. I am already convinced of that. But I am still waiting conviction regarding the first part—that Theism is Pantheism.

AGNOSTIC. Well, you know, Catholic, a good many theologians have spent a good deal of time trying to elucidate the Problem of Free Will, without any marked success. And the difficulty there seems to be exactly the same as the difficulty that Atheist is trying to point out in regard to Theism generally. It is the difficulty of maintaining the independence of the finite creature in face of the omnipotence of his Creator.

CATHOLIC. I think that that difficulty will disappear if you consider what creation really involves. God wills all that is requisite for the things which He wills. And so He creates things with the contingency or necessity that is proper to them. It is therefore no argument against the freedom of men to say that God has created them and therefore they cannot be free. On the contrary, God has created men free because it is proper for them to be free.—And similarly with things generally. It does not follow that the things of this world have no existence apart from the existence of God, because He has created them. On the contrary, in creating them He has endowed them with an existence apart from His own. And thus, being their creator, God both transcends and is immanent in His creatures. That is the meaning of creation.

ATHEIST. Of course that is the meaning of creation. That is my objection: that the meaning of creation is self-contradictory. It cannot be true both that a thing is completely dependent on another thing and also that it is independent. And yet that is what you have to say of anything that you assert to be created.

PROTESTANT. But surely, Atheist, you can say that a thing is dependent on another thing in some respects and independent in some respects.

ATHEIST. Not if the other thing is God. You cannot say that the things of this world are independent of God in any respect. He is omnipotent. Otherwise you admit a plurality of gods.

CATHOLIC. But can't you see, Atheist, that your argument, so far from invalidating my defence of God's transcendence, actually strengthens it? You insist on God's omnipotence. Very well, then; surely that omnipotence would be denied if God's creation were limited to things of a certain sort. But it is exactly this limitation that you assert when you say that God could not endow His creatures with an existence distinct from His own. You argue that the Divine omnipotence is incompatible with transcendence. I retort that it would be incompatible with anything but transcendence.

PROTESTANT. And it is a good retort, too. I know, Atheist, that you regard this sort of discussion as a game or a contest. And so I discount a good deal of what you say. But it really is very painful to me to hear you laying down the law about what God can do and what He cannot do. You ought to reflect that there are a good many things that you don't know.

ATHEIST. But surely, Catholic, if God creates things with the sort of existence that is proper to them, He must also create them in the sort of way that is proper to Him. In His creation it is obvious, I should think, that He cannot lose His omnipotence. But how can he fail to lose his omnipotence if He creates things that are independent of Him?

AGNOSTIC. So far as I can see, both your arguments are sound. God wouldn't be omnipotent unless He *could* create things with an independent existence, and yet He won't be omnipotent if He *does*. If, then, God is omnipotent, it must be that He could but He doesn't. God's omnipotence can be maintained only if it is not exercised—like freedom of speech, you know, in times of disturbance.

*     *     *

CATHOLIC. It is sometimes difficult, I admit, to obtain an adequate statement of all the implications of Theism. But then you must remember what I said previously: that in this life we are unable to comprehend the nature of God in Himself and are dependent for our knowledge of Him on our knowledge of His effects. And while these effects reveal

G

something of their First Cause—sufficient to assert His existence and to say something about His nature—they do not reveal everything. And so there is bound to be some verbal difficulty when we try to describe Him in terms drawn from our experience of this world, although these are the only terms available to us.

AGNOSTIC. I think that there is a good deal to be said for that, Catholic: If God did exist, we could not expect the clear and distinct account of His relation to the things of this world that Atheist demands, simply because we ourselves are things of this world. And the fact, then, that this account cannot be given is not a conclusive argument against the existence of God. It would be conclusive if our minds worked *in vacuo*—completely unaffected by our relations—our other relations—to the things we are considering. But that is plainly not the case. In any observation we have to allow for the position of the observer.

PROTESTANT. That is very true, Agnostic. Just as the astronomer in observing the movements of the stars has to allow for his own position on the earth, so the philosopher in discussing God has to allow for his own position as a creature of God. Atheist's great mistake is that he forgets the limitations of the intellect. And he does that because he forgets that man is far more than intellect.

ATHEIST. Well, it is illuminating to see how you all line up as sceptics in opposition to Atheism.

CATHOLIC. Nothing of the sort. The suggestion is not that you should abandon the use of your intellect, but simply that you should recognize the limitations which attach to it when it is associated with a finite body tied down to a particular time and place. And if that is scepticism, then every astronomer and every physicist—every scientist —is a sceptic.

ATHEIST. But you are saying that we can *never* know God's relation to His creatures while we retain our creaturely position. You are not saying that we have a particular view of God in order to allow for the particular consequences that that has for our knowledge—which is the procedure in scientific observation. You are saying that we have a particular point of view in order to stop further inquiry—in order to deny that we can have any knowledge at all of God's relation to His creatures. And if that isn't scepticism, it certainly commits the typical fallacy of scepticism.

AGNOSTIC. What do you mean? What is the objection to scepticism?

ATHEIST. The old objection—that the sceptic contradicts himself in assuming the knowledge that he denies. Catholic is saying that our relation to God is such that we cannot know our relation to God. And so he, at least, has transcended the limitations which he asserts can never be transcended.

AGNOSTIC. That objection, I agree, may hold against Catholic and Protestant, but not, I think, against me. You may reasonably complain that while they recognize your intellectual limitations in refusing to allow you to deny the existence of God, they fail to recognize their own in asserting His existence. But I am quite impartial in the matter. I believe that the assertion and the denial of God are equally beyond us.

ATHEIST. But why? Catholic and Protestant contradict themselves when they say that we cannot know our relation to God because of our relation to God. But so far as I can see, you have no reason at all for doubting our competence to decide the truth or falsity of Theism.

AGNOSTIC. Well, I should have thought that this discussion itself provided ample reason. It certainly shows that Theism is obscure. And then there are three possible explanations of its obscurity: either it is obscure because it is false, or because it is true, or because we are incompetent to decide whether it is true or false. You say that it is obscure because it is false. But Catholic and Protestant say that it is obscure because it is true. We cannot, they hold, know all about God because we are God's creatures. And since I see no way of deciding between these conflicting explanations, I prefer simply to say that it is obscure and leave it at that.

ATHEIST. That amounts to saying that we are incompetent to decide the truth of anything which we have not decided unanimously. And if you really believe that, you will have to conclude that we are incompetent to decide the truth of nearly everything—including Agnosticism.—But it is no use trying to decide this issue by counting heads. You have to follow the argument. And I am not saying merely that Theism is obscure, I am saying that it is self-contradictory, like the scepticism which is used to bolster it up—like the idea of a square circle. And there is no more reason to believe that the idea of Theism is beyond our competence than the idea of a square circle—unless you begin by assuming that Theism is true.

AGNOSTIC. But surely, Atheist, you cannot really believe that the idea of God is to be disposed of in this summary way. Surely you cannot leave out of consideration altogether the millions of men whose lives have revolved round the worship of God, especially since we continue to feel in ourselves exactly the same impulse to worship. I am not arguing that the existence of the impulse implies the existence of its object. Any argument of that sort seems quite indefensible. But I cannot agree that the persistence of the impulse has no bearing on the matter. Surely the impulse could not have persisted unless it had sometimes been gratified. And surely it is at least possible that it has been gratified, as the worshipper believes, by the God he worships.

ATHEIST. Quite possible, until you investigate the matter. And then you find that God cannot exist becaue it is impossible to speak consistently about Him, and in particular about His relation to the things of this world. And in the face of that fact—the self-contradiction of Theism—it is immaterial how many men have believed in its truth.


## II

ATHEIST. The trouble with Theism, I repeat, is that it has to start with various statements about the things of this world and it has to finish by denying the truth of all those statements. It appears finally that there is only one subject about which true statements can be made at all. And that is God.

CATHOLIC. And I repeat, Atheist, that that is not true so far as Christianity is concerned. Whatever the position is in Platonism or Spinozism or Calvinism or Hegelianism, the independent existence of the things of this world is not denied by Christianity.

ATHEIST. Well, if it isn't, it ought to be. That is the logical outcome of any Theism.

CATHOLIC. It is no use repeating all that again. Nothing you say can possibly sound convincing to a Christian until you are prepared to consider Christianity on its own merits. And you can only do that by starting at the beginning with the *Christian* reasons for believing in the existence of God.

PROTESTANT. Well, I don't believe that it is any use discussing the proofs of the existence of God any further. Christianity is a religion— not a philosophy, and not even a theology. Theology is only an attempt to give an account of religion, just as physiology is an attempt to give an account of the body. And just as it would be absurd to suppose that the existence of the body is denied by the inadequacies of physiology, so it is absurd to suppose that the reality of religion is denied by the inadequacies of theology. Religion is a fact which cannot be denied merely because it has not yet achieved a foolproof philosophical statement. And so I don't believe that you are starting at the beginning of Christianity by starting with the consideration of the proofs of the existence of God. I don't believe that there is any point at all in trying to prove the existence of God in an impersonal, metaphysical way. Even if you were to succeed, it wouldn't help you to incline the hearts and lives of men to religion. And that, after all, is the only thing that matters.

CATHOLIC. I agree, of course, that it is necessary to distinguish between the practice of religion and the theory of theology. But I cannot agree that therefore all theological and philosophical discussion is useless. I cannot see how a man's practice can be sound unless his theory is sound. And I cannot see how a man can practise religion, or anything else, without some theory. How *can* you incline a man's heart to religion while he persists in denying the existence of God—the unique object of religion?

PROTESTANT. Well, I don't believe that anybody has ever really denied the existence of God in his heart. But if he persists in saying that he does, like Atheist, I would tell him that he doesn't know what he is denying—that he is ignorant of the true nature of God. Everybody, at some time or another, feels that his life is worth while—that he is doing what is right and enjoying what is good. I would remind him of these experiences and tell him that, then, he has been experiencing God.

ATHEIST. And suppose he doesn't believe you?

PROTESTANT. How can he fail to believe me? He will know what these experiences mean to him. He cannot doubt that they represent the highest and best in life. How can he doubt, then, that they are manifestations of God?

ATHEIST. Quite easily, I should think. He may doubt whether they are manifestations of anything.

PROTESTANT. Well, I don't see how anybody can doubt it. We have enjoyed some good things; we want to enjoy more; we try to find where they come from. And so, whether we like it or not, all our lives are spent in the pursuit of God, since God is the giver of all good things. God is Goodness itself. We are only its vehicles: He is its source. And we cannot be content until we know its source.

ATHEIST. Well, in the first place, Protestant, your statement is an argument for the existence of God. And in the second place it is a very bad argument. God is not only the giver of good things, He is the perfect creator of all things. And so even if you could show—which you can't—that there is one 'source' of the goodness of good things, you would still be as far as ever from showing that there is also a single 'source' of all things.—It is absurd to derive the adjective 'good' from a personification of the abstract noun 'Goodness'. You might as well derive 'cold' from 'Coldness' or 'red' from 'Redness'. And, on the other hand, if it is not absurd—if you are justified in postulating a personal Goodness to account for the fact that some things are good— I am equally justified in postulating a personal Evil to account for the fact that some things are bad. And will you say then that God is not only Goodness itself, but also Evil itself?

PROTESTANT. Of course not. I have defined God as the source of *good* things.

ATHEIST. But you can't do that unless you are prepared to say that anything that exists is *therefore* good. And that the source of good things is the source of all things. Otherwise you have to postulate a source of bad things which is not God, besides the source of good things which is God. And then God will not be the creator of all things.

\*     \*     \*

CATHOLIC. I think we may agree, Atheist, that it is impossible to prove that there is a creator of all things except through the consideration of all things. And although I believe, as a matter of fact, that all things are good, I also agree that we cannot demonstrate their createdness by considering only their goodness. It is necessary to broaden the basis of Protestant's argument from 'goodness' to 'being' in order to prove the existence of God.

ATHEIST. And how will you do that?

CATHOLIC. By showing that the being of the things of this world is so imperfect that they could not be at all unless they were supported —created and sustained—by a perfect being which is not of this world.—In the first place, the imperfection of things is evidenced by their change. They begin to be and they cease to be; they become different; they move. All the things of this world are in a state of perpetual flux. They are perpetually becoming, but they never finally become anything. You will not, I suppose, deny that.

ATHEIST. No, the flux is admitted. But where is the imperfection? What is the matter with the flux?

CATHOLIC. The flux itself. Things change because they are unable to support themselves as they are—because they are unstable. And they

are unstable because they lack something which their nature demands
—something, if you prefer the phrase, which is implied by their idea.
That is why changing things are imperfect: their being is limited.—But
they do not change themselves. They are changed by other things
with more stability, more being. And so finally their change implies
an unchanging end of change in which all their limitations are overcome—which *is* all that they have it in them to become. And that is
God—Unmoved Mover and Supreme Being.—The case for God, then,
is based quite simply on the evident fact that there cannot be change
everywhere. Change itself depends on the unchangeable—instability
on stability.

ATHEIST. Well, it is not at all evident to me that there cannot be
change everywhere. And I completely fail to see how anything but
change can be inferred from change. As far as I can see, the occurrence
of any change depends only on the occurrence of its cause. And the
cause of a change is always another change. I don't understand what
you mean by 'being'. And I can't even imagine what you mean by
saying that things which are changed have less being than the things
which change them.

CATHOLIC. I mean that change is the reduction of something from
potentiality to actuality. And that nothing can be reduced from
potentiality to actuality except by something else which is already in
a state of actuality. As, for example, the potential heat of wood is
actualized by the actual heat of the fire. And so I conclude that there
must be a Supreme Being who moves all things because He is the
actuality of all things.

ATHEIST. Well, that sounds like plain humbug to me. If there is
one thing certain in this world it is that nothing—absolutely nothing—
is known or can be known or is there to be known of any actuality or
potentiality of things *independently of the changes which they are supposed
to explain.* And so the explanation of changes in these terms is simply
a pretentious and quite unfounded attempt to look wise after the
event. It is the sort of wisdom professed by Molière's doctor: 'Opium
causes sleep because it has a soporific quality.'

AGNOSTIC. But is it so certain that even that statement is nothing
but humbug? No doubt it is impossible to know that opium has a
soporific quality until it is known to cause sleep. And no doubt the
bare statement that it has a soporific quality tells us no more than the
statement that it causes sleep. But all the same it must be true that
opium does have a soporific quality if it causes sleep. And all that is

required to transform the humbug into science is the specification of
that soporific quality.—It is impossible in science to accept the changes
of things at their face value as you apparently wish to do, Atheist. It is
always necessary to seek an explanation of their changes in the things
themselves. And that, I take it, is a sufficient reason why we should
continue to use terms like 'actuality' and 'potentiality' when we don't
yet know what it is in the things that brings about their change.

ATHEIST. But how exactly are you going to find an explanation
of the changes of things in things themselves? What specification, for
example, of the soporific quality of opium would you accept as an
adequate explanation of the fact that opium causes sleep?

AGNOSTIC. Well, I suppose the fact would be explained if we
knew exactly what it is in the opium that acts upon the nervous system
in causing sleep, and exactly how it acts.

ATHEIST. What you really want to know, then, is the precise cause
of sleep when opium is administered and something about the details
of the causation. And that is how you would explain the fact that
opium causes sleep—by stating in more detail and with greater precision
*how* it causes sleep? Well, then, you are not concerned at all with any
soporific quality in opium, but simply and solely with the fact that it
causes sleep. And that I suggest is always the case: the *explanation* of a
change is nothing but a more detailed *description* of the change, and
the only questions involved in the description of a change are questions
of causation.

PROTESTANT. But surely there is some reason why one change
always follows another change. You cannot simply say that it is so and
leave it at that. There is far more to be known about it than that.

ATHEIST. There is always far more to be known about the details
of the change—about *how* it occurs. But there is never anything more
to be known about any underlying reason *why* it occurs. And it will
never be possible to get beyond the flat statement, which can only be
verified by experience, that it is so.

*        *        *

AGNOSTIC. But even if that is so, it doesn't dispose of Catholic's
argument for the *existence of God*. It only disposes of his *characterization*
of God. Even if it is impossible to argue from the nature of an effect
to the nature of its cause, it certainly is not impossible to argue from
the existence of an effect to the existence of its cause. And so even if

you deny that an unmoved mover is required to account for motion, you cannot deny that a First Cause is required to begin causation.

ATHEIST. But how can you ever come to a beginning of causation without arguing from the nature of the effect to the nature of its cause? So far as I can see, something like Catholic's theory of change is essential even to the assertion of a First Cause.

CATHOLIC. I don't think so. I think the existence of a First Cause can be proved quite independently of any theory of change: If there were no First Cause there would be no intermediate causes, and hence no ultimate causes—no causation at all. But there is causation and so there must be a First Cause.

ATHEIST. That merely begs the question. You are proving that there is a First Cause by assuming that there is a First Cause.

PROTESTANT. But surely, Atheist, you must admit that the series of causes begins somewhere.

ATHEIST. Well, in the first place, we have no evidence that there is *one* series of causes. And in fact all the evidence we have is against such a supposition. Whenever we try to describe the causal conditions of any event we always find ourselves radiating from it along divergent series of causes. And in the second place, even if there were one series of causes, we have no evidence that it must have a *beginning*. Every cause we know is also an effect. And I see no reason to admit an exception to this rule in favour of a First Cause.

CATHOLIC. But if there were no First Cause, the series of causes would stretch to infinity and the attempt to trace it to its end would involve an infinite regress. We could never obtain a complete account of the causation of any event. We should always be seeking a cause beyond the cause we had without ever being able to stop.

ATHEIST. Well, why not? What is wrong with an infinite regress like that? It is true that we can trace the series of causes as far as we like. But it is equally true that we can stop whenever we have had enough. There is no need to go on indefinitely.

CATHOLIC. But that is not sufficient. It is not sufficient that we can stop at any cause we like. We cannot be satisfied until we reach a cause which *constrains* us to stop. As scientists we can go on indefinitely tracing the causes of causes of causes. But our job as philosophers is quite different. And everybody has to be a philosopher, whether or not he is also a scientist.—As philosophers we are not concerned with the detail but with the completeness of knowledge. We are concerned not with the links of the causal chain, but with the hook from which it must depend—the necessary condition of the existence of *any* causal chain. That is why we have to admit a cause which is not also an effect. And that is what is really involved in the idea of a First Cause. It is not a member of the series of contingent causes but the self-caused cause of the whole series—the necessary reason why there are contingent causes at all.

ATHEIST. But how do you know that there is anything but the series of contingent causes? Where do you get your information about the hook from which it depends? You may be dissatisfied with the endless prospect of detailed work that is involved in science. But why should you think that you are justified in demanding anything else from philosophy?

CATHOLIC. Because the problem of philosophy is quite different from that of science—and equally legitimate. You said, a minute ago, that explanation is nothing but description. And that, I agree, is true— *in science*. But that doesn't mean that there is no explanation which is not description. It means rather that we have to look for it beyond science—*in philosophy*. That is the justification for philosophy: that it asks not merely *how* but *why* things are as they are—that it considers why they are at all.—All the facts described by science might have been otherwise. They might not have been at all. They are not necessary but contingent. And so when we ask why they exist, we must answer that they derive their existence from something which is not contingent but necessary. We cannot always refer the contingent to the contingent—the relative to the relative. At some point or other we must finally refer the contingent to the necessary   the relative to the absolute.—That is where philosophy supplants, or rather supplements, science. And that is why we have to admit the existence of God. He is the only being who contains within Himself the reason of His own existence. And so He alone can complete our knowledge as it requires to be completed.

ATHEIST. But that only begs the question again. It is no use repeating your assertion of an explanation which is not science—of a *why* which is not a *how*. That is precisely what I am denying. And I shall continue to deny it until you produce it in working order.—And finally, you know, you can only do that by accepting the ontological argument which you have so far evaded. That is the only way in which you can show that any being is necessary—that it really contains within itself the ground of its existence. And until you can show that, you cannot maintain that there is any necessary being.

CATHOLIC. Not at all. We can still prove that there is a necessary being even although we are unable to verify its necessity. The limitations of our faculties may prevent us seeing how God's essence involves existence, but they do not prevent us seeing that the contingency of the universe demands a creator whose essence involves existence.

*    *    *

AGNOSTIC. But how do you know, Catholic, that the universe itself is not necessary? You may say, distributively, that ever fact of the universe is contingent. But you cannot conclude, collectively, that all the facts—the whole universe—is contingent without committing the Fallacy of Composition.—And why, then, shouldn't we regard the universe as necessary? If we must suppose that something is necessary, as I agree we must, why shouldn't we make the most economical supposition and suppose that it is the universe, which we know, rather than a creator of the universe, which we don't know at all?

CATHOLIC. Well, that supposition—the supposition of Pantheism —may have the merit of economy. But it certainly hasn't the merit of answering my question. I am asking why there are any contingent facts. And it is not sufficient to reply that there must be facts. It is necessary to state why there must be facts. The facts themselves do not provide a reason. And you don't get beyond the facts by talking about the universe which is nothing but the unrealizable sum of the facts.

AGNOSTIC. But surely a whole may have properties which are not shared by its parts. A thing, for instance, may be spherical without any of its parts being spherical. And why, then, may not the whole universe be necessary even although each of its parts—each of its constituent facts—is contingent?

CATHOLIC. The very fact that the universe consists of parts shows that it is not the necessary being for which we are searching, since that must be simple. If the necessary being were composed of parts, its existence would depend on the existence of its parts, and then it would not be necessary.—And there is a further fact to be observed about the universe which is even more decisive—the fact that it is impossible to reach the end of its parts since it is extended, and therefore infinitely divisible—in time and space. The parts of the universe, then, cannot even be summed into a whole. And so obviously it cannot provide the sufficient reason for its contingent parts. It is so far from being necessary that it cannot even be regarded as being at all.

AGNOSTIC. On the other hand, there is this advantage in regarding the universe as the necessary reason of contingent facts: that it explains them by including them. And the relation of inclusion is comprehensible. But if you find the necessary reason of contingent facts in some being completely beyond them, you have to say that it creates them. And the relation of creation we have already found to be quite incomprehensible.

CATHOLIC. But how can you explain anything by means of 'the universe' when you cannot even talk about 'the universe'? You cannot, surely, find the relation of inclusion comprehensible without a comprehensible includer. And the universe, I say, is not a comprehensible includer. It is not comprehensible at all—in itself.

ATHEIST. On the one hand, then, the universe cannot be the necessary being which is to explain the existence of contingent facts, because it is nothing but the unrealizable sum of contingent facts. And, on the other hand, the only way in which the existence of contingent facts can be intelligibly explained by a necessary being is through their inclusion in that necessary being. Contingent facts must be completely dependent on the necessary being which accounts for their existence. And complete dependence can only be provided by inclusion.—So far as I can see, both your arguments are sound.

AGNOSTIC. But how can they both be sound when their conclusions are contradictory? If a necessary being must account for contingent facts by including them, then it must be the universe that is necessary. But, if you agree with that, you cannot also agree that the universe is not necessary, since that rules out inclusion. You can't have it both ways.

ATHEIST. I think I can. Your conclusions are only contradictory on the assumption that there must be a necessary basis of contingent facts. The contradiction disappears if that assumption is not true. And the contradiction itself shows that the assumption is not true.—When you say that it is most reasonable to suppose that the universe is necessary, *if we must find necessity somewhere*, you are saying again what I have said all along—that Theism is an unstable position which inevitably spills over into Pantheism. But that is not inconsistent with the recognition that Pantheism is also an unstable position, as Catholic maintains. Pantheism is not a better doctrine than Theism because it states a better sort of Theism, but because it is a clear exposure of the contradictions of any sort of Theism. And so it provides an impossible but highly useful bridge between Theism and Atheism. Pantheists, of course, fail to recognize this. They indulge in the same worshipful phraseology as Theists. But it is impossible in practice to maintain a worshipful attitude to the universe and so there is little harm done.—The claim of Pantheism on the dying Theist is that it provides a necessary basis for contingent facts without going beyond contingent facts. But that, as Catholic has pointed out, is a claim which cannot be substantiated. All that Pantheism can achieve is the restatement of contingent facts with the emotional fervour that attaches to the term 'universe'. It cannot show that the universe is the necessary basis of contingent facts. It can only show that they have no necessary basis—that there is nothing beyond contingent facts.

*　　*　　*

CATHOLIC. But that is absurd, Atheist. The very contingency of facts shows that there *must* be something else, since contingency and necessity are correlative terms like cause and effect or substance and attribute. If you admit the one, you must also admit the other.—When you admit that facts are contingent, you admit that they might have been otherwise—that they might not have been at all. And then you have to admit that there is some reason why they are as they are and not otherwise—why they are at all. But it is impossible to find this reason in other contingent facts because a reason has also to be found for their existence, and you are no further forward.—The question is: Why are there any contingent facts? And that question obviously cannot be answered by any contingent facts or even by all contingent facts. It can only be answered by reference to something which is not a contingent fact at all but a necessary being—a being which contains within itself the reason of its existence and which could not therefore have been otherwise.

AGNOSTIC. I don't see how you can help admitting that, Atheist. Once we assume that anything exists we cannot avoid the inference that something exists necessarily. It is true that we can never get any further than this. We can never *demonstrate* that anything necessarily exists by means of the ontological argument. We cannot even say whether it is the totality of facts—the universe—that exists necessarily, or something that creates the universe. We cannot start to answer the simplest questions about *what* it is that exists necessarily without becoming involved immediately in a tangle of insoluble antinomies. But all these difficulties relate only to the *characterization* of the necessarily existent. And it would be quite illogical to regard them as evidence against its *existence*.

ATHEIST. Well, I should have thought that the impossibility of characterizing the necessarily existent provided ample grounds for suspecting its existence. I don't see how you can continue to say that you *must* think that something exists necessarily when you cannot identify it with anything in particular. It is only through identification —characterization—that you can verify your inference—your unique inference—from the existent to the necessarily existent. And if you can't verify it, I don't see how you can possibly know that it is true. You can only say what Catholic says—that you are dissatisfied with a universe that is nothing but an endless procession of contingent facts. And however enlightening that may be about you and Catholic, it is certainly not evidence about the universe.

CATHOLIC. That is very unfair, Atheist. I began by saying that we could never be satisfied with a universe of contingent facts because I couldn't say everything at once. But since then I have repeatedly stated the grounds of my dissatisfaction in completely objective terms. And you have repeatedly evaded those statements. I said that we have to postulate a necessary being in order to answer the question: Why are there any contingent facts? And the only way in which you can show that there is no necessary being is by answering that question in some other sense.

ATHEIST. But I have answered it—by saying that it cannot be asked.

PROTESTANT. But it has just been asked, Atheist—it is always being asked. What is the sense in saying that it cannot be asked?

ATHEIST. I mean that it can only be answered by denial. We are all agreed apparently that it cannot be answered by the quotation of any contingent fact. And that, I think, is obviously true. We cannot find the sufficient reason of facts in any facts or in all facts without contradicting ourselves. But while you conclude that there must therefore be some necessary being which is not a fact, I conclude that the question is unanswerable and therefore improper. I don't see how you can answer any question without quoting some fact—some contingent fact. And if, then, this question cannot be answered by the quotation of any fact, so much the worse—not for the facts, but for the question.

CATHOLIC. But I have told you—time after time—how the question may be answered without the quotation of any contingent fact. It can be answered and it has to be answered by the recognition of a necessary being. And you surely cannot infer the impropriety of the question from your prejudiced unwillingness to accept that answer.

ATHEIST. But even that answer denies the question. You say that there are contingent facts because there is a necessary being who creates them. And the being of that necessary being, you say, is not a contingent fact because it is implied by its nature. Very well, then, you confess your complete inability to demonstrate that there actually is any such being. But let that pass. Suppose that there is. Then that is a fact and a contingent fact. It is a contingent fact that there is a necessary being. And so even in saying that a necessary being is the sufficient reason of contingent facts, you are not answering your question but only contradicting yourself in trying to answer it.

CATHOLIC. Well, if you are reduced to that sort of thing, Atheist, I am afraid it is impossible to continue this discussion. Scholasticism may be humbug, but at any rate it doesn't assume that black is white in order to prove that black is not black. It doesn't argue that a necessary being is not a necessary being because it is a contingent fact. And it cannot understand anybody who does.

ATHEIST. I cannot say that the being of a necessary being is a contingent fact. But I can and I do say that *the being of its being* is a contingent fact. If there were a case of necessary being—that is, a case where essence and being are identical—it would be a contingent fact that there is such a case. Its occurrence would not explain itself. And so it would be necessary, on your premises, to ask why there is such an occurrence. What more do you want to characterize it as a contingent fact?—And since, then, the question, 'Why are there any contingent facts?' can never be answered without contradiction—even by a being which is postulated for that purpose and on no other grounds at all—the only thing to do is to disallow the question from the beginning. Unless we do that, we shall always be in the predicament of Locke's poor Indian. We may rest the universe on an elephant and the elephant on a tortoise, but sooner or later our ingenuity is bound to give out. And then we shall have to confess that the whole construction rests on something—we know not what.

CATHOLIC. But after all, Locke's poor Indian has only found himself in an infinite regress. And I don't see how you can regard that as an objectionable position—on your principles. If there is no necessary being—nothing but contingent facts—we shall find ourselves in an infinite regress whenever we start to think. You have admitted as much with regard to causation. And if you don't object to an infinite regress there, why should you object to it here?

ATHEIST. An infinite regress is unobjectionable when you can stop whenever you want to. And that is the case with any inquiry into causes because it aims only at the extension of knowledge by description and not at any final completion of knowledge by explanation. A scientist can be satisfied that Y is the cause of Z although he knows quite well that that is not the end of the matter. Somebody else will discover that X is the cause of Y and therefore of Z, and somebody else again that W is the cause of X and therefore of Y and therefore of Z. But that doesn't affect his discovery. It is still true that Y is the cause of Z, however far the investigation of any single series of causes is carried and however many series are involved.—But the genesis of an infinite regress in the inquiry after a necessary basis of contingent facts is quite a different matter. The very purpose of that inquiry, as you have repeatedly told us, is to transcend description in order to obtain a final completion of knowledge. And if you admit an infinite regress in that inquiry you admit that your inquiry has failed. You admit that however far you go there will always be something beyond—that no final completion of knowledge is possible. And so you admit that you haven't transcended description and that you can't transcend it—that any attempt to extend knowledge, in the name of philosophy, beyond the description of facts required in science, is a waste of time.

# V

## IS DIVINE EXISTENCE CREDIBLE?

### By NORMAN KEMP SMITH

IN residing, some years ago, at an American State University, one of the things that most impressed me was the prevalence, alike among the students and among members of the Staff, of the view that belief in God is no longer possible for any really enlightened mind. This point of view was naïvely militant in the student-body; among members of the Staff, with comparatively rare exceptions, it seemed to be assumed as a matter of course. That such a way of thinking should be thus widespread in America is not, indeed, surprising. It owes much of its strength to the yet wider currency of the Fundamentalist counter-position; each creates a field highly favourable to the other. This sceptical way of thinking finds, however, notable representatives in every university and in every age; and in our European universities—at least until the past decade—there has probably been more of it than there has ever been at any time in the past. You may recall the passage in the Encyclical Letter of the Archbishops and Bishops in session at the Lambeth Conference: 'We are aware of the extent to which the very thought of God seems to be passing away from the minds and hearts of many even in nominally Christian nations.'

What—I propose to ask—are the positive grounds that lend to this negative attitude its assured confidence? Why is it that what was, at the least, an open question for David Hume, is for so many no longer worthy even of debate?

We have, of course, to distinguish between crude-minded types of disbelief and the more refined questionings of those who, though well aware of the many-sided character of the issues involved, yet arrive with conviction at a negative answer. It is with the latter that I am mainly concerned; but the two are interconnected, and I shall begin by considering certain misunderstandings, which by intervening tend to prejudge the issues, and indeed so to conceal them, that they are never properly even raised.

The first and main type of misunderstanding I should trace to the fact that those who are of this way of thinking, however they may have

thrown over the religious beliefs of the communities in which they
have been nurtured, still continue to be influenced by the phraseology
of religious devotion—a phraseology which, in its endeavour to be
concrete and universally intelligible, is at little pains to guard against the
misunderstandings to which it may so easily give rise. As they insist
upon, and even exaggerate, the merely literal meaning of this phraseology, the God in whom they have ceased to believe is a Being whom
they picture in an utterly anthropomorphic fashion—a kind of Being
whom it is not wholly absurd to picture as seated on a throne—a kind
of Being who even if he were able to say to himself, 'All things are
due to me,' would still of necessity be pursued by the question, 'But
whence then am I?' Such a Being could not be otherwise than abashed
before the immensities of space and time for which, as Divine, he has
to be conceived as responsible. For whatever be the honorific attributes
assigned to him, he is in essentials finite; and as Hume has so convincingly argued in his Dialogues—in Philo's reply to Cleanthes—a limited
and finite God can meet the needs neither of religion nor of theology.

Connected with this first cause of misunderstanding is the assertion,
so frequently made in religious circles, that belief in God is easy, and
indeed almost self-evident. Belief in the existence of God is indeed
easy for those who already so believe. But this is true of any and every
belief. All belief, once acquired, is thereafter easy. But this proves
nothing as regards the ease or difficulty of first acquiring it. And as a
matter of fact, is it not the case that there is no belief more difficult to
acquire than belief in the existence of God? If we avoid non-committal
terms, such as 'the Absolute', and if we profess to believe in a Being
who has the attributes customarily assigned to the Divine, and who is
at the same time a Being with whom we may have personal relations,
can there be any belief more difficult to acquire, for those who do not
find themselves already possessed by it? To believe in such a Being is
not a minimum belief, to be counted upon whatever else the believer
may or may not accept; it is a maximum belief, and commits us to all
the many other beliefs congruent with, and consequent upon, itself.
To represent such a belief as easy of acquisition is to set it in a misleading light, and is to discourage precisely those who are most sincere in
their approaches to it.

One main reason why the situation has been thus falsely represented
is, I think, the continuing influence of the eighteenth-century view
that the existence of God can be demonstrated from the facts of Nature
and history—the actual situation being—is it not?—that the existence

of God cannot be demonstrated in any such manner. If we come to Nature and to history with an *antecedent* belief in the existence of God, they may be shown to be, conceivably, not incompatible with such belief; but they never suffice to demonstrate it.

I can best lead up to the points upon which I wish to dwell by an examination of this usual assumption that God, if God exists, must be demonstrable from the facts of Nature and history. But before I do so, allow me to interpose a further word of general explanation. Dr. F. R. Tennant, in the second and concluding volume of his *Philosophical Theology*, contends that belief in the existence of God cannot be justified either from *a priori* premisses or from purely ethical data. So far I find myself in agreement with him. Now there are, he says, only two other methods of justifying belief in the existence of God. We may attempt to do so either by way of direct experience of the Divine or else by some form of the argument to design. Again I should agree; but I am unable to follow him in the alternative which he proceeds to adopt. Dr. Tennant holds that we have no direct acquaintance with the Divine, and that the argument to design is by itself valid and sufficient. The position from which my paper is written is that the argument to design can play no such part as he assigns to it, and that if certain important qualifications and reservations be made, we are justified in maintaining that belief in God does ultimately rest upon immediate experience.

Hume and Kant deal with the argument to design in a strangely hesitant manner. Thus Kant begins by eulogizing it as 'the oldest, the clearest, the best suited to ordinary human reason', and then straight-way proceeds to show that as argument it is the least satisfactory of the traditional proofs, involving not only those fallacies which, as he teaches, render the more speculative types of argument impossible of acceptance, but in addition a number of fallacies peculiar to itself.

This is also the manner in which Hume has argued in his *Dialogues concerning Natural Religion*, only in his case the inconsistency, if incon-sistency it be, is rendered the more flagrant in that he reverses the sequence. Instead of beginning with praise and ending with criticism, he first gives a quite devastating criticism of the argument and evidence for design—criticism placed in the mouth of Philo—and then in the concluding section of the *Dialogues*, and again through the mouth of Philo, in violent contradiction with the results previously arrived at, he proceeds to allege that 'a purpose, an intention, a design strikes everywhere [in Nature] the most careless, the most stupid thinker; and [that] no man can be so hardened in absurd systems, as at all times to reject it.'[1]

Recently Sir Arthur Keith has made a somewhat similar pronouncement. After stating the influences which have led to the destruction of his belief in a personal God—'a superbeing endowed with human attributes'—stating more particularly the irresistible body of evidence which shows that creation does 'not work from without but from within', and that 'the human soul is but the manifestation of the living brain, as light and heat are the manifestations of a glowing bar of steel', he none the less arrives at the following conclusion:

> The human brain is a poor instrument to solve such ultimate problems. We have to recognize its limitations. Yet it perceives how well-ordered all things are and how wonderful are the inventions of nature. *Design is manifest everywhere.* Whether we are laymen or scientists, we must postulate a Lord of the Universe—give Him what shape we will. But it is certain that the anthropomorphic God of the Hebrews cannot meet our modern needs.[2]

Now why is it that Hume, Kant, Sir Arthur Keith, and so many others, proceed in this manner? Why do they thus, while rejecting the *argument* to design, none the less still accept the *fact* of design? Is their formal inconsistency a real inconsistency? Are they in their own persons nullifying their own conclusions? Or are they no more than recognizing the conflicting requirements of the complex situation with which they are attempting to deal? As I shall try to show, their procedure cannot be defended against the charge of inconsistency. As I shall also try to show, the inconsistency is for them unavoidable. For however they may agree that it is not possible to prove God's existence from the facts of Nature and of history, they still have not been able to clarify their minds in regard to certain immediate experiences, which, as they believe, are undeniably aroused in them by the contemplation of Nature.

I shall dwell briefly on each of these two points. What are those defects in the argument to design which constrain us to reject it? In the first place, it ignores the radical character of the distinction between the natural and the artificial. The existence of an artificial product is only possible in and through the existence of an external artificer: the

---

[1] Op. cit., Pt. XII, at the beginning.
[2] *The Forum*, April 1930, p. 225. Italics not in text.

natural, on the other hand, is, *qua* natural, self-evolving and self-maintaining; that is to say, its form is as native and natural to it as the matter of which it is composed. Indeed the argument is at its weakest precisely in those fields in which it professes to find its chief evidence—the evidence upon which Paley, for instance, mainly relied—the amazingly complex and effective adjustments exhibited in vegetable and animal organisms. The hinge of a door affords conclusive proof of the existence of an artificer: the hinge of the bivalve shell, though incomparably superior as a hinge, affords no such proof;[3] it is as natural in its origin as anything in physical Nature can be known to be.

This brings us to a second, even more fundamental, objection, namely, that to conceive God as a Designer is to conceive God in terms of attributes proper only to a creaturely being. The concept of 'purpose' is so bound up with the distinction between present and future, and with the distinction between means and end, that when we combine it with the further concepts involved in the notion of 'design', we are really endeavouring to conceive God in terms of that part of our human experience which is least appropriate thereto. Design implies foresight. But when do we possess foresight? In our repetitive activities. When our activities are describable as being creative, then precisely in the degree in which they are so, they tend to be tentative, purposive indeed, but proceeding by trial and failure. Such activities are not conceivable save in reference to a being who is faced by an external environment which determines the possibilities among which he may choose, and supplies the materials through which they can be realized.

To state the point in the manner of Hume. Design involves a plan, and only if the plan be granted as pre-existing, can the designing activities act with foresight, namely, in accordance with the plan. But how does the plan itself originate? If we say that the plan must itself be planned, we are landed in an infinite self-defeating series. We must perforce admit a first stage, in which there is action that is not dependent upon a previously planned plan. To do so, however, is to conceive God not as a Designer but as a Creator. For we are then conceiving him, not as planning his plans, but as creating them; and if so, if we thus admit that design is not necessary to the creation of a plan (and the plan to be effective must be complete, down to the minutest details), we are no longer justified in requiring design as a stage preliminary to

---

[3] Cf. *The Life and Letters of Charles Darwin* (1887), ed. by Francis Darwin, Vol. I, p. 309.

the creation of Nature. Either, therefore, we have no right to the assumption of a Creative Being, even in respect of a plan; or if we have, it is as a Creator, not as a Designer, that he must be conceived.

In what respects, then, does the concept of creation differ from that of design? As already stated, only our repetitive activities can be designed, that is, performed with foresight. They are conditioned, therefore, by some prior activity that is not repetitive; and this prior activity, in being creative, is by no means out of line with other everyday happenings. As Whitehead teaches: Nature is constantly advancing into novelty. *Nature is made up*—with supplementary factors no less enigmatic—*of events which, as one-time occurrences, are unique.* Thus should I move my hand, the movement has never occurred before and will never occur again; events are not repeatable in being but only in type. I can say that I repeat the *same* motion of my hand; but it is not the same motion; it is a quite new motion; it is the *same* only in type or kind, not in being. It is in and through creativity, in and through one-time occurrences, that any continuing modes of being which we may have to recognize are maintained in existence.

It is commonly supposed that we can avoid this conclusion by resorting to the concept of substance, as that in and through which change is alone possible—this substance being conceived either as matter, or as energy, or as spirit. But even so, we do not really escape the acceptance of creativity. Substance, as thus postulated, is in all three forms an enigmatic type of existence; and in conditioning change it still exhibits that very creativity with which we are professing, by its means, to dispense. Substance is doubtless one of the factors conditioning creativity; it cannot be a substitute for it. For consider, again, the motions of my hand: at least, it may be said, the hand that makes the motions is the same throughout them all. But what is the hand? Like a vortex in water, it is the fixed form taken by certain changing constituents; and even as such a form, it is only relatively fixed. It too is always in process of passing; it too is a one-time occurrence, and so far unique. The change from caterpillar to butterfly is indeed 'a gesture in creation', but is not on that account a departure from Nature's ordinary course.

Now we do not possess even the beginnings of an understanding of creative activity: whenever and wherever it occurs—and it is occurring at every moment in all places—we are presented with something to which we can find no analogy in anything other than itself. Though it is thus omnipresent, exemplified in all that occurs, it is abidingly mysterious. It is one of the many opaque elements with which reason has to reckon when it endeavours to define the situations in which we find ourselves to be placed. If, with Samuel Alexander, we define the *a priori* as being not what is due to mind but as what is pervasive of all reality, creativity may be so described; and like all other ultimates, it has to be used in explanation, while remaining itself unexplained.

The typical attitude of the eighteenth-century thinkers in regard to the argument to design may perhaps be stated thus. The self was taken to be a self-subsistent being, naturally immortal, and capable of exercising purposive activities. In regard to it no further questions of a metaphysical character were asked. Creation might be spoken of in the Creeds: it was tacitly ignored, as hardly respectable, in philosophy. God was accordingly conceived as a magnified self, related to the natural world in what was supposed to be the easily understandable relation in which man stands to the works of his hands. God is the Divine Artificer, doing on the cosmic scale precisely what man is capable of doing in his own smaller world. On this view neither the self nor God is mysterious; they differ only in degree, and both are adequately known for what they are. The shift which has taken place in Hume and in Kant is precisely that further questions have been asked in regard to the self, both in regard to the nature of its purposive activities, and in regard to its supposedly self-conditioned existence, and mysteries are discerned where none had been suspected. The self is in fact not self-maintaining; it is upheld by the body, and the body is integral to its natural setting. The self is indeed, like all other exis- tences, capable of creativity; but it is a conditioned and delegated creativity; and if we are to believe in a Divine Being on analogy of the self, we must carry over into the conception of it all that is thus mysterious in the self, at the same time recognizing its possession of a creativity which is not thus conditioned and creaturely, and which is therefore proportionately the more mysterious. Certainly in this and that attribute the Divine must allow of being known to us—otherwise we should have no right to entitle it the Divine—but precisely in being thus known it will still be known as abidingly mysterious. For the concepts which we employ are problematic concepts; their function is to enable us to locate and to specify the mysteries of Divine Existence, not to resolve them.

This may be illustrated by reference to the attributes of 'omnipo- tence', 'omniscience', 'eternity' and 'omnipresence'—leaving aside for later consideration the question as to the general nature of the evidence upon which they may be predicable of the Divine. There is nothing in our human experience adequate to the concept of omnipotence. We do, of course, experience power in ourselves; but when we pass from the concept of power to that of omnipotence, the concept of power is modified in ways which presuppose for their possibility the existence of a Being quite other than the creaturely. All our powers are upheld and made possible by conditions which they do not themselves provide; they are conferred or delegated powers. Our power of knowing, for example, is conditioned by the brain, and the brain in turn by the whole natural order. Accordingly omnipotence remains a problematic concept. It is theomorphic, not anthropomorphic. It *presupposes* the possibility of the Divine; it can be allowed as possible only to the extent to which the Divine can be alleged to be itself possible.

So also with the attribute, omniscience. In two respects it presupposes what no human experience ever manifests. In us conscious experience is conditioned by the possession and use of sense-organs; God, if God there be, must be able to apprehend physical and other existences in some immediate, non-sensible manner. Secondly, we have no power of looking into the minds of others, and so of knowing their thoughts and feelings by direct inspection. In this regard also, omniscience is no mere enlargement of our human powers of knowledge. It too is theomorphic; it is conceivable only in a Being who in these fundamental respects is quite other than ourselves; and it therefore *presupposes* the independently established existence of that Being.

So also with eternity; as predicated of the Divine, it cannot mean merely endurance throughout all time. God, so conceived, would apprehend creaturely existence mainly through memory and foresight. In memory he would reach back into the 'immemorial' past, and through foresight would anticipate the interminable ages still to come. A Being, thus conceived, would be in creaturely subjection to the conditions of time. Should a Being thus situated claim to be Divine, he would be an upstart, posing in a role for which he is unfitted. Either Divine Existence is an utterly incredible mode of Being, or we must be prepared to allow that God transcends the present in some other manner than merely in this human fashion by memory and anticipation. This, I take it, is one main reason why my colleague, Professor Taylor, has recently been maintaining,[4] in agreement with Whitehead, that the problem of time is a central problem in present-day philosophy,

[4] *The Faith of a Moralist*, Vol. I, p. 66; Vol. II, p. 320.

and especially in theology. As a clue in terms of which we may endeavour to conceive such transcendence of time, we have the apprehension of the specious present, as in reading a poem or listening to a piece of music—a present which is 'a slab of duration' made up of the just-past and of the not-yet, as well as of the 'actually' present. But the step from durational time to eternity is precisely the step which has to be justified, and for the possibility of which such apprehension, in and by itself, affords no sufficient evidence.

Similarly with the attribute of omnipresence. Admittedly, we can find nothing analogous in the physical realm. Thus should we, speaking in the manner of the older physics, say that ether is present throughout all space, we mean only that its parts are external to one another and that there is enough of it to supply a distinguishable part corresponding to each distinguishable space. Obviously this is not omnipresence in the theological sense. But neither do we find any sufficient analogy in the dynamical efficacies whereby bodies exert influence on other bodies, or even in the cognitive processes whereby we apprehend what is distant in space and past in time. These are modes not of omnipresence but at most only of compresence; and even so, they rest on a number of highly specific limiting conditions. The step from compresence to omnipresence is again precisely the step that has to be accounted for, and for which our experiences of the creaturely can yet afford no sufficient support.

Thus in respect of each and all the ontological attributes the Divine is not known through analogy with the self, or with any other creaturely-mode of existence. These divine attributes *presuppose* God's existence, and save in this reference even their bare possibility cannot be established. If, without any antecedent or independent apprehension of the Divine, we have to start from the creaturely, as exhibited in Nature and in man, and by way of inference and of analogy—on the pattern of what is found in the creaturely—through enlargement or other processes of ideal completion, to construct for ourselves concepts of the Divine, then the sceptics have been in the right; the attempt is an impossible one, condemned to failure from the start. We cannot reach the Divine merely by way of inference, not even if the inference be analogical in character. By no idealization of the creaturely can we transcend the creaturely. To this extent, therefore, Hume's and Kant's negative criticisms of the argument to design must, I am contending, be accepted as unanswerable.

We may now turn to the second main point, the attitude of Hume and Kant to certain immediate experiences which, as they assert, induce belief which is independent of evidence, and which indeed transform the traditional argument from being an argument *to* design into being an argument *from* design. Hume and Kant are here, I shall further contend, guilty of a flagrant inconsistency—an inconsistency due to their failure to clarify their minds in regard to the modes in which the direct contemplation of Nature does and does not reinforce belief in Divine Existence. Faced by Nature and the overwhelming impression which in certain situations it generates in us, they see no option save to cast doubt upon their own conclusions. In Hume this is the less surprising; in his eyes it is merely one more instance of the non-rational character of our natural beliefs, which arise independently of evidence and persist in despite of logical refutation. In Kant, however, it is, I should say, a sheer inconsistency.

To quote from Hume's *Dialogues* the words of Philo—they express, we may believe, the personal attitude of Hume himself:

> You, in particular, Cleanthes, with whom I live in unreserved intimacy; you are sensible that notwithstanding the freedom of my conversation, and my love of singular arguments, no one has a deeper sense of religion impressed on his mind, or pays more profound adoration to the Divine Being, as he discovers himself to reason, in the inexplicable contrivance and artifice of Nature. A purpose, an intention, a design strikes everywhere the most careless, the most stupid thinker; and no man can be so hardened in absurd systems as at all times to reject it.[5]

Kant's statements, while less definite, are in similar terms: '[The argument from design] is the oldest, the clearest, and the best suited to ordinary human reason. It enlivens the study of nature, just as it itself derives its existence and gains ever new vigour from that source.'[6]

The question to be answered is therefore this: how far is it true to say that 'a purpose, an intention, a design [in Nature], strikes everywhere the most careless'? Certainly we receive an overwhelming impression of inexhaustible fertility in the generation of elaborate types of existence, mutually adjusted the one to the other, but of 'a purpose, an intention, a design', surely we have no discernment!

---

[5] Op. cit., Pt. XII.        [6] *Critique of Pure Reason*, A 623.

Consider the following comment upon Wordsworth's attitude to Nature:

The Wordsworthian adoration of Nature has two principal defects. The first . . . is that it is only possible in a country where Nature has been nearly or quite enslaved to man. The second is that it is only possible for those who are prepared to falsify their immediate intuitions of Nature. For Nature, even in the temperate zone, is always alien and unknown, and occasionally diabolic . . . [Wordsworth will not admit that a yellow primrose is simply a yellow primrose—beautiful, but essentially strange, having its own alien life apart. He wants it to possess some sort of soul, to exist humanly, not simply flowerily. . . . Our direct intuitions of Nature tell us that the world is bottomlessly strange; alien, even when it is kind and beautiful; having innumerable modes of being that are not our modes; always mysteriously not personal, not conscious, not moral; often hostile and sinister; sometimes even unimaginably, because inhumanly, evil. . . . A voyage through the tropics would have cured [Wordsworth] of his too easy and comfortable pantheism. A few months in the jungle would have convinced him that the diversity and utter strangeness of Nature are at least as real and significant as its intellectually discovered unity. Nor would he have felt as certain, in the damp and stifling darkness, among the leeches and the malevolently tangled rattans, of the divinely anglican character of that fundamental unity. He would have learned once more to treat Nature naturally, as he treated it in his youth; to react to it spontaneously, loving where love was the appropriate emotion, fearing, hating, fighting whenever Nature presented itself to his intuition as being, not merely strange, but hostile, inhumanly evil. . . . Europe is so well gardened that it resembles a work of art. . . . Man has re-created Europe in his own image. Its tamed and temperate Nature confirmed Wordsworth in his philosophizings.[7]

Hume (again in the person of Philo) can be cited against himself:

Look around this Universe. What an immense profusion of beings, animated and organized, sensible and active! You admire this prodigious variety and fecundity. But inspect a little more narrowly these living existences, the only beings worth regarding. How hostile and destructive to each other! How insufficient all of them for their own happiness! . . . The whole presents nothing but the idea of a

[7] Aldous Huxley, Do what you Will (1929), p. 116.

blind Nature, impregnated by a great vivifying principle, and pouring forth from her lap, without discernment or parental care, her maimed and abortive children![8]

This may be over-statement, but whatever qualifications may have to be made, do we not find ourselves in some degree approving the terms employed? Man himself, like all other animal existences, is a parasite. He lives parasitically upon vegetables and upon other animals; and in their absence could not survive. Bread, which we entitle the staff of life, itself consists of thwarted seed. The practice of the old-time gardener was to plant five seeds in each hole:

> One for the raven, one for the crow,
> Two to die, and one to grow.

There is a passage in Leopardi's *Dialogues*,[9] in which an Icelander who has wandered over the Earth in search of an answer to these and similar questions, propounds them to a Sphinx in the heart of Africa. The answer came in the form of two lions that crept up out of the desert. The beasts were so enfeebled and emaciated with long fasting that they had scarce strength left to devour the Icelander. And even so, he was sustenance to them for only one more day.

As Cardinal Newman has declared in the same general connexion, though more specifically in regard to the world of men: 'All this is a vision to dizzy and appal; and inflicts upon the mind the sense of a profound mystery, which is absolutely beyond human solution.'[10]

Undoubtedly, Hume and Kant are correct in maintaining that when the mind, freed for a time from its practical preoccupations, allows Nature to be the object of its contemplation, then no matter whether it be the complexities of animal existence or of our own bodies, or the immensities of the heavens that occupy our attention, Nature produces an overwhelming impression upon us. As John Stuart Mill has said: 'To a mind thus occupied it seems unutterable presumption in so puny a creature as man to look critically on things so far above him.'[11] Does this amount, however, to the apprehension of 'a purpose, an intention, a design'? That it did so in the minds of Hume and of Kant, their sceptical questionings notwithstanding, there is no reason to doubt. The best possible testimony to the sincerity of their statements is that they were surprised to discover these feelings, and were puzzled as to

---

[8] Op. cit., Pt. XI.    [9] *Operette Morali* (1928), ed. by A. Donati, pp. 81–82.
[10] *Apologia pro Vita Sua* (1864), p. 378.    [11] *Three Essays on Religion* (1874), p. 26.

how they could persist so obstinately when the evidence, impartially considered, points so very definitely in the opposite direction.

But something is evidently wrong in their statement of the situation. How can data which, when impartially considered, are found to be worthless as *evidence* of design, suffice for producing an overwhelming *impression* of design? The answer would seem to be that while undoubtedly Nature produces an impression which is overwhelming, the impression is being misinterpreted when described as being the impression of design. Minds which have been moulded upon the anthropomorphic Deistic ways of thinking so prevalent in the eighteenth century, and which in popular religious circles are still so usual, will indeed be apt to interpret the impression in this fashion. That Hume and Kant should have done so shows the extent to which they were still under their influence. Immediately the tension of their thought was relaxed, the accustomed ways of thinking resumed their sway.

When we turn to the spontaneous utterances of the religious mind, we find quite a different response to the impression made by Nature. We may take as typical the Old Testament writers. As A. B. Davidson has made so convincingly clear in his *Theology of the Old Testament*, 'it never occurred to any prophet or writer of the Old Testament to prove the existence of God'.[12] For them that was quite needless. They moved among ideas that presuppose God's existence—a Being with whom they stood in relations of religious fellowship. This conception of God already possessed is used by them to explain the world. In Davidson's own words:

> The Hebrew thinker came down from his thought of God upon the world; he did not rise from the world up to his thought of God. . . . There seems no passage in the Old Testament which represents men as reaching the knowledge of the existence of God through nature or the events of providence, although there are some passages which imply that false ideas of what God is may be corrected by the observation of nature and life.[13]

If we are in danger of likening God to any of his creatures, or of measuring his powers by the powers of man, then the knowledge which we otherwise have 'may be refreshed, and if needful corrected by the contemplation of Nature'.[14] In the words of Isaiah:[15] 'To whom then will ye liken me? . . . Lift up your eyes on high, and see who hath

[12] Op. cit. (1904) p. 30.
[14] Op. cit., p. 78.
[13] Op. cit., pp. 32–33.
[15] Isa. xl. 25–26. Revised Version.

created these, that bringeth out their host by number.' Or as in the 8th Psalm:

> When I consider thy heavens, the work of thy fingers, the moon and the stars, which thou hast ordained; what is man, that thou art mindful of him? and the son of man, that thou visitest him?[16]

But just because their belief in God was not based on evidence obtained by study of Nature and human life, they used it the more freely, and with greater assurance, to interpret both Nature and history. As God is for them the Being upon whom all things are dependent, nothing in Nature or history *can*, on their view, be contrary to his Will. And the facts which they choose to enforce this teaching are often precisely those that are a stumbling-block in the way of any argument to design. In the words of the Psalmist, God creates the darkness 'wherein all the beasts of the forest do creep forth. The young lions roar after their prey, and seek'—precisely Leopardi's counter-instance—'their meat from God'.[17]

As A. B. Davidson has also pointed out,[18] the nearest approach to an argument to design is in a passage in one of the Psalms:[19]

> They break in pieces thy people, O Lord, and afflict thine heritage. They slay the widow and the stranger, and murder the fatherless. And they say, The Lord shall not see, neither shall the God of Jacob consider. Consider, ye brutish among the people: and ye fools, when will ye be wise? He that planted the ear, shall he not hear? He that formed the eye, shall he not see? He that chastiseth the nations, shall he not correct, even he that teacheth man knowledge?

This is by no means an argument to design. The argument here is that the Being who *has been* able to plant the ear and to form the eye, who *is able* to instruct the nations and to teach men knowledge—all of which is taken as being beyond question—that such a Being must surely be omniscient, with powers which utterly transcend those of any of his creatures.

Hence, too, the kind of facts cited as witness of God's *providential* care. They were so assured of the existence of God, and *therefore* of his providential rule, that in all times of trial and disaster, to however contrary a conclusion the events, taken by themselves, might seem to point, the assurance remained unshaken. Not being obtained by

[16] Ps. viii. 3.          [17] Ps. civ. 20.
[18] Op. cit., pp. 79–80.   [19] Ps. xciv. 5–11. Revised Version.

reflection upon the course of events, it could not be overthrown by them.

The position, then, as regards the convictions of religious writers, whether in the Old Testament or elsewhere, is this. In and through their religious experience of fellowship with God, they have belief in God, and coming to Nature and history with this belief in their minds, they interpret Nature and history freely in accordance therewith. They do not observe order and design, and *therefore* infer a Designer: they argue that order and design must be present even where they are not apparent, because all existences other than God have their source in him. They start, that is to say, from an *immediate* experience of the Divine; and only so are their methods of argument and modes of expression possible at all.

Now Hume and Kant entirely overlooked this fundamental difference in standpoint. They took it as a matter of common agreement that there is no immediate experience of the Divine, and that the existence of God must be established, if it is to be established at all, in and through inference, that is, in and through study of what is other than God. And accordingly when they found religious writers interpreting Nature as divinely conditioned, they were confirmed in the view that Nature, in and by itself, yields the impression of intention and design, and in this fashion generates belief. Had they been as thorough in their scepticism as they professed to be, the experiences which they continued to have would have ceased to find lodgment in their minds.

But if the Divine cannot be reached by way of inference, if it cannot be gathered from any antecedent knowledge of the phenomena of Nature and of the events of history, and if also it cannot be arrived at through analogical reasoning, by magnification of attributes and processes which we experience in the self—if, in other words, it cannot be gathered from any knowledge antecedent to itself—then either we have no right to claim belief in the existence of God, or the one remaining alternative must be accepted, that we experience the Divine in a direct and immediate manner. It is to this alternative that I shall devote my remaining remarks.

'Immediate experience' is a phrase which calls for a good deal of explanation. As a mode of experience, it involves all the conditions that are required for the possibility of experience; and had I in this lecture been engaged in an epistemological discussion much would have to be said in regard to the *a priori* factors which, as I believe, enter into all experience, conferring upon our human consciousness its persistently questioning and characteristically metaphysical outlook. I cannot here do more than indicate, in passing, certain *negative* features of immediate experience.

Immediate experience is not equivalent to exhaustive knowledge. We have, it will probably be granted, immediate experience of the self; and the self, as I have already suggested, is an abidingly mysterious mode of existence.

Nor does it follow that what we immediately experience, we experience in isolation from what is other than itself. We may, or may not, do so. Each of us, for instance, experiences his own body in distinction from the bodies of his fellows. But in regard to the self, it is quite otherwise. If we attempt to isolate the self from all that is other than the self, then, as Kant long ago pointed out, nothing whatsoever is left. Though we experience the self directly, we never experience it sheerly in and by itself. At most we experience situations, past and present, and the self as integral to them; the attempt to locate the self at points within such situations—at points in which nothing but the self is present—is doomed to failure. This, it would seem, is likewise true of our experience of the Divine. We never experience the Divine sheerly in and by itself: we experience the Divine solely through and in connexion with what is other than the Divine.

There is no such temptation in regard to *other* selves, as there is in regard to the self, to hold that we can experience them in isolation. Indeed in the past the tendency has been all the other way. The prevailing view has been that our knowledge of other selves is indirect and inferential, consisting in the interpretation of signs and indications —consisting, indeed, in some mode of reasoning by analogy from the self. Observing the *bodies* of others, and noting that in their actions, as disclosed to us through the senses of sight and hearing, they behave as do we ourselves, we infer—so it is alleged—that accompanying their bodies there are inner conscious experiences analogous to our own. This is the point of view which the argument to design carries over into the theological domain, contending that it is by similar processes of analogical reasoning that we infer the existence of a Divine Being. Now it may be agreed that we do not experience other selves—any more than we experience the self—in isolation from all else, and certainly not independently of their bodily actions; but while doing so, we may still maintain that through, and in connexion with, these bodily activities other selves are experienced with the same immediacy with which we experience the self, our conviction as to their existence being based on directly experienced fellowship, and not upon inference. There is, indeed, growing agreement among philosophical thinkers on this point.

In consequence of this altered theory of knowledge, there is readiness to recognize, as is done by such different thinkers as Cook Wilson, Samuel Alexander, and C. C. J. Webb, that this is likewise true of our experience of the Divine. Should this position be accepted, our grounds for believing in the self, in other selves, and in the Divine will so far be identical in type. In all three cases, the question under discussion will be a *question strictly of fact*—namely, as to whether there is or is not any such type of immediate experience, *not a question as to the adequacy of argument from facts otherwise unquestioned.*

But in restating the issue in this manner, we must at the same time allow that the problems which emerge in connexion with our experience of the Divine are much more difficult than any which arise in connexion with our experience of the self and of other selves. I have already emphasized that what we immediately experience need not be, and indeed when properly envisaged never is, other than mysterious. If we try to define the nature of the self, or even of natural events, we are at once in the midst of controversy; immediate experience, while it justifies belief, yields belief only in what, in proportion as we become enlightened and self-critical in our beliefs, are admittedly highly problematic types of existence. But while this problematic, that is to say, mysterious character is, so far as regards the self and natural events, a late discovery, due to philosophical reflection and critical analysis, and save for occasional experiences in this and that individual, is almost entirely absent from the minds of the unsophisticated, in the case of the Divine, from the very start, mystery is a chief and prominent characteristic.

You are acquainted with the distinction between feeling and emotion. Feeling, such as pleasure or pain, is in itself a purely subjective experience; emotion implies an objective situation within which there is something which arouses the emotion, and towards which the emotion is directed. The Divine is, it would seem, first experienced in such a situation; and is initially apprehended solely and exclusively as that which arouses certain types of emotion. If the emotion be awe, then the Divine is so far apprehended as the awesome, what Otto has so helpfully entitled the numinous.

I

Even apart from the *a priori* factors—to which I have already referred, and which equip the mind for apprehending what is thus experienced—the considerations involved are extremely complicated. I may draw attention to four that are of chief importance. First, we have to recognize one main difference between the experience of other selves and the experience of the Divine. Owing to the fact that we experience other selves only through, and in connexion with, their bodies, other selves are experienced by us only in the situations in which these bodies are found; and whenever these bodies, or the indirect manifestations of such bodies, are apprehended, we have the immediate experience that other selves are there. In the case of the Divine, on the other hand, there are no such *isolable and constant* accompaniments. Potentially any situation may yield an immediate awareness of the Divine; actually there is no situation whatsoever which invariably yields it.

Secondly, consciousness of the Divine seems to have been first aroused through, and in connexion with, Nature and its occurrences, not in connexion with our specifically human modes of life. If we take Nature not only in its larger physical aspects, but also as exhibited in birth and death, and particularly in the dead body of the once-living man—the object of such awesome dread among primitive peoples—we would seem to be justified in saying that in the beginnings of civilization the natural world alone has the strangeness and mystery, the unfamiliar otherness, in the degree necessary to arouse the religious sentiment. It is only later, through the institution of impressive rites and ceremonies, and through the choice or provision of an artificial environment, such as the cave of Altamira or the temples of Carnac and Stonehenge, that the sentiment is brought under social control, being canalized in the direction of, and aroused in connexion with, the specifically human activities of the group life.

Thirdly, when religion is considered historically, in reference to its origins, we are faced by the strangely ambiguous character of its infant stages. Religion begins as a not very promising, and indeed highly questionable, set of rites and practices. The underlying conception of the Divine is quite indefinite. To quote a description which, according to Marett, is typical and applies almost universally: speaking of the Masai, a people very low in the scale of culture, an authority has said: 'Their conception of the deity seems marvellously vague. I was *Ngai*. My camp was *Ngai*. *Ngai* was in the steaming holes. His house was in the eternal snows of Kilimanjaro. In fact, whatever struck them as strange or incomprehensible, that they at once assumed had some connexion with *Ngai*.'[20] And the initial experience of the Divine is not only thus vague in conception; it is also highly ambiguous in its *practical* bearings. Since it is predominantly emotional, and so is more instinctive than reflective, it easily degenerates into the orgiastic, and tends to excesses and violences of every kind. When other sides of our nature, such as the sexual, join forces with it, it becomes an energy of extraordinarily high potential, and proportionately incalculable in its methods of release. Accordingly it stands in more imperative need of moralization than any other aspect of human life. And just as it starts by being other than morals, so it continues to the end to be more than morals. It has its own independent roots; and it is out of them, not out of morals, though with the favouring aid of morals, that it has to grow.

Fourthly, religion in any high form comes only late, when through mutual action and reaction religious experiences and social exigencies have, by mutual adaptation each to the other, brought into existence modes of group activity in which a way of life is prescribed to the members of the group—a way of life through which, in virtue of the discipline which it affords, they are given access to certain types of experience not otherwise possible to them—types of experience in which the Divine is apprehended no less directly than in regard to Nature and its occurrences, but which differ in that they reveal the Divine as not merely other than man but also as akin to man. The Mosaic Law of the Hebrews, for instance, with its prescribed ways of life and modes of worship supplied a discipline that made possible a society within which the Prophets could appear—what is specific in their teaching could not have appeared among the Polynesians or even among the Greeks—and could have those experiences in and through which the character of the Divine is further disclosed. The concepts of omnipotence, omniscience, eternity, and omnipresence are not, of course, part of any such experiences, taken in their first immediacy; they are the problematic concepts whereby we endeavour—it may be rightly or it may be wrongly—to define what the immediate experiences are to be taken as revealing. It is precisely in the control of these hazardous processes of interpretation, eventuating in this and that type of theology, that the great religious traditions exercise their distinctive functions; and they do so not merely by the guidance which they

[20] Quoted by R. R. Marett, *The Threshold of Religion* (1909), p. 12.

afford in matters of theory, but also, in a more radical fashion, by the supplementary, more specific data which they make accessible to us, and in the absence of which our reasoning faculties can have no sufficient material upon which to work.

These statements are too summary to be really definite; but they may suffice to indicate the thesis which is an essential part of my argument—that only by thus assigning a central role to the immediately experienced can we hope satisfactorily to account for the presence of religion already at the very beginnings of human civilization, for the ambiguous character of the first manifestations of religion, and for the part played by institutions and by tradition in determining its higher forms.

I come now to my last point, which is also my main point; it can be quite briefly stated. Though religion of any high type thus comes late, and is made possible only through and in connexion with our specifically human modes of activity, none the less the initial experiences in which religion takes its rise continue to be the source from which we can still best learn, and from which indeed we can alone learn, one all-important side of Divine Existence. It is, we may still maintain, through and in connexion with the *cosmic* setting of our human life, that we can alone experience that aspect of the Divine which is so essential to its credibility, because so essential to its possibility, and which is also required in order to give proper perspective to all our other assertions in regard to the Divine—the otherness, the non-creatureliness, of the Divine, as a Being whose throne is the heavens and whose footstool is the earth. Unless we are to resort to the concept of a finite God—and that by very general agreement is insufficient to meet the needs either of religion or of theology—then by the Divine we must, at the least, mean that upon which all things rest. This is a prime condition required of any Being to which we can legitimately assign the title 'God'; and it is a condition which can be fulfilled only by a Being endowed with attributes other than any to which the creaturely can lay claim. The conception of the Divine as merely other than the creaturely, even if we add that the Divine also conditions all that is creaturely, is in itself, indeed, a jejune and savourless conception. Yet when retained and carried over, in the manner of the higher religions, into further assertions, it is precisely what gives these further assertions their supreme importance. Admittedly, power is not the highest of the Divine attributes. None the less it is fundamental, since only on the basis of such power can the other attributes have a sufficing efficacy—an efficacy which will justify us in looking for them alike in the works of Nature and in those of Grace. They are deeply hidden, and there may not be in us the virtue to discern them; none the less, relying on such power, we may still be justified in proceeding on the assumption of their universal presence. Certainly the Divine, to justify the title, must possess such further attributes—attributes in which the Divine exhibits kinship with man—but even these are *divine* attributes only as being the attributes of a *Divine Being*; and so again we are brought back to the non-creatureliness, that is, to the otherness of God, as that in reference to which alone any such assertions are legitimate and have meaning. And there is, I have argued, no other path to the apprehension of *this* aspect of Divine Existence save that by which it first breaks in upon the consciousness of man, namely, in connexion with the inexhaustibly varied, infinitely vast, and profoundly mysterious natural order, of which we are integral constituents and whereby we are upheld. To quote a favourite saying of Baron von Hügel: 'God is the God of Nature as of Grace. He provides the meal as well as the yeast.'

The answer to my question is therefore this: Divine Existence is more than merely credible: it is immediately experienced; and is experienced in increasing degree in proportion as the individual, under the discipline and through the way of life prescribed by religion in this or that of its great traditional forms, is enabled to supplement his initial experiences by others of a more definite character. And in Divine Existence, as thus revealed, the non-creatureliness, that is, the otherness of God, is fundamental, as that under assumption of which alone any further, more specific assertions can be made.

# VI

# BIRTH, SUICIDE AND THE DOCTRINE OF CREATION: AN EXPLORATION OF ANALOGIES

By WILLIAM H. POTEAT

*Prima facie*, nothing would seem to be more unlikely to clarify the peculiar nature of certain concepts in theological discourse than an analysis of the expression 'I was born' and an examination of the nature of a decision to take one's own life. Nevertheless, I believe that such an inquiry will be of value in explicating certain features of the language of 'beginnings' which is a familiar part of theological discussion, and one which has perhaps presented peculiar difficulty in the one hundred years since the publication of Darwin's *Origin of Species*.

One of the many things that Christians profess to believe about God is that he is 'maker of heaven and earth'—where this is taken to mean that before the divine act, through the utterance of God's Word whereby the world with which we have to do is thought to have become what it is, there was nothing. Hence the so-called doctrine of *creatio ex nihilo*. This view, it is supposed, is a characteristic of both Christian and Jewish belief which sets them apart from the beliefs of all religions—such as Hinduism, Buddhism, etc.—which are either explicitly or implicitly a-theistic, and also against metaphysical systems where either there is no God, in the theistic sense, or where, if there is, he is thought to be no more than an artificer, working upon some antecedently given matter.

Along with this belief, it is also asserted that man is made in the image of God. Let me, as preliminary, take this to mean, so far as the present inquiry is concerned, that man, himself a creature, stands to the created world (understood as the subject of our public, common sense, or even our scientific curiosity) in a way analogous to that in which those who believe in *creatio ex nihilo* suppose God to stand to this world.

Now, it is notoriously difficult to assimilate logically what is thought to be meant by *creatio ex nihilo* to the many other things that we say about the world (whether we interpret the concept 'world' here in the Kantian sense as a regulative principle for *cosmologia rationalis*, or merely as any given finite sum of synthetic propositions about phenomena that may be thought of as being 'in' the world, taken in the Kantian sense). Theologians have declared the notion to be a mystery,[1] and philosophers, beginning in the modern period with Kant's antinomies, have generally regarded it as having no definite meaning.

I propose to show that though *creatio ex nihilo* is indeed a queer conception, which leads theologians to speak of mysteries and philosophers to speak of nonsense, in fact the notion is not so remote as has been supposed from certain demands within what is nowadays called our ordinary ways of speaking; and that within these ordinary ways of speaking where we are talking in a logically extended way about matters which are both meaningful and important to us as persons, there are displayed analogies with the sort of thing the theologian has in mind when he uses 'creation' and 'image of God'. To anticipate later argument, I think it can be shown by an analysis of some of the things we normally say and think of ourselves as persons that what we mean when we say them is logically heterogeneous with certain other things we say about ourselves, and therefore they may be said to be both 'queer' (if we take as our paradigm for what is 'unqueer' these other things we say) and yet meaningful; and that in them some analogy with what one might mean by *creatio ex nihilo* is to be found.

While, of course, this does not necessarily accredit the use of analogies drawn from these tracts of our ordinary ways of speaking for describing God; and while it certainly does not authorize the use of theological language in general; it does give us some genuine insight into what it is that the Christian might mean when he uses them.

This, I propose to do by exploring suicide as in some sense an act of absolute and radical destruction; and by analysing certain features of the expression 'I was born'.

I

The impulse to see man as in the image of God, and especially to see that image manifest paradigmatically in a dark and violent gesture of defiance, destructiveness and nihilism is of such antiquity that we

---

[1] '. . . In the history of religion the idea of real creation first appears when God, instead of being considered a merely natural force, becomes a transcendent Being. We do not know this God through experience or reason but through faith, and we know of the mystery of creation by the same means.' E. Frank, *Philosophical Understanding and Religious Truth*, New York, 1945, p. 58.

cannot but wonder what kind of posture man is thought to achieve in relation to the world and to himself in these acts in which it seems so natural to see the image of God. Adam and Eve are promised that, if they will eat of the tree of the Knowledge of Good and Evil, they will become as God. While this is a calamitous act, it is nevertheless one in which man is felt to exhibit a real if perverted likeness to God. Man's act of rebellion is in certain respects logically like God's act of creation! The logical parallel between God's act of creation and man's act of destruction is clearly assumed. If this be so, it is necessary to explore some of the features of the way we think of ourselves that are built in to our talk about ourselves as persons.

St. Augustine, in his *Confessions*, reflecting in later life upon a boy-hood act of wantonly stealing pears which he did not want and could not possibly eat, and concluding that the only possible answer to the question 'Why did I do it?' was: 'It was forbidden', goes on to make even more explicit the curious logical connexion between God's creative activity and man's wilful rebelliousness. He says, 'And where-in did I, even corruptedly and pervertedly, imitate my Lord? Did I wish, if only by artifice, to act contrary to Thy law . . . so that . . . I might imitate an imperfect liberty by doing with impunity things which I was not allowed to do, in obscured likeness of Thy omni-potency?'[2] And then, elsewhere, doubtless having the same case in mind says: 'For souls in their very sins strive after nothing else but some kind of likeness to God, in a proud, preposterous, and, so to speak, servile liberty[3]'.

A similar tie between God the radical creator and man the radical destroyer is shown in Albert Camus's brilliant essay, *The Rebel*. He says of modern revolt: 'Metaphysical rebellion is the means by which a man protests against his condition and against the whole of creation. It is metaphysical because it disputes the ends of man and of creation. . . . When the throne of God is overthrown, the rebel realizes that it is now his own responsibility to create the justice, order and unity that he sought in vain within his own condition and, in this way, to justify the fall of God'[4]—that is, to become God himself.

Again, the American poet, E. E. Cummings, seems to suggest that man as a radical destroyer of the world is the most apt antithesis to

[2] *Confessions*, Bk. II, ch. vi.       [3] *On the Trinity*, Bk. XI, ch. v.
[4] *The Rebel*, trans. by Anthony Bower, London, 1953, pp. 29–31.

and hence the best source of analogies for God as creator *ex nihilo* when
he writes:

> when god decided to invent
> everything he took one
> breath bigger than a circustent
> and everything began
>
> when man determined to destroy
> himself he picked the was
> of shall and finding only why
> smashed it into because[5]

Finally, in Dostoyevski's novel, *The Devils*, we are confronted by
Kirilov who, believing that God does not exist, nevertheless so conceives of the God who does not exist and who therefore must be
replaced, that only an act of suicide by him is a genuine earnest that
he himself may be thought to have become this God. He says: 'Full
freedom will come only when it makes no difference whether to live
or not to live . . . a new man will come, happy and proud. To whom it
won't matter whether he lives or not. . . . Everyone who desires supreme
freedom must dare to kill himself.'[6] In other words, the indifferent
contemplation of suicide seems for Kirilov to exhibit a posture in
relation to oneself and the world that is in some way or other like that
which God has been thought to have to the world which is his creature.

Preliminary to analysing further the significance of these striking
parallels, it is necessary to consider what can be meant by the concept
'world', for it seems to me to be a very ambiguous one, and its am-
biguity is the source of much confusion concerning what is meant by
God as the creator of the world. Being perforce brief, this will be
vague.

Doubtless there are many more uses of the concept 'world', but let
us consider here only three.

'World' can be used, as Kant seems to have thought, as an idea of
the Transcendental Reason, and as such functions as a regulative
principle for a *cosmologia rationalis*. The concept in this use has no
content—in Kant's sense—but nevertheless provides us with guide-
lines in the pursuit of a goal which, though never to be achieved,
nonetheless governs the progress of scientific understanding. This use
of the concept is largely irrelevant to my present inquiry.

[5] *Poems:* 1923–1954, New York, 1955, p. 404.
[6] *Penguin Classics*, trans. by David Magarshack, London, 1953, pp. 125–126.

The world may also be thought of as that which can be exhaustively catalogued by a, practically speaking, infinite number of straightforward subject-predicate sentences in a language system which we will, in order to educe the distinction essential to my purposes, imagine as having no use of first personal pronouns, singular. In fact, of course, if we eliminate first personal pronouns, singular, it is difficult to imagine what pronouns like 'we' and 'you' could do in the language (where they are steadfastly held to be unanalysable into demonstratives like 'this', 'that', 'these', and 'those'); and therefore we may eliminate them as well. Now we have a language with only the demonstratives, and the third personal pronouns. But surely, a language which does not use the first personal pronoun would have to reduce even the third personal to 'it', i.e. 'he', 'she' and 'they' could only mean what could be catalogued in reports of behaviour (actually we should have to say 'events') or dispositions to behaviour. We now have a language in terms of which nothing can be said about persons.

In the language thus truncated, the world will be the sum of synthetic propositions that could conceivably be shown to be true or false. It would, in other words, be the world that could be known to us, and which is thought of in our scientifically dominated culture, as the world of common sense, and of all of the sciences themselves. Therefore it will be the world as it is 'known by science'. It will be objective, that is, it will be what can be catalogued exhaustively in a language having no personal pronouns. It will be in practice, a third person world, remembering that the only pronoun in the third person which remains is 'it'. It will be, in other words, the public world as it must be imagined to be apart from anyone actually experiencing it. It is the world as we would all agree it *must be*; all epistemological relativism aside, in the language of our model, it cannot be described as being experienced by anyone in particular.[7] It is a world in which there are no persons, because 'I' and 'my' cannot be used in the language that describes it. Therefore, it cannot be the world *of* or *for* anyone. No doubt a description of the world in this way would be a *tour de force*, and would involve a language which is very awkward, when compared with our ordinary ways of speaking about the common sense world. Nevertheless, I think it an imaginable one, and is in fact the ideal goal of all

---

[7] Given the purposes of my model, it is an irrelevant criticism to observe that modern physics has had to argue that an ideal observer or at least an observation point always has to be posited.

objective scientific knowledge, albeit the concepts that may be meaningfully used vary among sciences.

In contrast with this, and as our third use of the concept 'world', let us imagine what we could speak of in a language in which there *are* first personal pronouns. What differences would immediately appear?

First the world would be *of* and *for* someone. What I would mean by the world would be *my* world—though, committed as I believe we usually are to using 'world' in the second of our three senses, this may be obscured. What is meant by 'world' in this sense would include all of those features which could be catalogued in 'third person' language as in sense two. But by adding the first personal pronoun all of this would be radically transformed by the additional characteristic of the world being mine; not just the world as I experience it from a particular point of view in a third person way like the third person way in which you, from a different particular point of view, also experience it (in other words, the first personal pronoun does not merely introduce the possibility of epistemological relativism); but mine in the sense that I have a relation to the body, its behaviour and the environment of its actions (which is the world *for me*), which is part of what I mean by 'I', that can never be identical with the relation which *you* have, and that cannot be expressed in the language lacking the first personal pronoun singular. That this statement would seem to be analytic does not weaken the force of the distinction.

Perhaps this can be illustrated in the following way. In the terms set forth above, the expression 'I will die' when used by me cannot be exhaustively analysed into a purely third person reading of 'This body will undergo a radical change, including ceasing to behave in certain ways, etc.'. References by me to the body and its behaviour which is part at least of what I mean by 'I' can never be made to be logically equivalent to references by me to bodies and their behaviour which are not. 'I will die' can never mean for me just the same thing as 'There is a body in the world (in the second sense) which one day will cease to behave as it now does'. What is being asserted is not just about an object in the world (in the second sense) in the way that 'This body (as a component of the world in the second sense) will die' is about an object in the world. My body and its behaviour is not in the world *for me* in the same way that your body (to avoid the possessive pronoun, we'll call it 'Smith') and its behaviour is in the world for me. For me to describe my death as the end of certain kinds of behaviour in the world is not *for me* the description of an occurrence *in the world* at all like an account by me of Smith's death as an occurrence *in the world.* For myself, I am not *in* the world as Smith is in the world.

Now, taking as our paradigm Kirilov's suggestion that the act of suicide will be the earnest of his having achieved Godhead because it will exhibit a characteristic in himself which he conceives to be essential to Godlikeness, how may the posture of a man to himself and to his world as he contemplates suicide be likened in certain respects to the posture of God when he is thought to be the 'maker of heaven and earth'?—and it must be remembered that the parallel we are here drawing is between God as radical creator and man, as in some sense, a radical destroyer.

If we take seriously our distinction between the use of the concept 'world' in the second sense above, where what is meant in the nature of the case cannot be something that is *of* or *for* someone in particular; and its use in sense three, where it is always *my* world; then I think it is quite meaningful, using 'world' in sense three, to say that my suicide is an act of destroying *my* world. If, that is, we keep in mind how 'world' is functioning here, we may say that when I take my own life, I destroy the world! As destroyer of the world, in this sense, I stand to the world in my act of radical destruction, as God seems to be thought to stand in his act of radical creation. The posture I assume toward myself and the world (in sense three) as radical disposer is logically different from that I assume as disposer of this, that, or some other characteristic or feature of myself or the world. I am not destroying something or other *in* the world. I am destroying the world as a whole. I may be thought, in other words, speaking metaphorically, to take up a relation to myself and the world *as a whole,* to stand 'outside' myself (in our ordinary uses of 'myself'); and this bears some analogy to what the Christian seems to be believing about God's relation to the world when he declares him to be 'maker of heaven and earth'.

Or, to put the case in a slightly different way, in the act of suicide I am, with reference to what I name with the personal pronoun 'I', bringing something radically to an end. Just as Hamlet's question 'To be or not to be . . .' is logically not like 'To be or not to be a doctor, lawyer or merchant chief . . .', so contemplating the ending of my life is logically not like ending a job or a marriage. It is an end of *all* possibilities for something namely, for what I name with the personal pronoun 'I', and not just the ending of certain possibilities such as this or that. We can say 'After his divorce he was remarried', or '. . . he

was sadder but wiser'. To go with the expression 'After he died . . .'
there are no expressions logically like 'he remarried' or 'was sadder
but wiser'.

I want to say then that though the act of suicide may not be thought
of as destroying the world insofar as it is taken as an object for thought
in the third person, nevertheless, the world as *my* world, *in* which part
of what I mean when I use the pronoun 'I' of myself is to be found,
which is the environment of the acts of the body that is part of what
I mean by 'I', and is accordingly the world in our third sense, *is*
destroyed. And the posture which I have in relation to the world, thus
construed, is analogous to that which God is thought to have to the
world (in either of our first two senses) as its radical creator.[8] There are
three equally important features of this analogy to be emphasized.
First, as destroyer of the world (in sense three), I have a view of myself
as what may be called a radical agent. In the act of suicide, I perform
an act which makes nothing out of something. My act is the reverse of
God's who makes something out of nothing. A world which can be
imagined, in terms of the present analysis, to have an end can equally
be thought to have a beginning. When I imagine the end of the world
by imaging a state of affairs in which there is no longer the world
*for me*, I am thinking of a situation logically no more nor less queer
than when I think of the world as having been created.

Secondly, in thinking of suicide as an act of destroying the world,
I am thinking of the world as coming to an end, that is, as being
finite. There is in this the greatest possible contrast with the way that
we, quite properly, think of the world when using the concept 'world'
in sense two. The world in the third person, the subject of our purely
scientific curiosity, is in practice, and rightly so, open-ended, infinite,
and therefore not a possible object of experience, as Kant seemed to
imply in his refusal to make the concept either an empirical one or one
of the understanding. Accordingly we can derive no analogy for God's
relation to the world which is his creature, from our relation to the
world in sense two, for nothing ever radically begins or ends in *this*
world.

Thirdly, it is having this kind of relation to the world (in sense
three) which I have as a radical agent, that constitutes, for the Christian,
my being in the image of God.

[8] There is a dangerous pitfall in the analogy here, for we may be tempted to infer from
it, at this stage, that God and his world are identical. But this would be an invalid inference
for, as I shall show, I and *my* world are not identical either.

## II

It still remains for me to show that there are certain logical pressures within what we ordinarily say and think about ourselves as persons which are not less 'queer' than, because logically analogous to, saying of God that he is 'maker of heaven and earth'. To do this I will undertake to analyse the expression 'I was born'.

Frequently we find ourselves answering questions such as 'When were you born?' And we do not take these questions to be odd in any way. We answer by giving a date, such as 'In April of 1919' or 'Shortly after the First World War' or if the context is appropriate, we may say 'In the year of the great earthquake', etc., or we may be asked 'Where were you born?' and answer 'In Kaifeng, China' or 'In the Presbyterian Hospital'. If we are to take these questions as in some way mystifying we would probably be taken to be resorting to, perhaps suspicious, evasion, or to be mere trouble-makers. For the questions obviously presuppose possible answers in terms of straightforwardly datable and locatable events, which occur in the objective world which is spread out in time and space; and which, in practice, extends infinitely backward and forward from the event expressed by 'I was born'. As such, the event may be thought to have all the complexity that any of the events in this world has: one may, for example, consider it from the standpoint of historical chronicle, from the standpoint of biology and genetics, or from the standpoint of obstetrics. And saying that 'I was born' is true will certainly entail that certain historical, biological and genetic, or obstetrical propositions will be true. One may even wish to go so far as to hold that the proposition 'I was born' can be exhaustively analysed into all the propositions of the same logical sort as those above, the truth of which would be entailed by the truth of 'I was born'.

We take 'I was born' in this way most of the time, and quite rightly so, as is evinced in our willingness to answer the question 'When were you born?' by straightforwardly offering a date, and not precipitating any philosophical quarrels about it.

But if we take this legitimate because, in most cases, quite adequate interpretation to be the paradigmatic or only one, we are left with some serious puzzles. For this puts me in the curious position of *celebrating* a chronicle of events, or biological and genetic or obstetrical facts, and the like when I celebrate my birthday! To honour and observe duly with solemn rites only certain obstetrical facts seems a very odd form of behaviour. And in fact I do not think any of us is doing this when we celebrate our birthdays, however impossible it may be to conceive of there being something to celebrate unless there *were* or *had been* some obstetrical facts. If we analyse 'I was born' into the sum of true propositions about obstetrical and other facts, and the like, which are entailed by the truth of the proposition 'I was born', then there seems to be nothing left of the sort that as persons we celebrate—nothing, indeed, in which we could take other than a purely obstetrical interest.

Now, why is this so? I believe we can say that it is because concealed in the language in which we are asked 'When were you born?' and in the answer 'In April of 1919' is a subtle commitment to the objectivist language which possesses no personal pronouns or else does not take them seriously; and therefore a birthday can never be described as *my* birthday. Or to put it differently, if we take the question 'When were you born?' to be like 'When did you come into the world?', we answer the question in such a way as to predispose us to take the meaning of 'into the *world*' in the second of the two senses above. It is obvious that in this view, my 'coming into the world' is not a radical event. When do we start counting 'being in the world'? At conception? At the moment I leave my mother's womb? Or do we start with the gleam in my father's eye? Birthdays are celebrated only by persons, for a birthday is not what we understand it to be unless it is *of* and *for* someone, unless there is only one person who uses the pronoun 'mine' of it. Only what can be *of* and *for* someone can be celebrated; and nothing in a world described merely in a language lacking personal pronouns can be so described. The fact that we celebrate birthdays therefore suggests that 'I was born' cannot be exhaustively analysed into reports upon obstetrical events, etc., in our language having no personal pronouns.

If, however, 'I was born' thus analysed tells some of the story of my coming into the world because the proposition 'I was born' entails that there will be certain obstetrical and other facts, what is left out? The answer is of course that the world into which I am described as having come is the world in sense two above. And there is not *for me* any world in sense three until I use 'I' and 'mine'. With this act, the world in sense three comes into being, the world which is *my* world. And it is an absolutely novel act, for only I can use 'I' and 'mine' *for* and *of me* and *my* world. The absolute discontinuity between there being no world in sense three for me and there suddenly being such a world because someone uses 'I' and 'mine' of it is the same as the logical discontinuity between language two having no personal pronouns and language three which does have them. And this is paralleled in the ontological discontinuity between there being nothing and there being something which is involved in the doctrine of *creatio ex nihilo*. In the act of suicide I make nothing out of something, the reverse of God's act of creation. In using the first personal pronouns singular, I make something out of nothing. It is from this that our analogy for God as 'maker of heaven and earth' must come. To speak of God as creator is not the same as saying 'I was born', but it *is* in certain respects logically like this.

## III

Let us then ask in conclusion how some of the apparent conflicts between science and religion—with particular reference to the notion of creation—can be shown to be the result of a confusion concerning the logical status of their respective claims.

Earlier on, I suggested that the implicit ideal of all objective scientific inquiry is a catalogue of everything there is in a language from which we might imagine all the personal pronouns to have been dropped out, for such a catalogue yields a world which is as it is independent of its being known from any particular point of view or by anyone in particular. I also suggested that within limits imposed by the programme itself this is a perfectly legitimate enterprise. Let me now anticipate what is to follow and suggest that the putative conflict between science and religion—between Fred Hoyle and Genesis—respecting creation is the result of failing to notice the subtle commitment in this programme to the concept of 'world' as I have defined it as sense two above; and further because of a failure to notice that many of the things we say and think quite ordinarily about ourselves as persons rather operates with the concept in sense three. Finally, if our analogy for creation is to be drawn from the kind of discourse in which I say of myself 'I was born', where this expression is analysed as unassimilable to a language having no personal pronouns and therefore must be understood as at once saying more than can be said in such a language while entailing all of the sorts of things that can, a compounding of the confusion is always possible. For this means that what is named by 'I' and 'world' in our language possessing personal pronouns is not entirely unrelated to the body and its environment that is described in the language which lacks them, because the concepts

K

'I' and 'world' (in sense three) could not be used were not the concepts 'body' and 'world' (in sense two) already in use—while the converse is not the case. Our language having personal pronouns says more than one lacking them, but not more in the sense of adding further information of the same logical sort as already known through the pronounless language. Adding personal pronouns changes *the whole* picture, but it is an already familiar picture that is *transformed*, seen in a different light. This means that, in speaking by means of our analogy, of the world as having been created, we run the risk of misconstruing the relation of religious claims about creation of the world to scientific claims about the world in either of two ways: (1) supposing there to be absolutely no connexion between them;[9] (2) supposing the connexion to be of the sort obtaining between two propositions within one of the language systems in our model. To say that the world is created, using our analogy, is not to report an additional fact about it like saying that there are material objects in it. Saying of the world that it is created stands to the fact of its being extended in a way analogous to saying of a body that it is a person stands to its having three dimensions.

Now, perhaps the difficulties can be elucidated in the following way. Let my body—in so far as it is extended, an organism, and capable of what might be called directed activity—be the kind of being about which the physicist, biologist and psychologist speak. Within their conceptual schemes the notion of creation as the emergence of absolute novelty does not appropriately operate. Why? Because of everything that may be conceived as being reported in the concepts of the aforementioned disciplines we can imagine asking 'What was the cause of *that*?' (where 'cause' functions in a straightforward explanatory way), and we would expect to be given an answer by reference to some antecedents on a common logical footing with the events or behaviour reported by these disciplines, using a covering law which embodies the concepts of these disciplines. Each of them, in other words, takes any given event or piece of behaviour reported by means of their concepts to be continuous with other events or behaviour of logically the same order prior to the one reported and so on *ad infinitum*. While obviously the physicist, biologist and psychologist operate with differing concepts appropriate to their own modes of explanation; and even though one may wish to hold that for this reason there is logical discontinuity of

⁹ Karl Barth and Rudolph Bultmann, in different ways, seem to me to come very close to suggesting this view.

a sort among these modes of explanation, since, e.g. no complex of *physical* facts *qua* physical logically entails any biological fact; there *is* an analogy among these modes in the respect that within the limits of their explanatory interests any fact, event or piece of behaviour is preceded by a theoretically infinite series of facts, events or pieces of behaviour of the same logical order. And their explanatory interests, far from requiring a notion of a radical discontinuation of these series, would in fact be frustrated by it.

The implicit ideal of these accounts of the world is a catalogue in a language in which there are no personal pronouns.

When, however, we add the personal pronouns everything is changed. However much the use of this new and enriched language may imply the appropriateness, within the specified limits, of the truncated one, we are now speaking of the world as *my* world and *yours*. A body and its environment may be thought of as becoming *my* body in *my* world—which is to use 'world' in the third of our senses— when someone, namely you or I, can use of them the expression '*my* body in *my* world'. Since nothing in the truncated language logically implies the new components of the richer one, we may say that *my* body in *my* world is, as *mine*, radically discontinuous with *this* body, *a* body, *the* body, etc., in the world (taken in the *second* sense). And it is this fact that makes it possible to speak of *me* and *my* world as having come into being *out of* nothing, i.e. as having been created.

To have shown the source of the analogies by means of which the Christian speaks of God as 'maker of heaven and earth' is not the same as showing that these analogies ought to be used.

I have attempted here only to argue that the doctrine of creation *ex nihilo* is a logically queer notion; but that it is not as remote as is supposed from many things we say and think about ourselves in quite ordinary ways, and that an analysis of the kind of posture a man may be thought to assume to himself and his world in contemplating suicide and of the expression 'I was born' display this fact. Persuading a man that he ought to think of the world as having been created is not unlike persuading a man who speaks a language having no personal pronouns that there are persons.

# VII

# LOVE AS PERCEPTION OF MEANING

## By J. R. Jones

I Cor. xiii: portions of verses 9, 12 and 13. 'We know in part
. . . for now we see through a glass, darkly . . . (But) now
abideth faith, hope, love, these three. And the greatest of
these is love.'

THESE words might be rendered: 'Knowledge is fragmentary . . . for
at present we only see the baffling reflections in a mirror. But we have
faith, hope, love, these three. And the greatest of these is love.'

The object of knowledge is the world. The *world* is what we are
seeing. But it is only very imperfectly that we can be said to know it,
St. Paul is saying, inasmuch as we do not really know what it is that
we are seeing. We are looking at something, certainly,—we confront
a world—but our state of mind is rather as if we saw objects in a broken
or uneven mirror. We see them, in one sense of 'see', but we are
unable to make out precisely what they are. We 'see' 'baffling reflections
in a mirror'. This is Moffatt's translation and it is an attempt to bring
out the way St. Paul runs his metaphor of the mirror into another one
—the metaphor of a riddle or puzzle. His point is that we see what is
there, in as much as we are only seeing a bad reflection of it, 'in the
form of a puzzle—enigmatically'. In short, what we are seeing does
not make much sense to us.

And yet, I have said, what we are seeing is *the world*. Then, surely,
you will say, this is to count science out. For is not the most significant
fact of human knowledge that man has in science devised a way of
looking at the world which, by painful progress, perhaps, but nevertheless with increasing triumph, is making sense of the world? '—Knowledge is limited, fragmentary: we see, but what we are seeing is
mysterious, puzzling, enigmatical . . .'—what *can* this man be saying?
Surely, you will feel, he cannot be describing us.

It would be instructive to ask how scientists themselves and writers
on the philosophy of science estimate the limits of human knowledge.
One is struck by the sharp contrast with this questioning estimate of
St. Paul's. 'In principle', writes the author of a recent work, 'there are

141

no limits to our knowledge. The boundaries which must be acknowledged are of an empirical nature and, therefore, never ultimate; they can be pushed back further and further; there is no unfathomable mystery in the world.' There is no recognition here that we may be looking at something and *failing to make out what it is*. There is consciousness of gaps in our knowledge, of frontiers—limits to our comprehension—that have to be pushed ever further back. The enterprise of science is seen as painstakingly piecing together a picture that is only becoming cumulatively intelligible. But there is absolutely no sense of bafflement, no sense of confronting a riddle or an enigma. The whole temper of modern science is one of emancipation from bafflement. The dominant image is of an area of illumination that is being extended over wider and wider ranges of a territory in which, certainly there is darkness—the darkness of ignorance—but no incomprehensible mystery.

How does it come about that the scientist is so sure that there are no mysteries—that all his problems are problems which are in principle soluble, although he may not actually succeed in solving them? It could be said that the reason is that he is making a restrictive assumption as to the kinds of questions that can possibly be formulated in language. Either a question can be shown by analysis of its logical grammar to be a senseless question, or it can in principle be answered by empirical investigation, that is, *by looking at the world*. Questions which we are unable to answer are either problems as yet empirically insoluble or they are not genuine questions. This assumption at once empties the world of mystery.

But it seems to me that another and deeper assumption underlies this—an assumption as to how one is to look at the world, or establish a relation with the world. It seems to me that the whole procedure of empirical investigation is tied up with a particular way of looking at the world. It is this that, in part, defines the precise sense in which science is 'an investigation of the world'.

A contrast which St. Paul wishes to bring out in this passage will enable us to give an indication of the way the scientist regards the world and to suggest how there might be another, very different, way of regarding it. The distinction St. Paul is drawing is the one between the partiality and fragmentariness of our knowledge here, in Time, and the fulness and directness of the grasp of truth to which we may hope to attain in Eternity. He says (to give his words in Moffatt's translation): 'At present we see the baffling reflections in a mirror, but then it will be face to face. At present I am learning bit by bit, then I shall understand as all along I have myself been understood.' And as it is knowledge that is involved, the narrower and more fragmentary vision must necessarily disappear in the wider and fuller one. 'When the perfect comes, the imperfect will be superseded'—as the man's mature experience replaces the child's. 'When I was a child, I talked, thought and reasoned as a child, but now that I am a man I am done with childish ways.' This is why St. Paul says that knowledge, meaning our present fragmentary knowledge, has no finality about it. It will be taken up into a totally different way of regarding things in Eternity.

But what is the nature of the illumination that is to supersede it? You noticed that he ascribes two characteristic to this. One is *directness*—in Eternity, knowledge will be a confrontation: 'then it will be face to face.' The other characteristic he expresses by saying that then I shall '. . . understand as all along I have myself been understood.' St. Paul seems here to be thinking of the way I am now known or understood *from* Eternity, that is, by God. What is being suggested is that in Eternity I shall have the same comprehension of things that God has at this moment of me. And the point of that is to suggest that to see things as they will be seen in Eternity is to see them as God sees them. It is to see *the world* as God sees it, to see Time, and the world as it exists in Time, not from within Time, but from where God is looking at it, from Eternity. But now, a perceiver who perceives the world from Eternity is no longer a part of what he beholds. He no longer perceives objects, as it were from within their midst. He is abstracted to a point of view outside the world. And to see the world thus, without one's own involvement in it, is to see it as a single thing. It is to become aware of its existence as a whole.

I am not suggesting, of course, that we can actually place ourselves at the point of Eternity. Indeed, in so far as 'eternity' is a concept of religious discourse it makes no sense to talk of the literal occupation of its point of view. Philosophers, however, have talked of beholding objects in Time, as it were, in the light, or under the aspect, of Eternity. Spinoza, for instance, thought there was a way of looking at things, as he said *sub specie aeternitatis*.

And we find Wittgenstein using the same phrase. He moreover, shows what the consequences are for our awareness of the world of looking at it in this way. He wrote in the *Notebooks* 'The usual way of looking at things sees objects, as it were, from the midst of them, the view *sub specie aeternitatis* from outside. In such a way that they have the whole world as background.' And in the *Tractatus* he says: 'The contemplation of the world *sub specie aeternitatis* is its contemplation as a limited whole.' He also says: 'The feeling of the world as a limited whole is the mystical feeling.' And again, 'Not *how* the world is, is the mystical, but *that* it is.' These sentences contain the germ of a distinction I now wish to draw in regard to ways in which the world can be looked at.

In one sense, '*how* the world is' covers everything. And this means that, in that sense, all you have is science. The world is the totality of facts. And, looking as it were from the midst of this, how the world is, how it goes, the *facts* of it, will cover everything. And the scientist's assumption is that this totality is, in principle, uniformly open to, or penetrable by, his techniques. He regards his procedures of investigation as, in principle, extensible over the whole area of fact. There are no mysteries and there are also therefore no limits to our knowledge. The boundaries that have to be acknowledged simply mark the extent to which we have hitherto succeeded in bringing the totality of facts under our purview. And these are limits which can, in principle, be pushed ever further back.

What attitude to the world is operative here? I reply: an attitude of complete immersion in the facts of the world, of taking the world as given—as, in principle, completely explorable and yet, in a sense, as having no limits, and, accordingly, as completely unmysterious. Science restricts its questions to within the world. It only puts to itself such questions as are answerable by piecemeal investigation of the world. It looks at objects *from the midst of them*. And it is able to say (to echo St. Paul) 'I am learning bit by bit'—I am illuminating, conceptualizing, mapping the total area of fact bit by bit. I may not have got very far yet. I am still very ignorant. But I know I shall never be baffled. For how the world is is completely unmysterious.

And, as I said, in a sense, '*how* the world is' is everything. It is the totality of facts. *In a sense* then there is no place for religion. For religion is not concerned with facts, with 'how the world is'. That, I think, was the point of saying that 'to believe in God means to see that the facts of the world are not the end of the matter'.[1] It is a fundamental mistake to think that science could bring anything to light which might tend either to confirm or overthrow the belief in the existence of God. And it is in the same way a mistake, though a very common one, to think

---

[1] Wittgenstein: *Notebooks*, Oxford, 1961, p. 74.

of the belief in God as some kind of probable hypothesis. How can it be this when it does not touch the systematic empirical investigation of the world at any point? There is nothing that could constitute evidence for it and there is no sense in which it is an explanation of anything. No predictions follow from it. 'How the world is', says Wittgenstein, 'is completely indifferent to what is higher. God does not reveal himself *in* the world. . . . The sense of the world must lie outside the world. The solution of the riddle of life in space and time lies outside space and time.' This both explains why religion should seem so unrelated to the scientific undertaking and shows how misguided a whole generation of apologists have been who looked to the facts of the world for some wishful reconcilation of a supposed conflict between religion and science.

What I want to say is—Science is concerned with the totality of facts and, in one sense, this is everything. *In one sense then, all you have is science.*

On the other hand, as we face our lives and in those moments when the question arises for us whether our life has any meaning at all— when we suddenly have what might be described as an awareness of existence and the whole question whether existence *has sense* arises for us, then we know perfectly well that the world is not unmysterious. For in these experiences there is a 'feeling of the world as a limited whole'. We seem abstracted to a point outside the world and we see it without our own involvement in it—we see it as one thing. And when this happens to you (if it ever does happen), you *know* that 'how the world is' is not everything. There is something else—there is the existence of the world—'*that* the world is'. You suddenly see the world in a way which makes you conscious of the mystery of its existence— of the mystery of existence itself. And a question arises which could not have arisen before while you were investigating the facts and taking the fact that there are facts for granted—namely, the question of the *meaning* of this latter fact. What does it mean that a world should exist, that anything should exist, that there should be facts at all? This is not a question that further knowledge of the facts of the world would enable us to answer. It is a mystery. We can become aware of this mystery—deeply and disturbingly. But the paradoxical thing is that you can have this experience without detriment to your confidence as a scientist. For 'how the world is' remains untouched—the facts are unchanged—and '*how* the world is' remains completely unmysterious. In other words, what I am saying is that it both makes sense to be confident that there is no unfathomable mystery within the world and at the same time to recognize that the world itself is the profoundest mystery.

You can watch an animal at play and be struck only by the way it is made—the delicate structures of its frame; or perhaps you are pre-occupied with its importance for your needs, fears, interests or pursuits of the moment. It may be an intricate, a useful or a fearful thing for you, but it is not a mysterious one. Then can you not suddenly see it in a quite different light—can you not become aware of its *existence*, of the mystery of its existence? Why should there *be* this thing? Now you see it with the whole world as background to it—the whole existence of the world; why should there *be* anything, why should there be a world at all?

And it is here, where we become conscious of the existence of the world as a whole, and in regard to the meaning of its existence—in regard to what plain men perhaps call 'the meaning of life' or 'the sense of life'—that we face something which lies quite beyond the limits of our knowledge. Here it is that we are aware of knowing only 'in part', of seeing only the baffling reflections in a mirror, of confronting an enigma. For here there is not only ignorance but bafflement. When the fact of the existence of the world obtrudes itself in this way upon consciousness, we seem drawn down to a depth where nothing can be said. The language in which we describe how the world is—the language of precise question and clear, definitive answer—fail us. It fails us as an instrument of exploration of the mystery of the world. The mean-ings which are capable of illuminating the mystery are not expressible in this language. It is not to this language that they belong.

What St. Paul is saying then is that, in regard to *the sense of existence*, the sort of sense things would have for us in Eternity, from where it must have become apparent why the world should exist or why any-thing should exist, we are *now* groping, baffled-looking, certainly, at something (for life is there, the world is with us), but seeing what we do see darkly, brokenly, enigmatically as in a dull and distorting mirror.

'Nehklyudov went into the house. "Yes, yes", he thought, "the work which is carried out by our life, the whole work, the whole meaning of this work, is dark to me and cannot be made intelligible".'

But, says St. Paul, where we have thus to face the fact that we do not *know* the meaning of existence—the meaning of life—we have the means of arriving at some kind of understanding of its meaning. 'We have faith, hope, love—these three.'

'And the greatest of these is love.' Why did he say that? I think he said it because love can give perceptive understanding of the meaning of the world. When I say 'perceptive understanding', I still of course do not mean that we can come to *know* the meaning, particularly if it were meant that the meaning of the world could be known as its facts are known. Its *meaning* is not another fact. Love's perception of the meaning of the world is an understanding of its meaning, not a knowledge. It does not make men learned; it makes them wise. But I shall return to the way I think love is perceptive of meaning. I first want to say something about 'faith' and 'hope'.

Faith and hope are connected with an understanding of the meaning of the world which, in contrast with the perceptive understanding that love can give, I would describe as problematic. It is an understanding through affirmation, an understanding through believing. Faith is the 'evidence of things not seen'. It is 'being convinced of what we do not see', namely, that the world has meaning. For we do not *see* its meaning. Faith is to *believe* in a meaning that we do not see.

A fundamental mistake with regard to faith is to treat it as if it were a kind of rational belief. I have already referred to the quite inappropriate use of the language of probability in this connection. We do not believe in God because there is good evidence that He exists. I have insisted that, looking at the world, as it were, from the midst of it, looking at the facts of the world, nothing can constitute evidence for the existence of God. 'How the world is' is entirely unaffected by whether you believe in God or not. If, therefore, you do believe in Him, your belief is not rational belief. You did not arrive at it by the consideration of commensurate evidence. For where *was* your evidence?

Faith is a *leap*—'an objective uncertainty held fast in infinite passion'. Why should we be afraid of saying that in the belief that God exists there is a large element of hoping that He may exist, of wanting existence to be meaningful? For with awareness of the existence of the world as a limited whole arises inescapably the thought of its possible ultimate meaninglessness. How the world is, of course, is meaningful enough. That is precisely what science is showing. But 'that the world is' is a mystery and might be a meaningless mystery, I mean, something which does not in fact have sense. It is against this background that the leap of faith is taken. It is an affirmation of meaning in the teeth of possible ultimate meaninglessness. That is why genuine faith is so often compounded with a persistently threatening doubt. 'Lord I believe, help Thou mine unbelief.' Faith is 'holding fast the uncertain in passionate certitude'. And it is precisely because it is an *uncertainty* that you hold fast that the certitude with which you hold it has to be passionate. If God were an inference, you would affirm Him without passion. You would be standing on the firm ground of your evidence. But you cannot *leap* without passion, without anguish. It has been profoundly said that 'Those who believe they believe in God but without passion in their heart, without anguish of mind, without uncertainty, without doubt and even at times without despair, believe only in the idea of God, not in God himself'. It was the Basque writer Miguel de Unamuno who said that and he has gone further than anyone I know—particularly among Catholic writers—in making hope rather than inference the clue to faith. He writes: 'We do not hope because we believe but rather we believe because we hope. For it is not rational necessity but vital anguish that impels us to believe in God. To believe in God is to feel a hunger for God, to be sensible of his lack and absence, to wish that God may exist. Faith in God is based upon the vital need of giving finality to existence.' This may be exaggeration. But I think I can see what it means. I think I can see how (at least certain) minds who have felt the world as a limited whole and faced the possibility that it may be without meaning, are driven by some kind of vital anguish to affirm God. This may look very like creating God. But if I am right that no facts or features of the world constitute evidence for the existence of God, what other kind of faith can you have? ' "God exists" (wrote Kierkegaard) must remain as dubitable a proposition as ever it was. It is no less dubitable when we have made the leap than it was before. Does this mean that the leap achieved nothing? On the contrary, it has achieved everything. Now we *believe*.'

At the same time, we are only problematically related to the hidden meaning of the world through hope or, which is the same thing, through faith. We are simply believing in a meaning which we do not see—passionately wishing that there may be this meaning. But we have 'faith, hope, *love*. And the *greatest* of these is love.' I want to suggest that love is greatest because, although it too can only give understanding, as opposed to knowledge, of the meaning of existence, the understanding it gives is perceptive, not problematic. Here meaning, although not comprehended is somehow *experienced*—it is no longer something to which we are merely problematically related through belief. It is a perception, not a leap.

Love perceives the sense of things because it is when a thing is loved by us that we come closest to seeing it as God sees it. It is then that we see it, as it were, from Eternity, with the whole world as background to it. Where persons are concerned, what love of another gives is perception of his or her unconditional significance. To see a person as unconditionally significant is to see him as God sees him. And one of the fundamental difficulties of life is to be able to perceive the unconditional significance of *another*. We are naturally ego-centric, which means that we ordinarily only recognize our own unconditional significance. That is the point of saying 'Love thy neighbour *as thyself*'. It is love alone that can *show* us the unconditional significance of another. A person whom I love is somehow revealed to me. I no longer see him through the miasma of his mere relevance to my wants or mere usefulness for my plans and purposes. And when he ceases thereby to be a mere adjunct to my life, I, as it were, break through to him. I no longer see him 'through a glass darkly'. I begin to see what it means to understand as all along, from Eternity, I have myself been understood.

But it is not merely in our relations to persons that love can be perceptive of meaning. We can have love towards all living things, and towards the non-living as well. We may like or not like them, but it will be because of *how* they are—what properties they have— that we like or dislike them. We love them because they *exist*. And in that sense we can have love of everything that exists, love of the world, love of existence. That is the love of which I speak. It is seeing the loved thing with the whole of existence as background to it. It is seeing the miracle of the existence of the thing. And this means that it is the same as seeing things *sub specie aeternitatis*; it is seeing things as God sees them. And you cannot see living things in this way, without blessing them, without gratitude for their existence, without profoundly thanking God for the miracle which made them, for the miracle of their existence.

It is rarely that we become aware of the existence of things in the way I mean. For it involves going out to the thing in a very special kind of way. And we are mostly unable to do this because we have already drawn the thing, as it were, into the net of our own subjectivity and self-concern—we see only its utility, its exploitability, its availability for the satisfaction of our wants or the furtherance of our purposes. To love a thing is to see a thing as existing in its own right—to go out to its existence. And to go out to a thing in this way when it is a living thing, and particularly when it is a living person, is *fundamentally to have pity for it*. This is not inconsistent with giving thanks for its existence. For the insight into its existence which makes us rejoice in its existence is at the same time an insight into its suffering, its defence-lessness, its profound vulnerability. Life, consciousness, sensitivity is a profoundly pitiful thing. It is not rare to feel this deep pity for those who are kindly disposed towards you. The difficulty is to feel it for those who curse you or hate you or despitefully use you. Seeing in your enemy the profoundly pathetic, vulnerable, defenceless human being is the difficult thing. This is why only love is truly perceptive in human relations. Only love can *see* and where it sees it pities, irrespec-tive of whether or not it receives pity in return. And that is why it 'beareth *all* things, suffereth *all* things'.

There is a beautiful illustration of what I am trying to say in the *Rime of the Ancient Mariner*. You will remember the tale of horror the Mariner had to tell—how, at first, their ship had drifted into regions of ice and fog and they had had the company of a great friendly Albatross to break the terrible gloom and the terrible loneliness.

> As it had been a Christian soul
> We hailed it in God's name.

And you will remember that, for no reason except sheer devilry, the Mariner shot this bird and drew upon them the curse which carried them swiftly southwards to a region of absolute calm and a pitiless withering sun.

> We were the first that ever burst
> Into that silent sea.
> The very deep did rot, O Christ
> That ever this should be;
> And slimy things did crawl with legs
> Upon the slimy sea.

The seamen knew where the guilt lay and as a terrible token of it they slung the great rotting body of the bird round the Mariner's neck.

> Instead of the cross, the Albatross
> About my head was hung.

Then came the ship which looked at first as though it might rescue them but which turned out to be a ghastly apparition which struck a greater terror than the men could stand and one dead body after another crashed down on the deck—leaving the guilty man alone.

> Alone, alone, all all alone,
> Alone on that wide wide sea.

> I looked upon the rotting sea
> And drew my eyes away;
> I looked upon the rotting deck
> And there the dead men lay.

> I looked to Heaven, and tried to pray
> But or e'er a prayer had gush't
> A wicked whisper came, and made
> My heart as dry as dust.

Then in the silence under the blazing sun he began to look at what had earlier simply been an added loathsomeness—the slimy things which infested the water round the ship, and he began to be *aware* of them. A fascination with their sheer existence gripped him. His perception took on a timeless quality. The swarming water-snakes suddenly seemed to lie there with the whole world—the whole of existence— as their background. And this meant seeing them as they might be seen from Eternity. Something then welled up within him to which he could only give the name of 'love' and he *suddenly felt grateful for them.* Not because they were of any use to him, because they were not; and not necessarily because he *liked* them: he found them strangely beautiful but possibly not attractive. The experience was something quite different from this—it was a gratitude for their existence. It is said in Genesis that 'God saw everything that he had made, and behold it was very good'. Sunk as he must have been in the depths of despair, it was something of this very fundamental experience that came to the Mariner; he saw existence objectively, as God might see it, and he saw it to be good. He gave thanks for it.

> O happy living things! No tongue
> Their beauty might declare,
> A spring of love gushed from my heart
> And I blessed them unaware.
> Sure my kind saint took pity on me
> And I blessed them unaware.

For such a love as this, a change comes over the world as a whole. It is no longer an enigma:

> . . . the burthen of the mystery
> . . . the heavy and the weary weight
> Of all this unintelligible world
> Is lightened.

How the world is—the facts of the world—remain as they were. Objects seen 'as it were, from the midst of them' are unaltered. And the task of finding out about them—the task of science—is unaltered. Only now the world as a whole is a different world. It has ceased to be an enigma. It has not, of course, ceased to be a mystery. But somehow now one sees its sense. And 'understanding the sense of existence' and 'blessing it', 'thanking God for it', 'feeling gratitude for existence' are deeply connected experiences. They constitute what I have learnt to regard as absolutely the fundamental thing in religion. The view of religion as essentially obscurantist and joyless, is, therefore, false. For to be able profoundly to give thanks for existence is the same as acceptance of the world, acceptance of life. And this is what being happy *means*—being in agreement with the world. The cynic will point out that, on our own admission, the facts of the world are not altered. Quite so. But the facts of the world are not the end of the matter. There is also the question whether, looked at from a point of view outside it, the world has sense. And, as Wittgenstein says, the world of the happy is a different *world* from the world of the unhappy. It has changed as a whole—'as by an acquisition of meaning'. It isn't that those who live happy are having a happy time. That is quite a different thing. For *how* the world is remains unchanged; it is still a place of struggle and suffering. It is with the facts of 'life' in this sense as with the 'facts' in the theoretical sense—the change which comes over life when we see its sense does not alter its facts. It does not make these any less harsh, where they are harsh, than they were before. The point is that those whom love has made perceptive in the way I have tried to describe feel accepted by life, no longer estranged from its sources of power and meaning.

> With an eye made quiet by the power
> Of harmony, and the deep power of joy,
> They see into the life of things.

And this, I should want to say, is the important thing in religion because religion has to do fundamentally with a problem of liberation or release—the problem of drawing man out of the bondage of pre-occupation with himself—preoccupation with his own (to him) over-whelming misfortune or overwhelming grief or overwhelming guilt. That moment the Ancient Mariner 'saw into the life' of those creatures, and blessed them because they were there and because they were happy.

> The self-same moment I could pray
> And from my neck so free
> The Albatross fell off and sunk
> Like lead into the sea.

A Welsh hymn speaks of a 'load of guilt, heavy as the hills, turning at the Cross into song'—at the Cross, at the place where things are comprehended as only love can comprehend them and where particu-larly man is understood and man's rebellion and degradation is under-stood as only love can understand it. 'Father, forgive them for they know not what they do.' He prayed for them because, despite the unspeakable bestiality with which they were treating his broken body, He saw them through the eyes of love as objects of the profoundest pity. 'For they know not what they do.' He prayed for them because He *pitied* them, because He saw them not as the hard and pitiless monsters that they seemed but as the pitifully bemused and misguided human souls that they were.

'He knoweth our frame, he remembereth that we are dust.' In one sense, existence is dust, living things are dust, human beings are dust. And it isn't only of the good ones and the friendly ones that this is true but of the vicious and the cruel ones as well. *This* is why Love 'beareth all things, suffereth all things'. And this was why it then willed not that it might be spared that bitterest of bitter cups but 'endured the Cross, despising the shame'.

# VIII

## THE MIRACULOUS

### By R. F. Holland

Most people think of a miracle as a violation of natural law; and a good many of those who regard the miraculous in this way incline to the idea that miracles are impossible and that 'science' tells us this (the more sophisticated might say that what tells us this is an unconfused *conception* of science). I shall argue that the conception of the miraculous as a violation of natural law is an inadequate conception because it is unduly restrictive, though there is also a sense in which it is not restrictive enough. To qualify for being accounted a miracle an occurrence does not have to be characterizable as a violation of natural law. However, though I do not take the conception of miracles as violations of natural law to be an adequate conception of the miraculous, I shall maintain that occurrences are conceivable in respect to which it could be said that some law or laws of nature had been violated—or it could be said equally that there was a contradiction in our experience: and if the surrounding circumstances were appropriate it would be possible for such occurrences to have a kind of human significance and hence intelligible for them to be hailed as miracles. I see no philosophical reason against this.

But consider first the following example. A child riding his toy motor-car strays on to an unguarded railway crossing near his house and a wheel of his car gets stuck down the side of one of the rails. An express train is due to pass with the signals in its favour and a curve in the track makes it impossible for the driver to stop his train in time to avoid any obstruction he might encounter on the crossing. The mother coming out of the house to look for her child sees him on the crossing and hears the train approaching. She runs forward shouting and waving. The little boy remains seated in his car looking downward, engrossed in the task of pedalling it free. The brakes of the train are applied and it comes to rest a few feet from the child. The mother thanks God for the miracle; which she never ceases to think of as such although, as she in due course learns, there was nothing supernatural about the manner in which the brakes of the train came to be applied. The driver had fainted, for a reason that had nothing to do with the presence of the child on the line, and the brakes were applied automatically as his hand ceased to exert pressure on the control lever. He fainted on this particular afternoon because his blood pressure had risen after an exceptionally heavy lunch during which he had quarrelled with a colleague, and the change in blood pressure caused a clot of blood to be dislodged and circulate. He fainted at the time when he did on the afternoon in question because this was the time at which the coagulation in his blood stream reached the brain.

Thus the stopping of the train and the fact that it stopped when it did have a natural explanation. I do not say a *scientific* explanation, for it does not seem to me that the explanation here as a whole is of this kind (in order for something to be unsusceptible of scientific explanation it does not have to be anything so queer and grandiose as a miracle). The form of explanation in the present case, I would say, is *historical*; and the considerations that enter into it are various. They include medical factors, for instance, and had these constituted the whole extent of the matter the explanation could have been called scientific. But as it is, the medical considerations, though obviously important, are only one aspect of a complex story, alongside other considerations of a practical and social kind; and in addition there is a reference to mechanical considerations. All of these enter into the explanation of, or story behind, the stopping of the train. And just as there is an explanatory story behind the train's stopping when and where it did, so there is an explanatory story behind the presence of the child on the line at the time when, and in the place where, he was. But these two explanations or histories are independent of each other. They are about as disconnected as the history of the steam loom is from the history of the Ming dynasty. The spacio-temporal coincidence, I mean the fact that the child was on the line at the time when the train approached and the train stopped a few feet short of the place where he was, is exactly what I have just called it, a coincidence—something which a chronicle of events can merely record, like the fact that the Ming dynasty was in power at the same time as the house of Lancaster.

But unlike the coincidence between the rise of the Ming dynasty and the arrival of the dynasty of Lancaster, the coincidence of the child's presence on the line with the arrival and then the stopping of the train is impressive, significant; not because it is very unusual for trains to be halted in the way this one was, but because the life of a child was imperilled and then, against expectation, preserved. The significance of some coincidences as opposed to others arises from their relation to human needs and hopes and fears, their effects for good or ill upon our lives. So we speak of our luck (fortune, fate, etc.). And the kind of thing that, outside religion, we call luck is in religious parlance the grace of God or a miracle of God. But while the reference here is the same, the meaning is different. The meaning is different in that whatever happens by God's grace or by a miracle is something for which God is thanked or thankable, something which has been or could have been prayed for, something which can be regarded with awe and be taken as a sign or made the subject of a vow (e.g. to go on a pilgrimage), all of which can only take place against the background of a religious tradition. Whereas what happens by a stroke of luck is something in regard to which one just seizes one's opportunity or feels glad about or feels relieved about, something for which one may thank one's lucky stars. To say that one thanks one's lucky stars is simply to express one's relief or to emphasize the intensity of the relief: if it signifies anything more than this it signifies a superstition (cf. touching wood).

But although a coincidence can be taken religiously as a sign and called a miracle and made the subject of a vow, it cannot without confusion be taken as a sign of divine interference with the natural order. If someone protests that it is no part of the natural order that an express train should stop for a child on the line whom the driver cannot see then in *protesting* this he misses the point. What he says has been agreed to be perfectly true in the sense that there is no natural order relating the train's motion to the child which could be either preserved or interfered with. The concept of the miraculous which we have so far been considering is distinct therefore from the concept exemplified in the biblical stories of the turning of water into wine and the feeding of five thousand people on a very few loaves and fishes. Let us call the former the contingency concept and the latter the violation concept.

To establish the contingency concept of the miraculous as a possible concept it seems to me enough to point out (1) that *pace* Spinoza, Leibniz, and others, there are genuine contingencies in the world, and (2) that certain of these contingencies can be, and are in fact, regarded religiously in the manner I have indicated. If you assent to this and still express a doubt—'But are they really miracles?'—then you must now be questioning whether people are right to react to contingencies in this way, questioning whether you ought yourself to go along with them. Why not just stick to talking of luck? When you think this you are somewhat in the position of one who watches others fall in love and as an outsider thinks it unreasonable, hyperbolical, ridiculous (surely friendship should suffice).

*          *          *

To turn now to the concept of the miraculous as a violation of natural law: I am aware of two arguments which, if they were correct, would show that this concept were not a possible concept. The first can be found in chapter ten of Hume's *Enquiry Concerning Human Understanding*:

> Nothing is esteemed a miracle, if it ever happen in the common course of nature. It is no miracle that a man, seemingly in good health, should die on a sudden: because such a kind of death, though more unusual than any other, has yet been frequently observed to happen. But it is a miracle, that a dead man should come to life; because that has never been observed in any age or country. There must, therefore, be a uniform experience against every miraculous event, otherwise the event would not merit that appellation. And as a uniform experience amounts to a proof, there is here a direct and full *proof*, from the nature of the fact, against the existence of any miracle; nor can such a proof be destroyed, or the miracle rendered credible, but by an opposite proof, which is superior.
>
> The plain consequence is (and it is a general maxim worthy of our attention), 'That no testimony is sufficient to establish a miracle, unless the testimony be of such a kind, that its falsehood would be more miraculous, than the fact, which it endeavours to establish; and even in that case there is a mutual destruction of arguments, and the superior only gives us an assurance suitable to that degree of force, which remains, after deducting the inferior.' When anyone tells me, that he saw a dead man restored to life, I immediately consider with myself, whether it be more probable, that this person should either deceive or be deceived, or that the fact, which he relates, should really have happened. I weigh the one miracle against the other; and according to the superiority, which I discover, I pronounce my decision, and always reject the greater miracle. If the falsehood of his testimony would be more miraculous, than the event which he relates; then, and not till then, can he pretend to command my belief or opinion.

Hume's concern in the chapter from which I have just quoted is ostensibly with the problem of assessing the *testimony of others* in regard to the allegedly miraculous. This is not the same problem as that which arises for the man who has to decide whether or not he himself has witnessed a miracle. Hume gives an inadequate account of the considerations which would influence one's decision to accept or reject the insistence of another person that something has happened which one finds it extremely hard to believe could have happened. The character and temperament of the witness, the kind of person he is and the kind of understanding one has of him, the closeness or distance of one's personal relationship with him are obviously important here, whereas Hume suggests that if we give credence to some witnesses rather than others the reason must be simply that we are accustomed to find in their case a conformity between testimony and reality (§ 89). Maybe the weakness of Hume's account of the nature of our trust or lack of trust in witnesses is connected with the fact that in some way he intended his treatment of the problem of witness concerning the miraculous to have a more general application—as if he were trying to cut across the distinction between the case where we are ourselves confronted with a miracle (or something we may be inclined to call one) and the case where other people intervene, and wanting us to consider it all as fundamentally a single problem of evidence, a problem of witness in which it would make no difference whether what were doing the witnessing were a person other than oneself, or oneself in the role of a witness to oneself, or one's senses as witnesses to oneself. This anyway is the view I am going to take of his intention here.

I can imagine it being contended that, while Hume has produced a strong argument against the possibility of our ever having certitude or even very good evidence that a miracle has occurred, his thesis does not amount to an argument against the possibility of miracles as such. But I think this would be a misunderstanding. For if Hume is right, the situation is not just that we do not happen as a matter of fact to have certitude or even good evidence for the occurrence of any miracle, but rather that *nothing can count* as good evidence: the logic of testimony precludes this. And in precluding this it must, so far as I can see, preclude equally our having *poor* evidence for the occurrence of any miracle, since a contrast between good evidence and poor evidence is necessary if there is to be sense in speaking of either. Equally it must follow that there can be no such thing as (because nothing is being allowed to count as) discovering, recognizing, becoming aware, etc., that a miracle has occurred; and if there be no such thing as finding out or being aware (etc.) that a miracle has occurred, there can be no such thing as failing to find out or failing to be aware that a miracle has occurred either; no such thing as a discovered or an undiscovered miracle . . . *en fin*, no such thing as a miracle. So Hume's argument is, after all, an argument against the very possibility of miracles. I do not think his argument is cogent either on the interpretation I have just put upon it or on the interpretation according to which it would be an argument merely against the possibility of our having good evidence for a miracle. But before giving my reason I would like first to mention the only other line of argument which I can at present envisage against the conception of the miraculous as a violation of natural law.

Consider the proposition that a criminal is a violator of the laws of the state. With this proposition in mind you will start to wonder, when someone says that a miracle is a violation of the laws of nature, if he is not confusing a law of nature with a judicial law as laid down by some legal authority. A judicial law is obviously something which can be violated. The laws of the state prescribe and their prescriptions can be flouted. But are the laws of nature in any sense prescriptions? Maybe they are in the sense that they prescribe to us what we are to expect, but since *we* formulated the laws this is really a matter of our offering prescriptions or recipes to ourselves. And we can certainly fail to act on these prescriptions. But the occurrences which the laws are about are not prescribed to: they are simply *de*scribed. And if anything should happen of which we are inclined to say that it goes counter to a law of nature, what this must mean is that the description we have framed has been, not flouted or violated, but falsified. We have encountered something that the description does not fit and we must therefore withdraw or modify our description. The law was wrong; we framed it wrongly: or rather what we framed has turned out not to have been a law. The relation between an occurrence and a law of nature is different then from a man's relation to a law of the state, for when the latter is deviated from we do not, save in exceptional circumstances, say that the law is wrong but rather that the man is wrong— he is a criminal. To suggest that an occurrence which has falsified a law of nature is *wrong* would be an absurdity: and it would be just as absurd to suggest that the law has been violated. Nothing can be conceived to be a violation of natural law, and if that is how the miraculous is conceived there can be no such thing as the miraculous. Laws of nature can be formulated or reformulated to cope with any eventuality, and would-be miracles are transformed automatically into natural occurrences the moment science gets on the track of them.

But there is an objection to this line of argument. If we say that a law of nature is a description, what exactly are we taking it to be a description of? A description of what has happened up to now or is actually happening now? Suppose we have a law to the effect that all unsupported bodies fall. From this I can deduce that if the pen now in my hand were unsupported it *would* fall and that when in a moment I withdraw from it the support it now has it *will* fall. But if the law were simply a description of what has happened up to now or is happening now and no more, these deductions would be impossible. So it looks as if the law must somehow describe the future as well as the past and present. 'A description of the future.' But what on earth is that? For until the future ceases to be the future and becomes actual there are no events for the description to describe—over and above those that either have already taken place or are at this moment taking place.

It seems that if we are to continue to maintain that a natural law is nothing but a description then we must say that the description covers not only the actual but also the possible and is every bit as much a description of the one as it is of the other. And this only amounts to a pleonastic way of saying that the law tells us, defines for us, what is and is not *possible* in regard to the behaviour of unsupported bodies. At which point we might just as well drop the talk about describing altogether and admit that the law does not just describe—it stipulates: stipulates that it is impossible for an unsupported body to do anything other than fall. Laws of nature and legal laws, though they may not resemble each other in other respects, are at least alike in this: that they both stipulate something. Moreover the stipulations which we call laws of nature are in many cases so solidly founded and knitted together with other stipulations, other laws, that they come to be something in the nature of a framework through which we look at the world and which to a considerable degree dictates our ways of describing phenomena.

Notice, however, that insofar as we resist in this way the second of the two arguments for the impossibility of the violation concept of the miraculous and insofar as we object to the suggestion that it is possible for our laws of nature to be dropped or reformulated in a sort of *ad hoc* manner to accommodate any would-be miracle, we seem to be making the first argument—the Humean argument against the miraculous— all the stronger. For if we take a law of nature to be more than a generalized description of what has happened up to now, and if at the same time we upgrade the mere probability or belief to which Hume thought we were confined here into certainty and real knowledge, then surely it must seem that our reluctance to throw overboard a whole nexus of well-established, mutually-supporting laws and theories must be so great as to justify us in rejecting out of hand, and not being prepared to assign even a degree of probability to, any testimony to an occurrence which our system of natural law decisively rules out; and surely we shall be justified in classifying as illusory any experience which purports to be the experience of such an occurrence.

The truth is that this position is not at all justified, and we should only be landed in inconsistency if we adopted it. For if it were granted that there can be no certainty in regard to the individual case, if there can be no real knowledge that a particular event has occurred in exactly the way that it has, how could our system of laws have got established in the first place?

On Hume's view, the empirical in general was synonymous with the probable. No law of nature could have more than a degree of probability, and neither for that matter could the occurrence of any particular event. This is what gave point to the idea of a balance of probabilities and hence to his thesis about the impossibility of ever establishing a miracle. But while in the one case, that of the general law, he was prepared (in the passage from which I quoted) to allow that the probability could have the status of a proof, in the other case he was curiously reluctant to allow this.

Now if in the interest of good conceptual sense we upgrade the probability of natural laws into certainty, so as to be able to distinguish a well-established law from a more or less tenable hypothesis, it is equally in the interest of good conceptual sense that we should upgrade in a comparable fashion the probability attaching to particular events and states of affairs, so as to allow that some of these, as opposed to others, can be certain and really known to be what they are. Otherwise a distinction gets blurred which is at least as important as the distinction between a law and a hypothesis—namely, the distinction between a hypothesis and a fact. The distinction between a hypothesis and a fact is for instance the distinction between my saying when I come upon an infant who is screaming and writhing and holding his ear 'he's got an abscess' and my making this statement again after looking into the ear, whether by means of an instrument or without, and actually seeing, coming upon, the abscess. Or again it is the difference between the statement 'it is snowing' when made by me now as I sit here and the same statement uttered as I go outside the building into the snow and get snowed on. The second statement, unlike the first, is uttered directly in the face of the circumstance which makes it true. I can be as certain in that situation that it is snowing as I can be of anything. And if there weren't things of this kind of which we can be certain, we wouldn't be able to be uncertain of anything either.

If it were remarked here that our senses are capable of deceiving us, I should reply that it does not follow from this that there are not occasions when we know perfectly well that we are not being deceived. And this is one of them. I submit that nothing would persuade you— or if it would it shouldn't—that you are not at this moment in the familiar surroundings of your university and that in what you see as you look around this room you are subject to an illusion. And if something very strange were to happen, such as one of us bursting into flame, you'd soon know it for what it was; and of course you'd expect the natural cause to be duly discovered (the smouldering pipe which set fire to the matches or whatever it might be).

But then suppose you failed to discover any cause. Or suppose that something happened which was truly bizarre, like my rising slowly and steadily three feet into the air and staying there. You could *know* that this happened if it did, and probably you would laugh and presume there must be some natural explanation: a rod behind, a disguised support beneath, a thin wire above. Or could it even be done by air pressure in some way? Or by a tremendously powerful magnet on the next floor, attracting metal in my clothing? Or if not by magnetic attraction then by magnetic repulsion? I rise in the air then, and since it is no magician's demonstration you can and do search under me, over me, and around me. But suppose you find nothing, nothing on me and nothing in the room or above, below, or around it. You cannot think it is the effect of an anti-gravity device (even if there be sense in that idea) because there just is no device. And you know that, excluding phenomena like tornadoes, it is impossible for a physical body in free air to behave thus in the absence of a special device. So does it not come to this: that if I were to rise in the air now, you could be completely certain of two incompatible things: (1) that it is impossible, and (2) that it has happened?

Now against what I have just said I envisage two objections. The first is that my rising three feet into the air in the absence of some special cause can only be held to be an impossibility by someone who is ignorant of the statistical basis of modern physics. For example, the water in a kettle comprises a vast number of atoms in motion and anything I do to the kettle, such as tilting it or heating it, will affect the movements of these atoms. But there is no way of determining what the effect will be in the case of any single atom. It is no more within the power of physicists to predict that a particular atom will change its position in such and such a way, or even at all, than it is within the power of insurance actuaries to predict that a certain man will die next week in a road accident, or die at all. However, reliable statistical statements can be made by actuaries about the life prospects of large numbers of people taken together and somewhat similarly, statistical laws are framed by physicists about the behaviour of atoms in large numbers. Statistical laws are laws of probability and it gets argued that, since this is the kind of law on which the behaviour of water in a heated vessel ultimately rests, there can be no *certainty* that the kettle on the hob will boil however fierce the fire, no certainty that it will boil absolutely *every* time, because there is always the probability—infinitesimally small admittedly, but still a definite probability—that enough of the constituent atoms in their molecules will move in a way that is incompatible with its doing so. Vessels of water and rubber balls seem to be the most frequently used examples when this argument is deployed, but the suggestion has been made to me that it (or some similar argument) could be applied to the behaviour of an unsupported body near the surface of the earth, in respect of which it could be maintained that there is a certain probability, albeit a very low one, in favour of the body's having its state of rest three feet above the ground.

However, it seems to me that any such argument must rest on the kind of confusion that Eddington fell into when he said, mentioning facts about atoms as the reason, that his table was not solid but consisted largely of empty space. If you add to this that your table is in a continuous vibratory motion and that the laws governing its behaviour are laws of probability only you are continuing in the same vein. To make the confusion more symmetrical you might perhaps go on to say that the movements of tables in space are only predictable even with probability when tables get together in large numbers (which accounts for the existence of warehouses). Anyway my point is that, using words in their ordinary senses, it is about as certain and as much a matter of common understanding that my kettle, when put on a fierce fire, will boil or that I shall not next moment float three feet in the air as it is certain and a matter of common understanding that my desk is solid and will continue for some time to be so. The validity of my statement about the desk is not impugned by any assertion about the behaviour of atoms whether singly or in the aggregate; neither is the validity of the corresponding statements about the kettle and my inability to float in the air impugned by any assertion about the statistical basis of modern science.

The second objection grants the impossibility of a body's rising three feet into the air in the absence of a special cause and grants my certitude of this. But what I can never be certain of, the objection runs, is that all the special causes and devices that accomplish this are absent. So I am entirely unjustified in asserting the outright impossibility of the phenomenon—especially when I think to do so in the very teeth of its occurrence. My saying that it is impossible could only have the force here of an ejaculation like 'Struth!' *Ab esse ad posse valet consequentia.* Supposing the thing to have occurred, our response as ungullible people should be to maintain confidence in the existence of a natural cause, to persist indefinitely in searching for one and to classify the occurrence in the meantime as an unsolved problem. So runs the second objection.

However, the idea that one cannot establish the absence of a natural cause is not to my mind the unassailable piece of logic it might seem at first glance to be. Both our common understanding and our scientific understanding include conceptions of the sort of thing that can and cannot happen, and of the sort of thing that has to take place to bring about some other sort of thing. These conceptions are presupposed to our arguing in such patterns as '*A* will do such and such unless *Y*', or 'If *Z* happens it can only be from this, that or the other (kind of) cause', or 'If *W* cannot be done in this way or that way it cannot be done at all'. An example of the first pattern is 'The horse will die if it gets no food'. My rising steadily three feet in the air is a subject for argument according to the second pattern. The second pattern presents the surface appearance of being more complicated than the first, but logically it is not. Let us turn our attention to the example of the first pattern.

Suppose that a horse, which has been normally born and reared, and is now deprived of all nourishment (we could be completely certain of this)—suppose that, instead of dying, this horse goes on thriving (which again is something we could be completely certain about). A series of thorough examinations reveals no abnormality in the horse's condition: its digestive system is always found to be working and to be at every moment in more or less the state it would have been in if

the horse had eaten a meal an hour or two before. This is utterly inconsistent with our whole conception of the needs and capacities of horses;
and because it is an impossibility in the light of our prevailing conception, my objector, in the event of its happening, would expect us to
abandon the conception—as though we had to have consistency at any
price. Whereas the position I advocate is that the price is too high and
it would be better to be left with the inconsistency; and that in any
event the prevailing conception has a logical status not altogether unlike
that of a necessary truth and cannot be simply thrown away as a mistake
—not when it rests on the experience of generations, not when all the
other horses in the world are continuing to behave as horses have
always done, and especially not when one considers the way our conception of the needs and capacities of horses interlocks with conceptions
of the needs and capacities of other living things and with a conception
of the difference between animate and inanimate behaviour quite
generally. These conceptions form part of a common understanding
that is well established and with us to stay. Any number of discoveries
remains to be made by zoologists and plenty of scope exists for conceptual revision in biological theory, but it is a confusion to think it
follows from this that we are less than well enough acquainted with,
and might have serious misconceptions about, what is and is not
possible in the behaviour under familiar conditions of common
objects with which we have a long history of practical dealings.
Similarly with the relation between common understanding and
physical discoveries, physical theories: what has been said about the
self-sustaining horse seems to me applicable *mutatis mutandis* to the
levitation example also. Not that my thesis about the miraculous rests
on the acceptance of this particular example. The objector who thinks
there is a loophole in it for natural explanation strikes me as lacking a
sense of the absurd but can keep his opinion for the moment, since he
will (I hope) be shown the loophole being closed in a further example
with which I shall conclude.

I did not in any case mean to suggest that if I rose in the air now in
the absence of any device it would be at all proper for a religious
person to hail this as a miracle. Far from it. From a religious point of
view it would either signify nothing at all or else be regarded as a sign
of devilry; and if the phenomenon persisted I should think that a religious person might well have recourse to exorcism, if that figured
among the institutions of his religion. Suppose, however, that by rising
into the air I were to avoid an otherwise certain death: then it would

(against a religious background) become possible to speak of a miracle, just as it would in what I called the contingency case. Or the phenomenon could be a miracle although nothing at all were achieved by it, provided I were a religiously significant figure, one of whom prophets had spoken, or at least an exceptionally holy man.

My thesis then in regard to the violation concept of the miraculous, by contrast with the contingency concept, which we have seen to be also a possible concept, is that a conflict of certainties is a necessary though not a sufficient condition of the miraculous. In other words a miracle, though it cannot only be this, must at least be something the occurrence of which can be categorized at one and the same time as empirically certain and conceptually impossible. If it were less than conceptually impossible it would reduce merely to a very unusual occurrence such as could be treated (because of the empirical certainty) in the manner of a decisive experiment and result in a modification to the prevailing conception of natural law; while if it were less than empirically certain nothing more would be called for in regard to it than a suspension of judgment. So if there is to be a type of the miraculous other than the contingency kind it must offend against the principle *ab esse ad posse valet consequentia*. And since the violation concept of the miraculous does seem to me to be a possible concept I therefore reject that time honoured logical principle.

I know that my suggestion that something could be at one and the same time empirically certain and conceptually impossible will sound to many people ridiculous. Must not the actual occurrence of something show that it *was* conceptually possible after all? And if I contend, as I do, that the fact that something has occurred might *not* necessarily show that it was conceptually possible; or to put it the other way round—if I contend, as I do, that the fact that something is conceptually impossible does not necessarily preclude its occurrence, then am I not opening the door to the instantiation of round squares, female fathers, and similar paradigms of senselessness? The answer is that the door is being opened only as far as is needed and no farther; certainly not to instantiations of the *self*-contradictory. There is more than one kind of conceptual impossibility.

Let me illustrate my meaning finally by reference to the New Testament story of the turning of water into wine. I am not assuming that this story is true, but I think that it logically could be. Hence if anyone chooses to maintain its truth as a matter of faith I see no philosophical objection to his doing so. A number of people could have been quite sure, could have had the fullest empirical certainty, that a vessel contained water at one moment and wine a moment later—good wine, as St. John says—without any device having been applied to it in the intervening time. Not that this last really needs to be added; for that any device should have existed *then* at least is inconceivable, even if it might just be argued to be a conceptual possibility now. I have in mind the very remote possibility of a liquid chemically indistinguishable from say mature claret being produced by means of atomic and molecular transformations. The device would have to be conceived as something enormously complicated, requiring a large supply of power. Anything less thorough-going would hardly meet the case, for those who are alleged to have drunk the wine were practiced wine-bibbers, capable of detecting at once the difference between a true wine and a concocted variety in the 'British Wine, Ruby Type' category. However, that water could conceivably have been turned into wine in the first century A.D. by means of a device is ruled out of court at once by common understanding; and though the verdict is supported by scientific knowledge, common understanding has no need of this support.

In the case of my previous example of a man, myself for instance, rising three feet into the air and remaining there unsupported, it was difficult to deal with the objection that we could not be certain there wasn't some special cause operating, *some* explanation even though we had searched to the utmost of our ability and had found none. And I imagined the objector trying to lay it down as axiomatic that while there is such a thing as not knowing what the cause or explanation of a phenomenon might be there can be no such thing as establishing the absence of a cause. The example of water being turned into wine is stronger, and I would think decisive, here. At one moment, let us suppose, there was water and at another moment wine, in the same vessel, although nobody had emptied out the water and poured in the wine. This is something that could conceivably have been established with certainty. What is not conceivable is that it could have been done by a device. Nor is it conceivable that there could have been a natural cause of it. For this would have had to be the natural cause of the water's becoming wine. And water's becoming wine is not the description of any conceivable natural process. It is conceptually impossible that the wine could have been got naturally from water, save in the very strained sense that moisture is needed to nourish the vines from which the grapes are taken, and this very strained sense is irrelevant here.

'But can we not still escape from the necessity to assert that one and the same thing is both empirically certain and conceptually impossible? For what has been said to be conceptually impossible is the turning of water into wine. However, when allusion is made to the alleged miracle, all the expression "turned into" can signify is that at one moment there was water and at a moment later wine. This is what could have been empirically certain: whereas what is conceptually impossible is that water should have been turned into wine if one really *means* turned into. It is not conceptually impossible that at one moment water should have been found and at another moment wine in the same vessel, even though nobody had emptied out the water and poured in the wine.' So someone might try to argue. But I cannot see that it does any good. To the suggestion that the thing is conceivable so long as we refrain from saying that the water *turned into* the wine I would reply: either the water turns into the wine or else it disappears and wine springs into existence in its place. But water cannot *conceivably* disappear like that without going anywhere, and wine cannot *conceivably* spring into existence from nowhere. Look at it in terms of transformation, or look at it in terms of 'coming into being and passing away'—or just look at it. Whatever you do, you cannot make sense of it: on all accounts it is inconceivable. So I keep to the position that the New Testament story of the turning of water into wine is the story of something that could have been known empirically to have occurred, and it is also the story of the occurrence of something which is conceptually impossible. It has to be both in order to be the miracle-story which, whether true or false, it is.

That expression 'the occurrence of something which is conceptually impossible' was used deliberately just then. And it will be objected, no doubt, that to speak of something which is conceptually impossible is to speak of a nullity. To ask for an example of something that is conceptually impossible is not (I shall be told) like asking for a sample of a substance and you cannot in order to comply with this request produce anything visible or tangible, you cannot point to an occurrence. Indeed you cannot, strictly speaking, offer a description either: you can only utter a form of words. What I have been arguing in effect is that there is a contradiction in St. John's 'description' of the water-into-wine episode. But if so, then nothing has really been described; or alternatively something has been—one should not say misdescribed but rather garbled—since a conceptual impossibility is *ex vi termini* one of which sense cannot be made.

M

I would reply to this that sense can certainly be made of a conceptual impossibility in the respect that one can see often enough that there *is* a conceptual impossibility there and also, often enough, what kind of a conceptual impossibility it is and how it arises. We can see there is an inconsistency; and words, moreover, are not the only things in which we can see inconsistency. Human actions can be pointed to here quite obviously. And I am maintaining that there is also such a thing as making sense, and failing to make sense, of *events*. If the objector holds that in the case of events, unlike the case of human actions, sense must always be there although one perhaps fails to find it, I ask: how does he know? Why the *must*? It is not part of my case that to regard a sequence of events as senseless or miraculous is to construe it as if it were a sort of action, or to see the invisible hand of a super-person at work in it. I have contended that there are circumstances in respect to which the expression 'occurrence of something which is conceptually impossible' would have a natural enough use, and I have offered three examples. I think the expression 'violation of a law of nature' could also be introduced quite naturally in this connection, or we could speak of a contradiction in our experience.

# IX

## THE DEVIL

### By R. G. COLLINGWOOD

'From the crafts and assaults of the Devil, good Lord, deliver us.' So we pray; and the prayer certainly answers our need. We feel ourselves surrounded by powers of evil, from which we want to be defended, and the desire expresses itself in the form of a petition for help against the Devil. But most people who have responded to the prayer must have asked themselves how much more than this they meant; whether they believed in a Devil at all, and if so what they imagined him to be like. There is no doubt that common belief has long been tending more and more to discard the idea of a Devil; and yet the idea is orthodox. Does this mean that modern thought is drifting away from orthodox Christianity? Is the disbelief in a Devil only part of that vague optimism, that disinclination to believe in anything evil, that blind conviction of the stability of its own virtue and the perfection of its own civilization, which seems at times to be the chief vice of the modern world?

In part this is so. And a world rudely awakened once more to the conviction that evil is real may come again to believe in a Devil. But if it returns to the same belief which it has gradually been relinquishing, the step will be retrograde. For that belief was neither fully orthodox nor fully true. Orthodox Christianity believes in a Devil who is, as it were, the bad child in God's family; the 'Devil' in whom people of to-day are coming to disbelieve owes much if not all of his character to the Manichaean fiction of an evil power over against God and struggling with Him for the dominion over man's soul. It may seem surprising that popular thought should confuse Manichaeism with orthodoxy; and it certainly is surprising that theologians should so seldom come forward to correct the mistake. But it is hard for the uninstructed to follow technical theology, and it is perhaps equally hard for the theologian to follow the obscure workings of the uninstructed mind.

It is clear then that the vital question is not, Does the Devil exist? but rather, What conception have we of the Devil? Unless we first

171

answer this question it will not be certain whether the spirit into whose existence we are inquiring is the orthodox or Manichean or indeed any other devil. Further, it is important to determine in what sense we believe in him. A man may, for instance, believe in Our Lord in the sense of believing what history tells us about Him, but yet not believe in Him, in the sense of not believing in His spiritual presence in the Church. So one might believe in the Devil in the sense that one accepts the story of Lucifer as historical; or in the sense that one believes in Lucifer as an evil force now present in the world; and so forth.

This way of proceeding may be called the critical method; and it is this which will be adopted in the present essay. But much popular thought on the subject is of a different kind. It concerns itself immediately with the question, Does the Devil exist? without first asking these other questions; and the method it adopts is 'scientific' in the popular sense of the word, that is, inductive. It proceeds by searching for 'evidence' of the Devil's existence; and this evidence is nowadays drawn chiefly from psychology. As the eighteenth century found the evidences of religion chiefly in the world of nature, so the present generation tends to seek them in the mind of man; but the argument is in each case of the same kind.

This psychological argument plays such an important part in popular thought that we must begin by reviewing it; otherwise every step in our criticism will be impeded by the protest that an ounce of fact is worth a ton of theory, and that, however we may theorize, there are facts, positive facts, which prove the existence of the Devil.

Let us then begin by considering these facts; not *in extenso*, for they would fill many volumes and could only be collected by much labour, but in a few typical instances, in order to see what kind of conclusion they yield. The evidence is no doubt cumulative, like all evidence; but a sample will show in what direction, if any, the accumulation tends.

The two most striking groups of evidence may be described as obsessions and visions. By 'obsession' I mean not the morbid phenomena of demoniacal possession, or the '*idée fixe*' of mania, but the sense of the merging of one's own personality in a greater and more powerful self, the feeling that one is overwhelmed and carried away not by impulses within but by the resistless force of another will. This feeling is extremely common in all religious experience. The saint feels himself passive in the hands of God. 'This is a trait' (says Höffding, *Philosophy of Religion*, § 28) 'very frequently found in mystics and pietists; the more they retain (or believe themselves to retain) their powers of thought and will, the more they tend to attribute to their inmost experiences a divine origin.' Höffding's parenthesis looks almost like a suggestion that the feeling only occurs in persons whose will is really in process of decay. But if the suggestion is intended, it is quite indefensible. The weak man, like Shakespeare's Henry VI, may have this feeling; but St. Paul had it even more strongly, and he was certainly not a weak man.

This feeling of obsession by a divine power is in fact only an extreme form of the sensation, which everybody knows, that we are surrounded by spiritual forces which by suggestion or other means influence our wills for good. And the same feeling, both in its rudimentary and extreme forms, exists with regard to evil forces. Children come quite naturally to believe in good and bad angels which draw them in different directions; and this belief may pass through all stages of intensity until we think of our own personality, not as a free will balancing and choosing between suggestions presented to it by angels of light and darkness, but as shrunk to a vanishing-point, the moment of impact between two gigantic and opposed forces. Man becomes the merely sentient battlefield of God and Satan.

The case which immediately concerns us is that of the soul overwhelmed by a spirit of evil; and this is equally familiar to psychology. As the saint represents himself the passive instrument of God, so the sinner feels that he is the passive instrument of the Devil. The saint says with St. Paul: 'I live, and yet not I but Christ liveth in me.' The sinner replies, from the same source: 'It is no more I that do it, but Sin that dwelleth in me.'

Here, then, is the first group of evidence for the existence of the Devil; and we must try to determine what it is worth. It will be noticed that the same type of experience serves as evidence in one case for the existence of the Devil, and in the other for the existence of God. We believe in the Devil (it is suggested) because we immediately experience his power over our hearts; and we believe in God for the same kind of reason. But psychology itself, which collects for us the evidence, warns us against this uncritical use of it. It may be that the whole feeling is a morbid and unhealthy one; or it may be that in one case it is natural and healthy, and in the other unnatural and morbid. Psychology can describe the feelings which people actually do have; but it cannot tell us whether the feelings are good or bad, trustworthy or misleading, sanity or mania. Telepathy, self-hypnotism, subconscious cerebration, force of education or environment—these and a thousand other explanations are from time to time adopted; and each is, within the limits of psychology, possible, none certain. In point of fact, the psychologist takes whichever view for the moment suits him as a working hypothesis, but the supposed explanation is never more than this, and is generally much less. So the really vital point in the argument is a gap which can only be bridged by the gossamers of flimsiest speculation.

The second group of evidence appears at first sight more conclusive. The visions of God, of Our Lord, of angels and of saints which are found in all types of Christianity (and similar visions seem to occur in all other religions) are parallel to visions, no less authentic, of fiends and demons and of the Devil himself.[1] These sensational forms of religious experience often seem to carry special weight as evidence of the reality of spirits other than our own; but here too the whole argument turns on their interpretation. Are they, in the language of popular philosophy, 'subjective' or 'objective'?

In order to answer this question, an attempt is sometimes made to analyse them with a view to discovering what they owe to tradition, to the education or surroundings of the person who sees them. Thus it is found that a vision of the Devil is accompanied by a smell of brimstone, and that one's patron saint appears in the clothes which he wears in the window of one's parish church. But these details prove exactly what the interpreter chooses to make them prove. To the simple, they are corroborative; they prove that the apparition is genuine. To the subtler critic they are suspicious; they suggest that the alleged vision is a merely 'subjective' reproduction of traditional images. But the critic is at least no better off than the simple believer. For if my patron saint wishes to appear to me, why should he not choose to appear in a form in which I can recognize him? And if I see the Devil and smell brimstone, may not the coincidence with tradition be due to the fact that when the Devil appears he really does smell of brimstone?

---

[1] It is not necessary to encumber the text with instances of such familiar experiences; but I should like to refer here, since it has only appeared in a review, to the case of a Roman Catholic priest, described in a series of his own letters in the *British Review*, Vol. I, No. 2 (April 1913), pp. 71–95. 'On one occasion, when I had retired for the night, a being appeared who addressed me using the most vile language and rehearsing for me in a terrible manner many incidents in my past life. . . . I jumped up and ran at it, making a large Cross in the air, when the figure melted away like smoke, leaving a smell as if a gun had been discharged. . . . When it reappeared I began to recite sentences of the exorcism, and it seemed to me that when I came to the more forcible portions of it the voice grew less distinct. As I proceeded and also made use of holy water the voice died away in a sort of moan. . . . The voice claimed to be that of Lucifer.'

Thus the discussion as to the subjective or objective nature of these visions is involved in an endless obscurity, and whatever answer is given depends on a private interpretation of the facts, which is at once challenged by the opponent. Psychology can collect accounts of visions; but to decide whether they are real or illusory is outside its power. Such a decision can only be reached in the light of critical principles which psychology itself cannot establish. There is nothing in a vision itself, and therefore there is nothing in a thousand visions, to guarantee its truth or falsity; and therefore the uncritical use of such things as evidences is no more than a delusion.

There is, however, a second and less crude method of using psychological data. How, it is asked, do we account for the existence of all the world's evil? We are conscious in ourselves of solicitations and temptations to sin; and even if we are not in these temptations directly conscious of the personal presence of a tempter, we cannot account for their existence except by assuming that he is real. We do not, according to this argument, claim direct personal knowledge of the Devil, but we argue to his reality from the facts of life. There must be a Devil, because there is so much evil in the world. We know that our own sins make others sin, and it seems only reasonable to suppose that our sins may in turn be due to an Arch-Sinner, whose primal sin propagates itself in the wills of those who come under his malign influence.

Everything, we believe, must have a cause; and in assigning it to its cause we have, so far as we can ever hope to do so, explained it. A thing whose cause we have not discovered is, we say, unexplained, and one which has no cause is inexplicable; but we refuse to believe that anything is in the long run inexplicable. Evil then—so we argue—must have a cause; and the cause of evil in me can only be some other evil outside myself. And therefore we postulate a Devil as the First Cause of all evil, just as we postulate a God as the First Cause of all good.

But the parallel here suggested is entirely misleading. God and the Devil are not twin hypotheses which stand or fall together. God, as present to the religious mind, is not a hypothesis at all; He is not a far-fetched explanation of phenomena. He is about our path and about our bed; we do not search the world for traces of His passing by, or render His existence more probable by scientific inductions. Philosophy may demand a proof of His existence, as it may demand a proof of the existence of this paper, of the philosopher's friends or of the philosopher himself; but the kind of certainty which the religious mind has of God is of the same kind as that which we have of ourselves and of other people, and not in any way similar to the gradually strengthening belief in a hypothesis. The two kinds of belief must not be confused. I do not consider the existence of another mind like my own as a highly probable explanation of the voice I hear in conversation with a friend; to describe my belief in such terms would be entirely to misrepresent its real nature. The Devil may be a hypothesis, but God is not; and if we find reason for rejecting the above argument for the reality of the Devil we have not thereby thrown any doubt on the reality of God.

The belief in a Devil is supposed to be a hypothesis. But is it a good hypothesis? Does it explain the facts?

There are two questions to which we may require an answer. First, how do I come to think of this sin as a possible thing to do? Secondly, why do I desire to do it? To the first question the hypothesis does supply an answer: but no answer is really needed. My own faculties are sufficient, without any diabolical instruction, to discover that on a given occasion I might do wrong if I would.

To the second and much more important question the hypothesis of a Devil supplies no answer at all; and to conceal this deficiency it raises two other questions, each equally hard, and each in point of fact only a new form of the original problem. If evil can only be explained by postulating a Devil, in the first place, what explains the sins of the Devil himself? Secondly, granted that there is a Devil, why do people do what he wants them to do? The first of these questions is not answered by saying that the Devil's sin is a First Cause and needs no explanation; that is, that it was the uncaused act of a free being. The same is obviously true of our own actions; and it was only because this account of them seemed insufficient that we felt compelled to postulate a Devil. But if it is insufficient in our case, how can we guarantee its sufficiency in his?

The other question is even more unanswerable. If the Devil, by some compulsive power, forces us to act in certain ways, then these acts are not our acts, and therefore not our sins; and if he only induces us to act, the question is, why do we let ourselves be induced? If there is a Devil who wants me to do something wrong, his desire is impotent until I choose to fall in with it. And therefore his existence does nothing whatever to explain my sin. The hypothesis of a Devil explains nothing; and if the fact which it is meant to explain, the fact of evil, requires an explanation, then the Devil himself requires an explanation of the same kind.

The truth is that evil neither requires nor admits any explanation whatever. To the question, 'Why do people do wrong?' the only answer is, 'Because they choose to'. To a mind obsessed by the idea of causation, the idea that everything must be explained by something else, this answer seems inadequate. But action is precisely that which is not caused; the will of a person acting determines itself and is not determined by anything outside itself. Causation has doubtless its proper sphere. In certain studies it may be true, or true enough for scientific purposes, to describe one event as entirely due to another. But if the Law of Causation is a good servant, it is a bad master. It cannot be applied to the activity of the will without explicitly falsifying the whole nature of that activity. An act of the will is its own cause and its own explanation; to seek its explanation in something else is to treat it not as an act but as a mechanical event. It is hardly surprising that such a quest should end in a confusion greater than that in which it began. Evil, like every other activity of free beings, has its source and its explanation within itself alone. It neither need nor can be explained by the invocation of a fictitious entity such as the Devil.

In the absence of any results from the method of evidence and hypothesis, we must turn to the only other alternative, the simpler though perhaps more difficult method described above as the method of criticism. Instead of asking whether or not the Devil exists, we must ask what we understand by the Devil, and whether that conception is itself a possible and reasonable one. When we have answered these questions we shall perhaps find that the other has answered itself.

To this critical procedure it may be objected at the outset that the method is illegitimate; for it implies the claim to conceive things which in their very nature are inconceivable. Infinite good and infinite evil are, it is said, beyond the grasp of our finite minds; we cannot conceive God, and therefore neither can we conceive the Devil. To limit infinity within the circle of a definition is necessarily to falsify it; any attempt at conception can only lead to misconception.

Even if this objection were justified, instead of being based on a false theory of knowledge, it would not really affect our question. If the Devil is inconceivable, then we have no conception of him, or only a false one; and there is an end of the matter. But any one who maintains his existence does claim to have a conception of him; he uses the word Devil and presumably means something by it. The objection, if used on behalf of a believer in the Devil, would be no more than a confession that he attaches no meaning to the word and therefore does not believe in a Devil at all. So far as he does believe, his belief is a conception and can therefore be criticized.

Now the idea of God as an omnipotent and entirely good being is certainly conceivable. It is possible to imagine a person who possessed all the power in existence, who could do everything there was to be done, and who did everything well. Whether this conception can be so easily reconciled with others, we do not ask; we are only examining the idea itself. Further, it is an essential element in the conception of God that He should be not perfectly good alone, but also the sole and absolute source of goodness; that He should will not only good but all the good there is. Now it is essential to grasp the fact that whether such a will as this is conceivable or not depends on whether good things are all compatible with one another, or whether one good thing may exclude, contradict, or compete with another good thing. If they are all compatible, if the 'Law of Contradiction', that no truth can contradict another truth, applies *mutatis mutandis* to the sphere of morality, then all individual good things are parts of one harmonious scheme of good which might be the aim of a single perfectly good will. If, on the other hand, one good thing is incompatible with another, it follows that they are not parts of a single whole, but essentially in conflict with one another, and that therefore the same will cannot include, that is cannot choose, all at once. For instance, granted that A and B cannot both have a thing, if it is right that A should have it and also right that B should have it, God cannot will all that is good; for one mind can only choose one of two contradictory things.

It seems to be a necessary axiom of ethics that on any given occasion there can only be one duty. For duty means that which a man ought to do; and it cannot conceivably be a duty to do something impossible.[2] Therefore if I have two duties at the same time, it must be possible for me to do both. They cannot contradict one another, for then one would be impossible and therefore not obligatory. There can be a 'conflict of duties' only in the sense that from two different points of view each of two incompatible things seems to be my duty; the conflict disappears when I determine which point of view ought to be for the moment supreme. This does not mean that there is a greater duty which overrides the less; for the distinction between doing and not

---

[2] It is sometimes perhaps a duty to *try* to do an impossible thing. But in that case the claims of duty are satisfied by the attempt; and to attempt the impossible is not necessarily itself impossible.

doing, and between 'ought to do' and 'ought not to do', is not a question of degree. The one is simply my duty, and the other not my duty. No doubt the latter might have been my duty in a different situation; and it is often distressing to see what good things we might have done if the situation, created perhaps by our own or another's folly, had not demanded something else. But here again there are not two duties; there is one and only one, together with the knowledge that in other conditions some other duty would have taken its place.

If it is true that my duty can never contradict itself, it is equally true that my duty cannot contradict any one else's. A may feel it his duty to promote a cause which B feels it right to resist; but clearly in this case one must be mistaken. Their countries may be at war, and they may be called upon by the voice of duty to fight each other; but one country—perhaps both—must be in the wrong. It is possibly a duty to fight for one's country in a wrongful cause; but if that is so it is one's duty not to win but to atone in some degree for the national sin by one's own death.

A real duty, and therefore a real good, is a good not for this or that man, but for the whole world. If it is good, morally good, that A should have a thing, it is good for B that A should have it. Thus all moral goods are compatible, and they are therefore capable of being all simultaneously willed by a single mind. So far, then, the idea of God seems to be a consistent and conceivable notion. Is the same true of the idea of the Devil?

The Devil is generally regarded as being not only entirely bad, but the cause of all evil: the absolute evil will, as God is the absolute good will. But a very little reflexion shows that this is impossible. Good cannot contradict good, just as truth cannot contradict truth; but two errors may conflict, and so may two crimes. Two good men can only quarrel in so far as their goodness is fragmentary and incomplete; but there is no security that two absolutely bad men would agree. The reverse is true; they can only agree so far as they set a limit to their badness, and each undertakes not to thwart and cheat the other. Every really good thing in the world harmonizes with every other; but evil is at variance not only with good but with other evils. If two thieves quarrel over their plunder, a wrong is done whichever gets it, but no one Devil can will both these wrongs. The idea of a Devil as a person who wills all actual and possible evil, then, contradicts itself, and no amount of psychological evidence or mythological explanation can make it a conceivable idea.

Our first notion of the Devil must be given up. But we might modify it by suggesting that the Devil does not will that either thief should get the plunder; he desires not our success in evil projects, but simply our badness. He incites the two to fight out of pure malice, not with any constructive purpose but simply in order to make mischief. That one thief should succeed prevents the other thief from succeeding; but there is nothing in the mere badness of the one incompatible with the mere badness of the other. And the badness of each is quite sufficiently shown in the attempt, whether successful or not, to defraud the other.

This brings us to a different conception of the Devil as a person who does, not all the evil there is, but all the evil he can. He is an opportunist; when thieves can do most harm by agreeing, he leads them to agree; when by quarrelling, he incites them to quarrel. He may not be omnipotent in evil; whatever evil he brings about is at the expense of other possible ills; but at least he is consistently wicked and never does anything good. Is this second idea more conceivable than the first? In order to answer this question we must inquire briefly into the character and conditions of the evil will.

There are two well-established and popular accounts of evil, neither of which is entirely satisfactory. Sometimes evil is said to be the mere negation of good; nothing positive, but rather a deficiency of that which alone is positive, namely goodness; more commonly good and evil are represented as different and opposed forces.

The first view contains elements of real truth, and is supported by such great names as that of Augustine, who was led, in his reaction from Manichaeism, to adopt it as expressing the distinctively Christian attitude towards evil.

This view is generally criticized by pointing out that as evil is the negation of good, so good is the negation of evil; either is positive in itself but negative in relation to the other. This criticism is valid as against the verbal expression of the theory, though it does not touch the inner meaning which the theory aims at expressing. But unless this inner meaning is thought out and developed with much more care than is generally the case, the view of evil as merely negative expresses nothing but a superficial optimism, implying that any activity is good if only there is enough of it, that only small and trivial things can be bad, and (in extreme forms of the theory) that evil is only evil from a limited and human point of view, whereas to a fuller and more comprehensive view it would be non-existent. These sophistical conclusions are so plainly untenable that they force the mind to take refuge in the opposite view.

Good and evil, according to this view, are different and opposed forces. If the opposition is imagined as existing between an absolute good will and an absolute bad (as for instance in Manichaeism) we have already shown that it cannot be maintained, for an absolute bad will is inconceivable. The crude antithesis of Manichaeism therefore gives place to a different kind of opposition, such as that between body and soul, desire and reason, matter and spirit, egoism and altruism, and so on *ad infinitum*. To criticize these in detail would be tedious; it is perhaps enough to point out the fallacy which underlies all alike. That which acts is never one part of the self; it is the whole self. It is impossible to split up a man into two parts and ascribe his good actions to one part—his soul, his reason, his spirit, his altruistic impulses—and his bad actions to another. Each action is done by him, by his one indivisible will. Call that will anything you like; say that his self is desire, and you must distinguish between right desires and wrong desires; say that it is spirit, and you must add that spirit may be good or bad. The essence of his good acts is that he might have done a bad one: the essence of his bad, that he—the same he—might have done a good. It is impossible to distinguish between any two categories one of which is necessarily bad and the other necessarily good. We constantly try to do so; we say, for instance, that it is wrong to yield to passion and right to act on principle. But either we beg the question by surreptitiously identifying passion with that which is wrong and principle with that which is right, or we must confess that passions may well be right and that principles are very often wrong. The moral struggle is not a struggle between two different elements in our personality; for two different elements, just so far as they are different, cannot ever cross each other's path. What opposes desires for evil is not reason, but desires for good. What opposes egoism—a false valuation of oneself—is not altruism but, as Butler long ago pointed out, a higher egoism, a true valuation of oneself.

Evil, and therefore the Devil, is not a mere negation, not the shadow cast by the light of goodness. Nor is it identical with matter, body, desire, or any other single term of a quasi-Manichaean antithesis. It is something homogeneous with good, and yet not good; neither the mere absence of goodness nor the mere presence of its opposite. We do evil not through lack of positive will, nor yet because we will something definitely and obviously different from good. The first alternative breaks down because doing wrong is a real activity of the will; the second because doing wrong for the sake of wrong, if it happens at all, is a very small part of the evil that actually exists.

It is surely the case that the immense majority of crimes are done under a kind of self-deception. We persuade ourselves that this act, which is generally considered a crime, is really when properly understood, or when seen in the light of our peculiar circumstances, a fine and praiseworthy act. Such a plea is not in itself wrong. It is a duty, indeed it is the spring of all moral advance, to criticize current standards of morality and to ask whether this may not be a case where the current rule fails to apply. But though this criticism is not necessarily wrong but is the very essence of right action, it is not necessarily right but is the very essence of evil. To set oneself against current beliefs and practices is the central characteristic of all heroes, and it is equally the central characteristic of all criminals; of Christ and of Lucifer. The difference is not psychological; it is not that the hero has noble and exalted sentiments while the criminal gives way to ignoble and debased passions. The essence of crime is the pride of Lucifer, the feeling of nobility and exaltation, of superiority to convention and vulgar prejudice. When we do wrong, we believe, or persuade ourselves, that the opinion which is really the right one, really the expression of moral truth, is a mere fiction or convention; and we represent ourselves as rebels and martyrs for a noble cause.

It may be that some crimes have not this characteristic. At times, perhaps, we act wrongly in the clear understanding that we are doing wrong, while still attaching the right meaning to that word. But when we say, 'I know it is wrong, but I intend to do it', we generally mean by 'wrong' that which is commonly called wrong; wrong in public opinion, but to our own superior understanding right. Or, what is really the same thing, we admit that it is 'morally wrong' but hold that it has a value other than, and transcending, that of morality; a meaningless phrase if we recollect that morality is simply that kind of value which actions possess, so that to judge them by another standard is impossible. Any other standard we apply is morality under another name.[3]

[3] People say, for instance, 'So-and-so ought to think less about morality, and more about his neighbours' happiness,' or the like. But this language means that to consult his neighbours' happiness is a moral duty which So-and-so has been neglecting. Here, as in the similar case of polemics against 'morality', the word is misused for 'that which people wrongly imagine to be morality'. Those writers who expect or exhort mankind to develop into a life beyond good and evil do not quite realize that they regard it as a *good* thing to be 'beyond good and evil'. To believe that any standard is the right one to act upon implies believing, or rather is believing, that it is a moral standard.

The essence of evil, then, is that it should set itself up not in opposition, open and proclaimed, to good as good; but that it should set itself up to be the good, standing where it ought not in the holy place and demanding that worship which is due to good alone. Evil is not the absence of good nor yet the opposite of good; it is the counterfeit of good.[4]

Now if this is so, it follows that nobody can be entirely and deliberately bad. To be enslaved by a counterfeit of goodness we must know goodness itself; there must be an element of real good in a will before it can ever become evil. And that element of good persists throughout, and is the basis of all hopes of redemption. The force and life of evil comes from the positive experience of good which underlies the evil, which alone makes evil possible. Therefore the Devil, just as he cannot will all the evil there is, cannot be fundamentally and perfectly wicked; he is not a wicked angel but a fallen angel, preserving in his fall the tattered remnants of the glory that was his, to be at once the foundation and the abatement of his badness. It is this contradiction in the nature of the evil will that Dante has in mind when, coming to the centre and heart of the Inferno, he finds its lord not triumphant, not proud and happy in his kingdom, but inconsolably wretched.

> Con sei occhi piangeva, e per tre menti
> Gocciava 'l pianto e sanguinosa bava.[5]

[4] It goes without saying that counterfeit goods or false ideals, like true ones, are seldom the peculiar property of any one individual; they are often, though of course not necessarily, common to a family or class or sex or nation. This fact has, however, no bearing on the point at issue; and is only quoted here because of a false value very often attached to it. The ideals I act on are, wherever I get them from, mine; that they should happen to be shared by others is irrelevant. But, it is said, I get them as a matter of fact from others; I have them because others have them; the influence of a corrupt public opinion is of the utmost importance in any concrete account of the evil will—this language is so common that it is worth while to point out the fallacy it contains. It is another instance of a fictitious entity (in this case 'Society') posing as the 'explanation' of evil. The alleged explanation contains (1) a vicious circle and (2) a fatal gap. (1) 'Society' consists of Tom, Dick and Harry: if I 'get my ideals' from them, where do they 'get' theirs from? Presumably from me; unless it is supposed that ideals never change at all, but are simply transmitted en bloc from generation to generation. (2) If other people's ideals are bad, they may on that account equally well reproduce themselves in me, or rouse me to reject them. Man's relation to his moral environment is just as much negative as affirmative; and therefore no detail of his moral character can ever be explained by reference to such environment.

[5] Inferno, c. xxxiv. lines 53–54. 'With six eyes he wept, and down three chins trickled his tears and blood-stained slaver.' Stained, that is, with the blood of the traitors whose limbs he was mangling. Paradise Lost, c. 1.

And Milton knows that Satan's mind, in the thought of lost happiness and lasting pain, was filled with torments of huge affliction and dismay; confounded though immortal.

In these and kindred accounts of the Devil we recognize a very real and profound truth. But of what kind is this truth? Is it a true portrait of an actual, historical person called Lucifer or Satan who at some time in the remote past rose against God and set himself up as leader of an angelic rebellion? Or is it the true description of a real spirit who, whatever his past history, lives and rules the forces of evil now? Or lastly, is its truth mythical truth? Is Satan simply the type of all evil wills?

In answer to the first of these questions we can only say that such a thing may well have happened. There may have been, at some definite time in the past, war in heaven, Michael and his angels fighting against the dragon and his angels. We know of countless people who have at various times set up false ideals of truth and of right, and have worshipped those false gods, instead of the true God. And it may be that there was once a person, not a human being but a being of some kind, whose rebellion was of surpassing magnitude and weight, like Arianism among the Christian heresies; and that his name has somehow come down to us as Lucifer. If this is presented as mere history it is not possible to prove or disprove it. But in speaking of the fall of Lucifer do we really mean this, and only this?

It would appear that we mean both more and less. Less, because we hardly believe that Lucifer's fall took place at any actual date. It was 'before the beginning of the world'; it has no definite place in our time-series. To ask its date seems incongruous, not because we have no evidence for dating it, but because we do not regard it as quite an event in history. But we also mean more; for we regard Lucifer or the Devil not as a character in past history only, a pretender like Perkin Warbeck, but as a spiritual force about us here and now. His fall is somehow repeated and represented, not merely imitated, in the apparition and collapse of any great force working for evil. There may have been a historical Lucifer, but it is not he, it is no historical person simply as such, of whom we speak as the Devil.

Is he then the supreme evil power? Is he the Manichaean anti-God whose spirit informs the communion of sinners as the Holy Spirit informs the communion of saints? No; for we have already seen that there can be no supreme power which directs and controls all the forces of evil. That army is one without discipline, without a leader;

the throne of the kingdom of evil is empty, and its government is anarchy. Evil wills exist, but they owe no allegiance to any supreme spirit. They worship evil, they worship the Devil; but their worship is idolatry because they themselves create its god. If the Devil were a real ruler, then worship of him would be within its limits a true religion; but it is false religion, the worship of a phantom.

It remains that we should regard the Devil as a myth. This does not mean that the descriptions of him are untrue, or that they are the product of that fancy whose creations are neither true nor false but merely imaginary. A myth is capable of, and is judged by, a certain kind of truth. Mythology is to the naïve consciousness a form of history; the myth of Herakles to a simple-minded Greek was the biography of a real person. But, as such, it was false. Mythology does not contain historical truth, though it presents itself in a historical form. The truth it contains may perhaps be described as typical truth. Herakles is the type of all strong men who devote their strength to the bettering of human life; and the truth of the myth lies precisely in this, that the story truly presents the real character of the type. This is the difference between mythology and art, the work of the imagination. The mythical person is never quite an individual. He is always something of an abstraction, a type rather than a person. In art, on the other hand, the person is not a type but an individual. Hamlet is not typical of any class of men, as Herakles is; he is simply his unique self. An art which forgets the individual and presents the type, an art which generalizes, has forgotten its artistic mission and has become mythology.

The Devil is in this sense a myth. He rebels against God and sets himself up for worship, because all evil is rebellion against the true good and the worship of false ideals, of counterfeit goods, of idols. He rules over the kingdom of darkness, and yet his rule is only a mockery, because there is no real unity in evil, though there is a fictitious and spurious unity. He is a laughing-stock to the saints, because evil once seen as evil has no more power over the mind; it only controls those who worship it, who reverence it as good. He torments souls in hell, and is himself tormented, because the evil will is divided against itself and can never reach the unity and harmony which alone characterize the good. His strength lies in his infinite disguises; he comes in countless alluring forms, which at the word of power vanish leaving his own naked horror of impotent rage, because evil is never seen as evil by its worshippers; they clothe it in all the forms of beauty and sincerity and virtue, which must be torn away by the wind of truth leaving the

N

idolater face to face with the reality of the thing he has worshipped till he turns from it in loathing. Christian demonology is a storehouse of observations, not as to the life-history of a single Devil or even of many devils, but as to the nature, growth and development of the evil will.

Are there, then, no spiritual forces which influence man for evil? Are the malign spirits which surround us with temptations a mere mythological description of our own inner wickedness?

There certainly are spiritual forces of evil. But by 'spiritual' we do not necessarily mean other than human; still less do we refer to a class of ambiguous beings sometimes physical and sometimes 'dematerialized'; the 'spirits' of vulgar superstition. There may be personal minds other than those we know as God, man and the lower animals; and if so, they are doubtless good or bad. But, as we saw, no such beings need be postulated to account for human sin; nor would they account for it, if they existed. The spirits whose evil we know are human spirits; and the forces of evil with which we are surrounded are the sins of this human world. The Devil is an immanent spirit of evil in the heart of man, as God is an immanent spirit of goodness. But there is this great difference, that God is transcendent also, a real mind with a life of His own, while the Devil is purely immanent, that is, considered as a person, non-existent.

Nor is it even entirely true to say that the Devil is immanent. For that would imply that evil is a principle one and the same in all evil acts; and this it cannot be, for while good acts all form part of one whole of goodness, evil acts have no parallel unity. There is no communion of sinners; they live not in communion with one another, but in mutual strife. There is not one immanent Devil, but countless immanent devils, born in a moment and each in a moment dying to give place to another, or else to that re-entering spirit of good which is always one and the same.

The devils within us are our own evil selves. But this does not mean that they cannot come, in a sense, from without. When one man infects another with his own badness, it is quite literal truth to say that a devil goes from one to the other; and there may be a kind of unity, a kind of momentary kingdom of evil, when the same devil seizes upon a large number of people and they do in a crowd things which no man would do by himself. There may even be a more lasting kingdom where an institution or a class keeps alive for generations a false ideal. And since evil influences may affect us from books, from places, from the weather, we tend naturally to think of devils as inhabiting these things. Are we here back again in mythology? There really is a devil—a spirit of evil—in a bad person; is there one, in the same sense, in a wood or in the east wind?

It is a difficult question to answer, since it depends on how far each of these things has a self, and how far the selfhood which to us it seems to have is really conferred upon it by our own thought. To us the east wind is a definite thing; and so to us it can be a devil. But is it a definite thing to itself? Is the influence it exerts upon us its own influence, or is it only the reflexion in it of our own nature? Perhaps it is best to leave the question open. There may be devils in places and in things which we generally regard as inanimate; but those which we know exist in the human mind. Of these the Devil of orthodoxy is a type or myth; a myth not in the colloquial sense in which the word means a fiction or illusion, but in the proper sense which we have explained above. And the truth of the orthodox belief consists in the fact that it does with perfect accuracy describe the real nature of the evil will. But as soon as the mythical nature of the belief is forgotten, as soon as the Devil is taken not as a type of all evil wills but as their actual supreme ruler, then the step has been taken from truth to superstition, from Christianity to Manichaeism.

\*     \*     \*

How does all this affect the theory and practice of prayer? 'The Devil' in any given case is simply the person who is sinning; the wickedness into which he has made himself. Therefore devil-worship is first and primarily self-worship. Self-worship is not necessarily bad; the 'religion of humanity' may mean the worship of God as revealed in and through human goodness. But in that case it is not mere self-worship, but the worship of the God immanent in ourselves. Worship of the self pure and simple must always be devil-worship, for it is only the bad self that can be called self pure and simple. The good self is always something more than self; it is self informed and directed by the spirit of God. Man is only alone in the world when he has expelled the spirit of God from his heart and lives a life of evil; for there is no great central power of evil upon which he can then depend as in the alternative case he depends on God. The vacant sanctuary can only be filled with an idol created by man for his own worship; and this idol is the Brocken-spectre on the fog, the gigantic shadow of man himself when he turns away from the sunlight.

Idolatry, self-worship and devil-worship are one and the same thing; and they are identical with evil in general. For that false ideal which, in evil, takes the place due to the true ideal or God, is always our self, or rather a magnified reflexion of our self. Intellectual evil consists in setting up that which I believe as the standard of truth, whereas I ought rather to test and if necessary reject my beliefs by comparing them with reality. Moral evil consists not so much in yielding to desires which I know to be wrong as in erecting my moral standards and judgements into the sole test of rightness. In every case alike evil arises when man takes himself, exactly as he stands, for the measure of all things; for in that case he is setting up a god in his own image and worshipping idols.

True religion lies not in making God in our image, but in making ourselves in God's image; for God alone exists, and man is only struggling into existence for good or evil. In order to attain to any existence worth having, we must bear in mind that truth, reality, God, are real things existing quite independently of our individual life and private opinions; and an opinion is no less private if it happens to be shared by the whole human race. The type of all false religion is to believe what we will to believe, instead of what we have ascertained to be true; supposing that reality must be such as to satisfy our desires, and if not, go to, let us alter it. This is no ultimate, inexplicable fact; it follows necessarily from the truth that man's nature is as yet un-formed, incomplete; it is, in the great phrase of an English philosopher,[6] 'in process of being communicated to him'; and in that incomplete shape it is incapable of being the standard of anything. It is itself in need of a standard, and that standard, which for science is Reality, for religion is God.

Man's life is a becoming; and not only becoming, but self-creation. He does not grow under the direction and control of irresistible forces. The force that shapes him is his own will. All his life is an effort to attain to real human nature. But human nature, since man is at bottom spirit, is only exemplified in the absolute spirit of God. Hence man must shape himself in God's image, or he ceases to be even human and becomes diabolical. This self-creation must also be self-knowledge; not the self-knowledge of introspection, the examination of the self that is, but the knowledge of God, the self that is to be. Knowledge of God is the beginning, the centre and end, of human life.

[6] T. H. Green.

A painter makes his picture perfect by looking back from moment to moment at the vision which he is trying to reproduce. A scientist perfects his theory by testing it at every point by the facts of nature. So the religious life must come back again and again to the contemplation of its ideal in God. But God is a person, not a thing; a mind, not an object. We contemplate objects, but we do not contemplate persons. The attitude of one mind to another is not contemplation but communion; and communion with God is prayer. Prayer may not be the whole of religion, but it is the touchstone of it. All religion must come to the test of prayer; for in prayer the soul maps out the course it has taken and the journey it has yet to make, reviewing the past and the future in the light of the presence of God.

# X

## MORAL AND RELIGIOUS CONCEPTIONS OF DUTY: AN ANALYSIS[1]

### By D. Z. PHILLIPS

WHAT would it mean if I said that duties to God are given, whereas moral duties are not? Religious *and* moral duties seem to be given. We do not choose a religion in the sense of deciding that it should be the kind of thing it is, any more than we decide what our moral duties shall be. What morality is and what religion is does not depend on the individual will. All sorts of forces and influences have played a part in shaping our morality, most of which do not depend on any specific person. Similarly, an account could be given of the development of religious ideas, showing that there were contributory factors, not themselves religious, which played an important part in the development of religion. So it seems untrue to say that the duties we owe to God are given and that moral duties are not. Both it seems are given, in so far as they are not dependent on individual choices. On the other hand, this argument does not take us very far in the attempt to understand the concept of duty in the respective spheres. To do this one must view the matter from the inside. What must be considered is the grammar of these concepts. It is from the point of view of the grammar of the concepts that I suggest that there is some sense in saying that whereas duties to God are given, moral duties are not.

Moral duties are not given in the sense in which military orders are given. Despite the fact that one could give a justification of military commands in terms of discipline or strategy, and despite the fact that in war-time, for the sake of morale, the soldier is allowed an elementary glimpse of the importance of the order—the success of this mission is all important for our campaign—Britain depends on every man to do his duty—despite all this, the ideal characterization of military orders is, Do as you are told. Military orders seem to provide the most literal example of duties being given.

[1] I am indebted to Mr. Rush Rhees for the many discussions I have had with him on this topic.

Moral duties are not given in this way. Military commands are important for the soldier not because of what is said, but because what is said is an order. The mere fact that it is an order makes it a duty irrespective of what the order may be. In morality, however, it is the content of the duties which make them important.

Religious duties are more akin to military duties than moral duties are. I do not wish to press an analogy which has obvious limitations, but there is a similarity between the soldier's saying in reply to a question why he must perform an action, 'Because these are my superior's orders', and the religious believer's answering the same question, 'Because this is the will of God'. One might object to this by pointing out that the believer who has any insight at all into his Faith could proceed to say something of why he thinks it important to obey God's commands; he could distinguish between a life with God and a life without God. The believer and the unbeliever who is concerned with moral questions can give an account of the duties they obey, but there are important differences to be noted. When the unbeliever expounds the importance of moral duties, what he refers to is the importance of doing *this* action rather than *that* one. This is not what the believer does. When he says that it is important to do the will of God, he is not expounding the contents of God's commands, and as it were, their importance in human relationships, but rather, he is expounding the meaning of submission to the authority of the commands. The unbeliever is saying something about the role of the duties themselves; the believer is talking about *the role of the Giver of the duties*. In religious duties one has a distinction between the content of the duty and the authority of the duty which is absent in moral duties. The radical difference between doing one's duty in and outside religion rests, to a large extent, on the religious identification of duty with the will of God. This difference is illustrated in the following ways:

First, moral duties are not always present; we do not spend even the greater part of our time thinking about duty. On the other hand, the more one meditates on the law of God and disciplines oneself to it, the nearer one is said to be to God: 'But his delight is in the law of the Lord; and in his law doth he meditate day and night' (Psalm i. 2). If anyone talked of meditating on his duty day and night he would be an unbearable person and morally reprehensible. The moral life is not ruled by duty in the way in which the religious life is ruled by the will of God. One of the differences between the average believer and the saint is that the life of the latter is governed more by meditation and obedience than the life of the former. In morality, on the other hand, the admirable person would be the person who acted admirably in given situations. The characteristic of thinking constantly about duty should be absent in such a man.

Secondly, what is to be done in the performance of one's moral duty is usually quite specific. In the profounder kinds of moral perplexity, the question is not, 'How much shall I do?' but 'What ought I to do?' Many moral problems do bring in the former question. One often says, 'I could have done more had I been prepared to sacrifice'. There are always levels of achievement in this respect beyond the level attained by the individual. There are other situations, however, usually involving more intimate human relationships, where the person involved does not know what he ought to do. Sometimes the situation is such that whatever one does one will hurt someone. There is no question here of attaining higher and higher ends, since the person involved says, 'I wish I knew the answer', or in other words, 'I wish I knew what my duty was here'.

In religion, on the other hand, apart from the negative duties of 'thou shalt not . . .', almost all the duties do present one with this indefinite area of achievement. In the command to love and to forgive one's neighbour, one is not given a limit at which to stop. In morality, whether the question is 'How much shall I do?' or 'What ought I to do?' it makes sense to say at some stage, 'I have done enough'. We say of a third person, 'He has done his duty admirably'. One cannot say of someone in religion, 'He has done his duty' and mean by this, 'He has done enough'.

The two differences between moral and religious conceptions of duty which we have considered are based on a third, more fundamental, difference, namely, that moral duties, unlike religious duties, are often thought of in relation to needs. I recognize that it is my moral duty to do something in face of a need for that particular action to be done which makes up my duty. If a duty is done in relation to needs it at least makes sense to suppose that the need can be met. In so far as the people who benefit from the performance of religious duties get what they needed, it makes sense to talk of answering needs in the perform- ance of religious duties. Yet, the *meaning* of the religious conception of duty resides in the fact that the deed was not done as a duty towards these people, but as a duty towards God, and as a duty to God the divine requirement is never met. The reason for this difference is that religious duties are not done because God needs them. What would it mean for the believer to say that he had helped him on whom he believed himself to be utterly dependent? Or as Kierkegaard has it,

> ... God needs no man. It would otherwise be a highly embarrassing thing to be a creator, if the result was that the creator came to depend on the creature (*Concluding Unscientific Postscript*, Book II, part ii, chap. i, p. 122).

Many people would want to say that God does need the fulfilment of duties. They want to say that it makes sense to attribute specific needs and emotions to God. Disobedience offends God; obedience pleases him. Biblical covenants seem to take the form of conditional agreements: 'If you'll do this, I'll do that.' This makes the promises of God less profound than human loyalty which endures irrespective of whether it is deserved or not. This argument assumes that human promises and divine promises are essentially the same. But is this so? In answering this question we come to a fourth difference between moral and religious conceptions of duty.

Failure to keep one's promise to another person often leads to an injury to that person. If one fails to do the will of God does one injure God in some way? The sorrow that a thoughtless act can cause is inextricable from the kind of life that human beings live; we do misunderstand one another, and by so doing cause pain and sorrow. But God does not exist in this way. God does not have ups and downs! If one injures another person seriously enough, one can never, despite being forgiven, begin again as if nothing had happened. As a result of God's forgiveness complete reconciliation is said to be possible. What was lost between the sinner and God can be found again, whereas in morality, what was lost through injury can often never be restored.

Again, the ignoring of moral duty can lead to an accentuation of distress. A person's distress could be increased by his discovering that those who could help would not. Disobedience as an offence against God cannot be understood in this way. The fulfilment of religious duties is an expression of the believer's love of God. The horror of sin consists not in any injury done to God, but in the sinner's realization of his rejection and violation of the love which God has shown to him.

The idea of religious duties as expressions of love of God might suggest an analogy with certain human relationships where, although duties are involved, one would not normally speak of duty as a motive for action. I refer to relationships such as those which exist between husband and wife, child and parent, friend and friend. The fulfilment of the marriage vow seems akin to religious duties, since this too is an expression of love. There are, however, important differences to take account of. The love found in marriage, in friendship, and in the family, is essentially particular. By this I mean that it is the separation of these people from everyone else, which to a large extent, makes these relationships what they are. In marriage it is the taking of *this* man and *this* woman which is the source of much of its importance. Again, if everyone were one's friend, friendship would not be the kind of thing it is. The love which exists between the believer and God is not of this order, since it does not depend on the particularity of the individual relationship to God. Love of the child for the parent does depend on the particularity of the relationship, since if we were all children of the same parents, the love of the child for the parent would be radically different. But all men are said to be the children of God.

Having a relationship with God is very different from having a relationship with another human being. The fulfilment of duties in morality often makes possible a participation in certain relationships, and the answering of specific needs. The fulfilment of religious duties makes possible a relationship with God, but what such a relationship entails is a certain attitude to life, and seeing what one's life ought to be. One important aspect of such a relationship is the possibility of giving thanks for one's existence. In morality there need not be anything like an attitude to one's existence as a whole. There would be no contradiction in holding that moral values are important, while believing that life is a hopeless mess. One could not believe in God and assert that life is devoid of hope.

To understand, then, what is meant by the religious conception of duty, one must understand what it means to believe in God. This must be recognized in any analysis of religious conceptions of duty, and it brings one to perhaps the most important difference between them and moral conceptions of duty.

In morality, adherence to certain values often involves a recognition of why these values are important. True, moral standards are often observed without any particular insight into their importance. Moral perplexity, however, usually calls for moral and psychological insight. One cannot possess such insight unless one has thought one's way through to an appreciation of a moral analysis of various situations. If God is important to the believer, and if it is all-important that God's will is done, this is not because the believer has somehow thought his way through to God. That is why St. John of the Cross makes such radical assertions as the following:

'. . . if any among you seemeth to be wise let him become ignorant that he may be wise; for the wisdom of this world is foolishness with God.' So that, in order to come to union with the wisdom of God, the soul has to proceed by unknowing rather than by knowing (*Ascent of Mount Carmel*, Book I, chap. iv, p. 19).

The idea of 'the way of unknowing' is important for our analysis and for philosophy of religion generally. Morality is part of the way of knowing; it involves an appreciation of values. The profound believer does not arrive at his belief in a way akin to the unbeliever's arrival at a moral decision. It is only when he realizes that he does not know the answers that the believer finds the grace of God. In finding God the believer has not thought his way through to a meaning in his life or in life in general, but has accepted, without reservation, the will of God. What Job came to know was that he did not know the answers about himself or about the world.

The above argument which contrasts religious acceptance with moral understanding should be understood as a corrective, rather than as an independent thesis. I am anxious to avoid a position in which religious language seems to be a special language cut off from other forms of human discourse. Religion would not have the kind of importance it has were it not connected with the rest of life. Religious discourse has much in common with moral discourse. The naked are clothed and the starving are fed whether the motive is moral or religious. Religion, in the form of prayer, can often help to resolve moral difficulties. More important is the fact that we say that the later stages of a religion are *deeper* than the earlier stages; we say too that one person's faith is deeper than the faith of another person. These judgements can be made by non-believers, which suggests that religious concepts are not inaccessible to non-religious understanding.

On the other hand, I also want to avoid the view that religious concepts can be accounted for in moral terms. My emphasis on the differences between moral and religious conceptions of duty was meant to combat such a view, an example of which is seen in Gilbert Murray's position:

. . . the various bodies who have accepted or put into articulate shape these moral ideals always have some difficulty in accounting for them. Man has known that he wished to be good and do good, but has never quite found a satisfactory answer to the question why he wished it. He nearly always had to invent what I will venture to call a mythology (*Myths and Ethics*, p. 18).

The concept of God must be central in an analysis of religious conceptions of duty. This centrality is illustrated by the way in which the analogy between military duties and religious duties breaks down. Military commands or commands of the state can be challenged. Other obligations may be thought to be more important; for example, obligations to one's family (cf. Antigone). It does not make sense to assume that in certain situations other duties might be more important than one's duty to God. God's commands cannot become of secondary importance without being abandoned.

The distinction between the moral and religious conceptions of duty is not one of degree. As Kierkegaard says,

> Concerning the spiritual relation one cannot—if he wishes to avoid speaking foolishly—talk like a shopkeeper who has a best quality of goods, but also an intermediate quality which he also ventures to recommend as very good, as almost equally good (*Works of Love*, p. 38).

The distinction between the concepts is one of grammar; that is to say, what it makes sense to say of one, it often does not make sense to say of the other. This is no trivial matter.

# XI

## 'I WILL DIE': AN ANALYSIS

### By William H. Poteat

### INTRODUCTION

The concept of death, as is well known, has been a central preoccupation of much of contemporary so-called Existentialist thought—whether that is expressed through discursive philosophical analysis, or in the novels, plays and other literary devices associated with this movement. Man is not only pictured as the creature who dies, perhaps the only creature who dies; and death is not only seen as the peculiar threat to all human meaning which it is. Man in the face of death is believed to reveal not merely the ultimate human value of courage, so that, for example, Sartre and Camus have chosen in their novels and plays to place their protagonists in the presence of death. When in the presence of its threat, the hero's actions are decisive: he is thought to become human or to fail his humanity in a paradigmatic way. All this may be caught in Heidegger's expression *Sein Zum Tode*—the mark of the human as such.

But if the Existentialists are simply telling us what every man knows, even though he may be in flight from his knowledge, namely, that he will die; or even if they exhort us to see and to incarnate the moral value of courage; they can hardly be said to have performed any very striking philosophical service—though they may have done what all great literature does: make us *engage*.

But what is actually involved is, as it seems to me, something at once more radical and more definitive of their over-all philosophic objective. The preoccupation with death is not merely an interest in reminding us of the most unpleasant of all 'empirical' facts; or of enjoining us, as Plato suggested it to be the philosophic task *par excellence* to enjoin, namely, to practise to die.

The interest is, in fact, at bottom a conceptual one, although the Existentialists themselves have not explicitly acknowledged this and may not even have realized it.[1]

[1] To be sure, M. Heidegger has sought to distinguish his own programme from those of Kierkegaard, Jaspers and Marcel, as he sees them, by the use of the categories 'existential' and 'existentiel', the one being soteriologically oriented, the other being primarily a 'scientific' task—a step toward a fundamental ontology.

By this I mean that implicitly it is recognized that to understand what it is to be a self, a subject, *dasein*, a *pour soi*, authentic, radical freedom is to understand what it is for me to die. Or, to put it in the idiom of the linguistic analytic branch of contemporary philosophy: to understand how the concept 'death' functions is to understand more about how the concept 'self' does; to observe how these two correlate with each other and how *they* in turn correlate differently with other (in relation to them) logically heterogeneous concepts is to understand the difference between being a man and being just a thing.

Finally, Bultmann's confused and naïve proposal to substitute the Heideggerian myth for the New Testament myth implicitly recognizes at least that the difference between the modern scientific or even the modern common-sense view of the world and that of the Christian Faith, whose central claim is that Jesus Christ has overcome sin and death, is a profound conceptual difference and that, by further implication, the difficulties can only be removed by a clearing away of conceptual underbrush.

But this interest, though certainly dominant here, is not limited to the so-called Existentialists. In a quite different way, and within a context where conceptual analysis is an explicit programme, there has been and perhaps is now a growing interest in the concept 'death' among the Anglo-American analysts.

As long ago as 1921 when the German edition of his *Tractatus* appeared, Ludwig Wittgenstein, the father of the Vienna Circle positivists, at the end of his discussion of the philosophy of logic, made a brief but exciting remark upon the logical peculiarities of the concept of death. He says: 'As in death, too, the world does not change, but ceases. Death is not an event in life. Death is not lived through.'[2] Subsequently in his classic article on 'Meaning and Verification',[3] Moritz Schlick indicates some of the logical issues involved in the concept of death in the course of investigating the general principle of verifiability, formulating them in terms of whether it is meaningful to wonder if 'I can be a witness at my own funeral'.

More recently, A. G. N. Flew,[4] asking 'Can a man witness his own funeral?', is not primarily concerned with general questions of meaning

---

[2] *Tractatus Logico-Philosophicus*, London, 1949, 6.431, 6.4311.

[3] *The Philosophical Review*, 45, 1936.

[4] *Hibbert Journal*, LIV, April 1956. Ian Ramsey has undertaken to meet Flew's argument in *Hibbert Journal*, LIV, June 1956.

but with the concept of death, and concludes that the suggestion that we survive death is self-contradictory.

It is my conviction that the analyses so far made have failed to appreciate what is really significant about the logical puzzles surrounding the concept of death, and have not noticed, what I believe to be implicit in Wittgenstein's dark saying and to be even more hidden in the quite different descriptions of the Existentialists, namely, that important connections hold among the words 'I', 'death', 'world', 'human', and 'last things', 'the end of history', 'the end of the world'. And not only so: that when we discern something of the logical behaviour of these terms we shall see something of the role of theological language in general and of its legitimation—indeed of its inescapability. I propose therefore to analyse the expression 'I will die'. As I do so, I urge you to think of what I will be saying in the first person. That is, whenever I use the expression 'I will die', think '*I* will die', not 'He will die'. I believe this to be essential to seeing what I hope to have you see.

Now then, what I want to argue is the following: (1) Flew, in holding that to think of the survival of death is to think a logical contradiction, is quite right, though trivially right, because analytically so, *if 'death' is a concept that simply correlates with or is logically assimilable to reports or predictions of events* (bio-chemical, social, physiological, auditory, etc.) *and 'acts' and behaviour.* Further, this correlation of 'death' with more or less straightforward reports or predictions of events in the common-sense spatio-temporal world is, with *a certain amount of not very plausible forcing,* possible. I want to show, however, that in our ordinary use we do not force and that *then,* in certain circumstances, the concept 'death' has an extension and hence an acceptable use beyond reports and predictions, about acts and ordinary events. (2) That this extension of the concept is not recognized when the verb 'to die' is conjugated merely in the second or third persons, but is clearly to be seen when I *use,* not just mention, 'I will die' of myself. (3) That when I use the expression of myself what I am asserting is not assimilable to reports or predictions of events or behaviour in the common-sense world, but is nevertheless perfectly—though, no doubt, strangely—meaningful. (4) That even if Flew were to say, e.g. 'After I have died, there will be nothing'—and says it thoughtfully of himself, he is himself using the concept 'death' in an equivocal and logically peculiar way, that is to say, in a way not assimilable to reports or predictions of events or behaviour in the common-sense world, and, furthermore, in

o

a way which is, *in the respect of its unassimilability*, logically like 'death' as it functions in what a Christian might say: for example, 'When I die, I shall have fellowship with God'. (5) Finally, that when we observe the peculiar behaviour of 'death' in the first person singular, we shall be struck by the logical peculiarity of 'I' itself—which is, I believe, one of the points which the Existentialists try rather misleadingly to make.

If such an ambitious programme can be made to 'come off', it may be possible to suggest something about the meaning of eschatological concepts in general, such as 'end of history', etc. I want to show, in short, what I believe to be the case, namely, that 'death' in certain of its common-sensically acceptable uses is a logically extended use and is hence an, if you will, eschatological concept; and that 'I' when it is coupled with death, in this logically extended use is also logically extended, and hence may be thought of as a kind of meta-concept; and finally (without trying here to display its complicated logic) we may say that these logically extended concepts require and therefore legitimize and properly function within the structure of what I'll call myth.

## I

*Prima facie*, the expression 'I will die' is a possible candidate for classification only as a performatory proposition[5] (where the saying of something is itself the doing of it) or as a straightforward empirical prediction. A third view which would hold it has certain logical affinities with each of these seems hardly possible.

But it cannot be construed as performatory, for uttering the expression 'I will die' is not the same thing as dying in the way that uttering the expression 'I promise to so and so' is the same thing as promising to so and so.

We must ask, then, whether it is possible to construe it, as the import of Flew's analysis would seem to demand, as a statement to the effect that at a certain time in the future some behaviour now observable in the world will no longer be observed, and nothing more.[6]

Let us first concede that my saying 'I will die' entails certain quite ordinary empirical propositions of a predictive sort—propositions about bio-chemical, social, physiological, auditory and other events or

---

[5] J. L. Austin, 'Other Minds', in *Logic and Language*, 2nd Series, ed. A. G. N. Flew, Oxford, 1953. See pp. 143 f.

[6] I take M. Schlick to be putting a similar case about the type of proposition we are to take our example as being.

behaviour in the experienceable world. It does not follow, however, from this entailment that 'I will die' is assimilable to a finite number of such propositions, in the sense that the meaning of 'I will die' as I use the expression of myself can be analysed without remainder into propositions of this sort. Neither does it follow that it cannot be so analysed. Flew, if I understand him, is holding that it can: that when I say, 'I am alive', I mean there is observable behaviour of a certain sort, and nothing more; and when I say, 'I will die', I mean that a time will come when there will not be any such behaviour, and nothing more. We then must determine on other gronnds whether or not such an assimilation is licit.

How shall we proceed? Let us begin by assuming, even if it requires an implausible forcing, that 'self' or 'I' may be exhaustively analysed in terms of a finite number of reports about behaviour (in the ordinary sense). I use the term 'behaviour' rather than 'acts' because on the surface—though probably not in the long run—'acts' is a more question-begging term, since a world in which there are acts but no actors is a logical impossibility, and the question we are facing here is just that of whether there are actors over and above acts (behaviour).[7] Further, let me assume that these reports about past and present behaviour are being given in the first person singular. What are the characteristics of the verbs which I might be imagined as using, for example: to run, to think, to wonder, to justify.[8] If I use any of these or even others to report upon myself or to predict about myself, I will find no difficulty whatever in conjugating these verbs in every possible tense, every possible person. I can with perfectly good sense say: 'I wondered, I wonder, I will wonder.' There is in the English language a vast number of verbs which I may use to report and predict in the first person in any tense and which are like our examples above and like one another in the respect that they make perfectly good sense when conjugated in the first person in any tense. This suggests that the first person singular can simply be accommodated to the verbs of our language in any tense and that my reporting, 'I wondered', is logically precisely like my

[7] One may certainly wonder whether it really makes any better sense to speak of behaviour with no behavers—although our sense of linguistic propriety is not so obviously violated; and this may account in part for the fact that a reductionistic behaviourism has a superficial plausibility.

[8] I use some of these examples, because Gilbert Ryle, *The Concept of Mind*, has given a logical behaviouristic analysis of mental concepts so that to say 'Jones thinks he is God Almighty' is to say something that can be analysed into reports on actions and dispositions of Jones, relieving us of having to posit 'ghostly occurrences behind the scenes'.

reporting 'Jones wondered'; and that if someone should ask what I meant in these two cases, I would submit further reports on Jones which I took to be evidence that 'Jones wondered' is true, which would display what I took myself to be meaning when I said it; and that I would submit further reports, logically of the same sort, where the pronoun 'I' would be substituted for 'Jones' in order to show what I meant by 'I wondered'. In other words, the pronoun 'I', when it is actually put to use with the verbs with which we report or predict in the experienceable world, behaves in precisely the same way that the proper-name, 'Jones', does: all the verbs are conjugable in all tenses, etc. When I use 'I' to report on Poteat, the verbs I use are governed by the same rules as when I use 'Jones' to report on Jones. Jones, being for me, no more than the sum of the things I can report on him, using these verbs, it follows, by parity of reasoning that I am for me no more than the sum of things I can report on myself, using these verbs.

Is the case, though, really as impressive as this? No! Of the verb 'to die' these things cannot be said. It makes perfectly good sense for me to sensibly say, 'Jones is dying', 'Jones has died', or 'Jones will die'. I cannot sensibly say: 'I died.' This verb cannot be meaningfully conjugated in the past tense, first person singular—or, if it is, it cannot be *used*. The parallel between the case of I reporting or predicting about myself and I reporting or predicting about Jones breaks down here. This verb behaves quite differently in the two cases. There is no apparent difference when we look at 'I will die' and 'Jones will die'. The role of 'die' in these two expressions seems to be identical. When, however, we try to conjugate 'to die' in all persons in the past tense its odd role becomes quite clear. It cannot be used in the past tense, first person singular. Though it can be used in the future tense, first person singular, its curious status and role in the language must not be overlooked. 'To die' is not an activity on logical all-fours with 'to run', 'to think', 'to wonder', 'to justify'. Not only so. 'I' is also logically peculiar. It does not behave consistently like the proper name, 'Jones' (unless 'I' and 'Jones' happen to be naming the same person). First, 'Jones' is not a part of the English language as is 'I'; 'I' is not a proper name; yet 'I' is never used without becoming exactly equivalent to someone's proper name. Secondly, there is at least one case where 'I' cannot be meaningfully coupled with a verb in the English language in every tense, whereas there is *no* case where 'Jones' (when Jones does not name the same person as 'I') cannot be so coupled. In other words, it is significant that the odd behaviour of 'to die' occurs only in the first person. It points to the logical unassimilability of 'I' to reports or predictions about behaviour (in the ordinary sense).

Now we must ask whether this linguistic fact concerning the behaviour of 'I' and 'to die' can be shown to have the significance which it must, if it is to bear the weight of my argument. Does this lack of symmetry here show that Flew's and Schlick's implied proposal to construe 'I will die' as analysable into reports or predictions about certain forms of behaviour, and nothing more not only fails, but fails in a way that permits me to conclude that 'I' is what I have called a kind of meta-concept and that 'to die' has in certain circumstances a logically extended though common-sensically meaningful use: that, in short, it means certain empirical predictions—and something more.

To begin with we may observe a further and perhaps trivial fact about these terms: that when we couple them in the present tense, first person singular, 'I die', 'I am dying', the expression generally appears in a quite different kind of context from that in which 'I will die' is uttered. If you will imagine hearing me say 'I will die', I think you will feel that I am saying something quite different—and not merely by reference to tense—from what you would feel that I would be saying if I were to say 'I am dying'. I think you would not imagine me in the former case to be primarily making reference to certain future contingent empirical facts that might be expressed in propositions about bio-chemical and physiological events in the way you might imagine me to be if you heard me say 'I am dying'—not even that there is now a body which emits the sound 'I' which one day will not emit that sound. If you heard me say, 'I am dying', I think you might be inclined to ask, 'Have you received a mortal wound? Does your pulse grow weak? Is your sight getting dim?' etc. Whereas when I say, 'I will die' you are not apt to think in these terms. You are perhaps more apt to reflect, 'Yes, I will die, too'.

Nevertheless, let us give this, as I have called it, somewhat forced analysis its full credit. Let us assume that 'I will die' is just a statement about my body and its behaviour in the future tense. Suppose we take it to mean that there is a certain organism which at some indefinite future time will undergo a radical change, including ceasing to behave in certain ways, etc., known as death. There seems to be nothing problematical about saying this, even though inevitably there will be an *end* at some point to my actually experiencing this process of change, even if an end which I do not experience, just as I do not experience the end of being awake.[9] There is nothing problematical about this, for there is no respect in which the occurrences predicted in my statement, so construed, are not about experience in a straightforward way. All of us have experienced occurrences *like* this all around us. All that I am saying is that *this* body (Poteat's) will one day cease to behave in certain ways, and that its ceasing to behave in these ways, including emitting the noises 'I', 'here', and 'now' and also the noises 'I will die' will be taken as signs that I am dead and that when I say 'I will die' I am only predicting that there will be a time when all this will be true. Is there any logical embarrassment in any of this which would lead one to resort to all this talk of 'death' being a logically extended concept? I think there is and that it can be shown by taking a closer look at the expression 'this body'.

Usually 'this' is a demonstrative pronoun which a speaker uses to make an identifying reference to a particular. My hearers understand the reference because 'this' is tied to a particular place and time by relation to the body from which the word 'this' is emitted. When I make a reference to a particular object in the world other than my body, let us say, by my pointing a finger at it, the identity of the particular being called 'this' is established for my hearers because it has a certain spatio-temporal relation to my body which emits the noise 'this', and because they too have a spatio-temporal relation to my body. But I want to urge that 'this' when used to pick out the body of the speaker functions differently *for the speaker*. Of course, it is obvious that the object of my identifying reference has not the same kind of relation to my body when the object is my body as when it is not. What is important here is that, when I say, '*This* body will undergo a radical change, including ceasing to behave in certain ways, etc.', I am making a reference to something in the experienceable world which has the unique status among such objects of being at least part of what I mean by 'I'. There is only one 'this' in the world of which W. H. Poteat can use 'I': When he uses 'this' to make reference to the body and its behaviour to which he may also make reference by using 'I', the term 'this' functions in a unique way. Even if one wanted to say that there are other extended objects in the world besides the one called 'my body' to which I could make reference either with 'this' or 'my'—any object belonging to me—I do not think that any other

---

[9] It is not an accident that we use the expression 'He is asleep' as a euphemism for 'He is dead', since there are real parallels between the relation of 'going to sleep' and 'experience' and 'dying' and 'experience'.

object may be said to be 'mine' in the same way that my body may be said to be. The characteristic of qualifying as 'this' (having a certain determinate *relation* to a body from which the sound 'this' is heard to come) is not the same characteristic as that of being the body from which the sound 'my body' is heard to come and to which the expression '*my* body' is recognized by myself as applying. One cannot assimilate '*my* body' to '*this* body'. And I recognize that everyone else has a similarly unique relation to the object which is his body.

Therefore reference by me to the body and its behaviour which is part at least of what I mean by 'I' can never be made to be logically equivalent to references by me to bodies and their behaviour which are not. Hence, 'I will die' can never mean for me the same thing as 'There is a body in the world which one day will cease to behave as it now does.' What is being asserted is not just about an object in the world in the way that '*This* body will die' (where the body in question is *not* mine) *is* about an object in the world. My body and its behaviour is not in the world *for me* in the same way that Jones' body and its behaviour is in the world for me. For me to describe my death as the end of certain kinds of behaviour in the world is not *for me* the description of an occurrence *in the world* at all like an account by me of Jones' death as an occurrence *in the world*. For myself, I am not *in* the world as Jones is in the world. For me therefore to say of myself that I will no longer be in the world is to use logically extended concepts. Thus, again we see the asymmetry of the logical grammar of 'I will die' when I use it of myself and 'Jones will die' when I use it of Jones. From the fact that 'Jones will die' seems assimilable to reports or predictions of a straightforward empirical sort it does not follow that 'I will die', when I use it of myself, can be so assimilated. From this we also see that 'I' and 'death' in certain circumstances, namely, when I use them of myself, are logically extended concepts in the sense demanded by my thesis; and that attempts to assimilate them, are, as I have said, forced. Finally, this means that Flew and Schlick would not be able to make a case for 'I will die' being analysed into predictions about behaviour, and nothing more; and that unless Flew is willing altogether to deny himself the privilege of thoughtfully using of himself the expression 'I will die', he must involve himself in the use of what I am here calling myth. To say, 'when I have died, there is nothing', is not the use of the Platonic myth nor of the Christian myth, but myth it is, nonetheless; which is to say a resort to the use of logically extended concepts. A strain is being put upon the very language within which Flew has, quite rightly, argued that the expression 'I will survive my death' is a contradiction. It is this pressure which produces and legitimizes—indeed, makes inescapable—the language of myth or meta-concepts, if we are going to accord any meaning to an expression which each one of us does in fact find meaningful, namely: 'I will die.'

Insofar, then, as any of us thoughtfully says of himself, 'I will die', he is involved in making a statement about himself which cannot be exhaustively expressed in reports or predictions about behaviour, actions or events of a straightforward sort. My dying is for me not *just* doing or ceasing to do certain reportable things, though it certainly *entails* my doing or ceasing to do these things. When I use 'I' of myself, something is being named which is *for me* not just the spatio-temporal speaker or behaver from whom the noise 'I' has come. If you ask me what it is that is named, hoping to have an answer given in reports of behaviour alone, then of course I can't say. You are asking a question which on your terms, as I have been trying to show, it is impossible to answer. If you do not ask what it is that is named *in these terms*, then my answer is quite simple: myself! Dying, therefore, (and this is true analytically) in the sense of what *I* will do, in the sense, that is to say, which is displayed by the analysis of this logically peculiar verb 'to die', is something done only by selves, only, that is, by *users* of the first personal pronoun singular. In this peculiar sense, objects don't die, only subjects die. In a world only of objects (a logical impossibility when you consider what 'object' means, and one incidentally which gives us a clue to the logic of the concept 'world') there is no death. This is at once why it makes sense to say: 'By man came death'; and also why the Platonic tradition lacks the same anxiety over death which is characteristic of contemporary culture with its concept of a radically self-transcending subject, and with its emphasis upon subjectivity. Dying is a private affair, because being a self is. Death, then, is an eschatological concept. To say 'I will die' is to say something which entails that certain empirical propositions about the experienceable world will at a certain time be true. But it is to say something *more* than and different from just this. Death in certain circumstances is a concept which applies to the experienceable world, but also extends beyond it. It is quite definitely anchored in and applies to the world of common sense, but it also stands in a different relation to that world. If my analysis will hold up, everyone believes when he says thoughtfully of himself, 'I will die', that he is saying something which is true and something which is about 'reality', but not just about the public world of experience. His language is being put under an unusual kind of pressure, a pressure which gives rise to a system of discourse which I am for brevity's sake calling myth. While firmly anchored in the common-sense world by the entailment of certain empirical propositions, the concept extends beyond this common-sense world. And as I have held, this is true whether one says, 'When I have died, there will be nothing', 'When I die my soul will become discarnate and abide eternally in a realm of forms', or 'When I die, I shall have fellowship with God'.

Lest you think that these three cases are not logically of the same sort, I will just observe that the man who says, 'When I have died, there will be nothing' is not saying anything about the world of common sense at all like, 'When I have run, I will be tired'. In other words, when he asserts that death is the end, he does not exactly 'know' what he is saying. Yet in another sense he and all of us know very well what he is saying. And if a dispute over alternative myths arises between ourselves and him, though we shall certainly feel that both he and we are saying something genuinely meaningful about reality, what we will be respectively saying is not about reality in the way that reports upon or predictions of observable behaviour are about it. It is dubious whether we can call this a dispute, since it is not clear that there are any rules common to the disputants by reference to which a settlement might be made. But, if it is a dispute, it is not one between those who have, in my sense, an eschatology and those who do not. It is a dispute between rival eschatologies; and the apparent economy of one in which we say only, 'When I have died, there will be nothing' is not as such a reason for preferring it. Indeed, one wonders whether the expression 'reason for preferring' has any definite sense here.

## II

I want to conclude by making a few suggestions concerning the implications of all this for our understanding of the Christian interpretation of death. To put it another way, when we allow the extended concept 'death' to operate within the structure of the Christian myth, what happens?

First, I think it is important to recognize that the overwhelming majority of people in the contemporary world, Christian and non-Christian, take the essence of the Christian claim (as Flew seems to) to be a belief to the effect that 'I will survive my death'; and further, that they are culturally conditioned by the same forces which induce Flew to take as his paradigm for meaningful discourse the language we use about the common-sense world; and finally that on their own premises, Flew's demonstration of the contradictoriness of 'I will survive my death' must be devastating. If 'death' is the kind of concept which he holds that it is, then to speak of surviving it *is* utter nonsense.

Secondly, earlier on I suggested that there is a profound difference between 'death' as it is understood in the broadly Platonic tradition and death as it is understood in contemporary western culture; and that this is a function of the concept of a radically self-transcending self. Now it is in this context that we will have to interpret the doctrine of the Resurrection. That is to say, if Resurrection is the concept or system of concepts comprising the Christian myth within which the logically extended concept 'death' is to be operative, then 'death', insofar as it is anchored in the experienceable world, while extending beyond it, will have to be anchored in what the contemporary man understands by the common-sense world, if, that is to say, Resurrection is to have any real meaning for him. In short, 'death' insofar as it operates within the discourse of common sense alone will have to operate in accordance with the rules governing its use within that discourse. And this means precisely that whatever else the Christian may be claiming when tying the logically extended concept of death to the myth of the Resurrection, he is not claiming and could not claim that there is any *survival* of death, since, as we saw above, even this logically extended concept is so related to the empirical world that to say, 'I will die', is to say something which *entails* certain empirical propositions being true at some future time, and that these propositions being true entails that we cannot believe that there *exists*, in any ordinary sense of the word, something or other, not even a ghostly something or other, after these empirical propositions will have become true. And this, for the simple reason that the condition of the possibility of something, even a ghostly something, existing is that the empirical propositions are *not yet* true. That is, either 'I exist' means nothing more than that certain empirical reports about behaviour, etc., are true, in which case it is logically contradictory to speak, in any sense, of my existing after my death (i.e. after the kind of behaviour reported has ceased); or it means this, plus something else, which cannot be expressed in empirical existence language; in which case, I no longer exist, insofar as my existence entails certain kinds of reportable behaviour, and inasmuch as the something more was precisely what cannot be assimilated to these reports. Or to put the matter differently, even though our analysis of the concept 'death' demands that we give it and therefore the concept 'I' as well an extension beyond ordinary empirical language that does not mean that what is *beyond* in the concept 'I' is a ghostly *thing*, for 'thing' is itself a concept which can be cashed only in empirical language. If I understand 'I' to mean not just the something more than what can function in straightforward empirical language, but what *can* so function *and something more*, then it is meaningless to speak of my surviving death when it is no longer possible to identify certain familiar types of behaviour in the experienceable world as Poteat's animated behaviour. On the basis of the Platonic account, this would not be the case, for in this account, Poteat's quite commonplace historical activity is not really thought to be any part of what it is to be Poteat. Therefore, we can meaningfully talk about Poteat surviving death even though there is no longer any animated historical behaviour of Poteat. This perhaps sad state of affairs is a logical consequence of the whole body of Christian myth which connected its logically extended concepts to propositions about the empirical world in such a way as to make it quite certain that we could no longer separate Poteat from his commonplace historical acts. One may even go so far as to say that the doctrine of the Resurrection of the body, when once it is taken seriously, makes it impossible for us any more to believe that *I* can survive my death in the sense that there is a *something* to which death does not write a *finis*.

If the Christian, then, when he uses the concept 'death' uses it, as do others, in a logically extended sense; and if he understands 'I' to be similarly extended; and if he insists that though 'I' be extended, what it means to be Poteat cannot be separated from his historical acts and animated behaviour in the experienceable world; how can he embody the logically extended concept 'I' in a myth in such a way that he can say something about the curious experience of death, say that it has been overcome, has lost its sting, etc., *while at the same time* holding both that I do not survive death and that nevertheless my historical acts are redeemed from death along with the something more which the concept 'I' is thought to cover?

First, he will have to use myth. Second, the myth cannot be construed as asserting or implying that he does not die, nor that his resurrection will be a beginning all over again exactly as before, but yet in such a way as to take his historical acts into a structure of meaning *along with the something more* covered by the logically extended concept 'I'. It would be impossible to invent such a myth. In fact, I have posed the problem in this way because I have started with the myth of the Resurrection of the body as given.

Here we must be reminded that the myth of the Resurrection of the body has its status within the whole fabric of the concepts of Biblical thought. Let us suppose that the key to this thought is the concept of a relation between man and God which is an I-Thou relation. In an I-Thou relation all that makes me the person I am—both what in other circumstances can be cashed in terms of ordinary empirical reports of behaviour, and the something more—is involved with another fully personal being. In the discourse in which we try to exhibit this relation, there is no place for language about body and soul, etc., but only for such notions as love, fellowship, responsibility, forgiveness, freedom, etc. And to know and be in fellowship with a person cannot be analysed in terms of just knowing their behaviour or empirical reports about their behaviour or even this *and something more*. These concepts do not function in this game at all. In an I-Thou relation the distinction between me and my body disappears. Equally it is one in which the distinction between 'happens' because the relation is in time and 'doesn't happen' because it is in a timeless eternity does not apply. This kind of a relation does not occur because we are doing something extraordinary with reference to the world of space and time. Nor do we talk of it as though it were spaceless and timeless. Our analogy is drawn from a quite different quarter—one where we know ourselves not as 'inside' our bodies, not as souls transcending them, not as dualisms of this sort at all. Here we know ourselves quite independently of these distinctions. Here we act as a unity 'knowing' the difference between ourselves and our acts (i.e. knowing the difference between what could be given in empirical reports and the something more that cannot) only in that we can say of them that they are *our* acts—'I did it'—which is to say, we know ourselves as responsible.

If someone asks, 'What then is eternal life? Is it living in some strange way forever? Or is it rather a quality of this life?' we reply that these questions cannot be asked in this universe of discourse. There is a more radical break with our common-sense discourse involved. We cannot say either that it is like or analogous to our present life, only it goes on forever; nor can we say that it is just a heightening of this life.

When the Christian says that he believes in the Resurrection of the body, this is one way he has of saying that he—that part of him which in other circumstances can be cashed in empirical language *and* the something more that cannot—will have fellowship with God. And if he is asked whether this takes place *in* history or at the *end* of history, he will reply, 'at the *end of history*', but then he will have used another eschatological concept, in some ways like that of 'death'. But that is another story.

The Christian myth of the Resurrection of the body, then, is legitimized in the same way that any system of discourse for embodying the logically extended concepts of 'death' and 'I' is. In this myth what the Christian asserts about the meaning of his own death is that he will have fellowship with God as a fully personal being. 'Fellowship' is a notion that can function only in discourse about the relations between personal beings. The logically extended concept 'I' which refers to the something more than just what can be cashed in straightforward empirical language is embodied in the myth by means of person-concepts such as 'love' and 'fellowship'. But the anchorage of this concept in the empirical world is preserved in the mythically transformed symbol of a resurrected body. What is thought to have personal fellowship with God is, in this myth, a being about which we speak in analogies drawn from our normal person-talk. Therefore, the myth is not something free-floating in an extra-existent realm, but is about the existential reality which I am, though not literally about it. None of what has been said in any way constitutes an argument for preferring the Christian myth to other possible myths. Indeed, one wonders what an argument of this sort would be. All that has been attempted here is to show that when we analyse an expression like 'I will die' we discover at certain points a pressure within our ordinary language; that this pressure is felt at so commonplace a point as when we speak of our own death; that when we do, we quite naturally resort to myth; and finally, that the Christian myth is fundamentally different from alternative ones and is at least as well grounded.

# INDEX OF NAMES